Margaret River

Frances Andrijich, Peter Forrestal, Ray Jordan

*This book is dedicated to the memory of Di Cullen (1923–2003),
matriarch, pioneer, a woman for all seasons.*

*For my loving parents Nikola and Jagoda Andrijich
and my wonderful daughters Annaliese and Mikhaila.
FA*

*In loving memory of my mother, Enid Forrestal (1917–1992), who loved the work of Fremantle Arts
Centre Press and would have been well pleased with this book; and for my tolerant wife, Elaine: as the
current Fremantle Arts Centre Press catalogue describes her, 'outstanding and much-loved'.
PF*

*To my understanding and supportive family, Jennifer, Daniel and Jack;
and to neurosurgeon Dr Charlie Teo, whose incredible skill has kept us together.
RJ*

Margaret River

Frances Andrijich, Peter Forrestal, Ray Jordan

Fremantle Arts Centre Press
Australia's finest small publisher

First published 2003 by
FREMANTLE ARTS CENTRE PRESS
25 Quarry Street, Fremantle
(PO Box 158, North Fremantle 6159)
Western Australia.
www.facp.iinet.net.au

Copyright photographs © Frances Andrijich, 2003.
Copyright text © Peter Forrestal and Ray Jordan, 2003.

This book is copyright. Apart from any fair dealing for the purpose of private study,
research, criticism or review, as permitted under the Copyright Act,
no part may be reproduced by any process without written permission.
Enquiries should be made to the publisher.

Consultant Editors Ray Coffey and Cate Sutherland.
Designer Marion Duke.
Printed by South Wind Productions, Singapore.

National Library of Australia
Cataloguing-in-publication data

Andrijich, Frances.
Margaret River.

ISBN 1 920731 61 X.

1. Wine districts - Western Australia - Margaret River Region.
2. Wine and wine making - Western Australia - Margaret River Region.
3. Margaret River Region (W.A.) - Guidebooks.
I. Forrestal, Peter. II. Jordan, Ray. III. Title.

641.22099412

The State of Western Australia has made an investment in this project
through ArtsWA in association with the Lotteries Commission.

Previous page: Mammoth Rock near Contos Beach.
Above: Prevelly Beach at sunset.
Overleaf: Bunker Bay.

Acknowledgements

Many thanks to our major sponsors: Fujifilm Australia, who supplied the film used in photographing the book, and Churchill Colour Laboratories, who processed it. At Fujifilm, we acknowledge the support of Jacques Guerinet, David Norton, Peter Taylor and Kevin Cooper; while at Churchill Colour Laboratories, we are indebted to Berenice and Peter Carter.

Frances Andrijich would like to thank Duncan Dodd of Maxwell Opticals (Nikon) for the loan of the Nikkor 600mm f4 lens used for the surfing shots.

In exploring the Margaret River area, Frances had four wonderful guides who gave freely of their time and expertise to help her understand the region, some of its secrets and its best locations: thanks to Shelley Cullen, Michael and Roslyn Andrijich and Michael Whyte.

The authors also thank the following for their contribution to this book: Frances Ah Chee, Mary Andrijich, Shaun Atkinson, Jeff Bell, Amy and Jeff Burch, Mike Calneggia, Aaron Carr, Claire Codrington, Mandee Collins, Maggie Conrad, Kay Craze, Vanya Cullen, Moya and John Dempster, Kate Dick, Dotty, Ian Dowling, Claire Finucaine, Gillian Forsyth, John Gladstones, Tim Gill, Shane Gould, Guy Grant, Judi Halliday, Don Hancey, Duncan Hancock, Gene Hardy, Noreen Hackett, Katrina Hawley, Heather Jenkins, Deirdre and Malcolm Jones, Jack Jordan, Rob and Karen Karri-Davies, Alexandra Kemp, Michael Kerrigan, Uta and Stefan Kurys-Romer, Kitty and David Lewis, Fiona McQuisten, Amber and Matthew Miller, Barbara and Gordon Mitchell, Terri and Steve Mitchell, Andrew Moore, Clare and Keith Mugford, Kathy and Philip Pain, Kate Parry, Barbara, Shirley and Zoe Peirce, Michael Peterkin, Karolina Puchalka, Peter Rigby, Frida Rossi, Trevor Todd, Jenny Spencer, Tom Stannage, Sam and Sascha Watson, Lauren Waye, Bill and Vilma Webb and Michael Wright.

We acknowledge the importance of the following in researching this book: Margaret River Tourist Bureau, JS Battye Library at the State Library of Western Australia, Eagles Heritage, Augusta Historical Museum and Western Australian Museum. The help which we were given by the staff of these institutions was greatly appreciated.

The process of collaborating in the production of this book has been made much easier by the enormously supportive staff at Fremantle Arts Centre Press. We pay tribute to the talents of Ray Coffey, Clive Newman, Marion Duke, Cate Sutherland, Janet Blagg and Stephanie Green.

Above: The rocks at North Point, Gracetown.
Overleaf: North Point, Cowaramup Bay.

Contents

1. A brief history — 15
2. The landscape — 43
3. The flora and fauna — 67
4. The sea — 83
5. The architecture — 113
6. The people — 131
7. The food — 149
8. The wine — 169
9. The great sites — 207

1. A brief history

The Wardandi

Margaret River is in the land of the Wardandi — the people of Wardan, the Ocean Spirit — one of the fourteen Nyungar tribes that live in the South-West. Their land extends from the coast at Stratham (near Capel) to Nannup and down the Blackwood River to the sea at Augusta. Stories passed down among the Wardandi people tell of a time when the coastline near Margaret River extended about seventy kilometres further than it does today. Dreamtime stories refer to the 'Great earth shaking' in which as many as eighty per cent of the Wardandi perished in an earthquake. This led to the earth subsiding and the coastline finding its present position. The long association between the Aboriginal people and the Margaret River region can be seen in archaeological evidence from the Devil's Lair cave, which suggests that it was occupied for the best part of sixty thousand years, though not for the past two thousand. The Wardandi story of a disaster that took place when the entrance to the cave fell in offers a logical explanation for the absence of recent occupation.

Before European settlement, the Wardandi moved around the different parts of this abundant land over the six seasons of their calendar, fishing and hunting and gathering fruit and berries. They were — and are — conservationists with a strong sense of the importance of preserving a balance with nature.

In the view of elder Bill Webb, the coming of white people has been disastrous for the Wardandi, and their numbers have fallen dramatically since the settlers first arrived. Although historians disagree about precise numbers, the best contemporary estimates give the number of Aborigines living in the South-West in the 1830s — from Perth to Albany to Augusta — as between five thousand and twelve thousand. Sylvia Hallam cites reports from settlers in the 1830s which suggest that there was a greater concentration of people in the coastal area around Bunbury and Vasse than in the dense inland forests of the South-West. The Margaret River valley was generally avoided by the Aboriginal people because of its deep limestone caves which contained important mythological sites.

The expansion of European settlement in the South-West was accompanied by the displacement of the Nyungar people from this area to fringe camps and missions, so that by 1900 their traditional lifestyle had all but disappeared. Although Aboriginal people no longer live as they did two hundred years ago, their strong sense of identity with the land remains unbroken. As Bill Webb says, tribal lands, with their sacred areas, major camp sites and burial places, are clearly delineated and do not change over time.

Previous page: Torpedo Rocks looking towards Smiths Beach.
Right: Redgate Beach in a big swell.

Early explorers

The first Europeans to encounter the west coast of Australia were the Dutch who were conducting a lucrative trade in spices and textiles during the seventeenth century with what is now Indonesia. Slight miscalculations led to many Dutch ships sailing too far east and reaching the coast of Western Australia — in the case of the *Batavia* (1629) and the *Vergulde Draeck* (*Gilt Dragon*, 1656), with disastrous consequences. The *Leeuwin* (1621), the name of whose captain is not known, was the first to see the south-west coast.

In the late eighteenth century, the French were intrepid explorers keen to unlock the secrets and the riches of the Great South Land. François St Allouarn in the *Gros Ventre* (1772) visited Flinders Bay as part of a survey of the west coast, which prepared the way for the important scientific expedition of Nicholas Baudin in the *Geographe* and Jacques Hamelin in the *Naturaliste* (1801).

Baudin and Hamelin spent nine days surveying and exploring the Geographe Bay area, collecting scientific data. In attempting to salvage a longboat in rough weather, second-class helmsman Timothée Vasse was swept overboard and drowned near the river that today bears his name.

The Wardandi people tell a different story, of Vasse surviving to live among them for three weeks before dying of toxemia from drinking brackish water.

Baudin returned two years later and more accurately charted the south-west coast, coming upon the safe harbour where Bunbury is today, while his French scientists continued to document the natural history of the continent. According to historian Leslie Marchant, this early French exploration of Australian waters was to spark interest in establishing a penal colony on the west coast of Australia in post-Napoleonic France of the early 1820s. However, Louis Duperrey and Hyacinthe Bougainville, who were sent to explore the possibilities of such a venture, failed to follow orders. But for this twist of fate, the colonisation of Australia's west may have been vastly different.

Previous page: Sugarloaf near Cape Naturaliste.
Left: Dawn at Yallingup Beach.
Overleaf: Redgate Beach — popular with abalone gatherers.

Early settlement

The first European settlement in the Margaret River region was established by Lieutenant-Governor James Stirling at Augusta in 1830 because there was not enough suitable land near Perth for new settlers to the colony. However, the dense hardwood forests were a major obstacle to agriculture and horticulture in the area. Poor soil and the inability of many of the settlers to adapt to growing conditions in Australia made even subsistence farming difficult in the early years.

In the late 1830s several of the families (including the Molloys and the Bussells) moved further north to better land around the Vasse. Only a few of the original settlers remained in Augusta, maintaining a small settlement there until a second (and much more successful) wave of settlers came in the late 1860s, leading to the establishment of some successful beef and dairy farms.

Aboriginal settlement was heavy near Vasse because of the good drinking water and excellent fishing. The pasture, which was regularly fired by the Aborigines, provided a steady food source for kangaroos. The early settlers surmised that what was good pasture for kangaroos would be ideal for cattle. In 1839 Captain John Molloy gave as one of his reasons for moving to Vasse the fact that it had the 'most numerous native population'. As Sylvia Hallam points out in *Fire and Hearth*, it was not the Aborigines who were attracted to European settlements in Western Australia but the other way round.

As elsewhere, conflict between Aborigines and the settlers was resolved brutally. At Vasse, punitive expeditions in 1837 and 1838 resulted in the deaths of five Aborigines. The second of these followed the spearing of one of George Chapman's heifers. Three years later, twenty-nine year old George Layman pulled the beard of an Aboriginal elder during a confrontation and was speared in retaliation. The elder, Geewar, and four of his tribe were pursued and killed. Two other Aborigines were brought back to the settlement and shot.

The best known of the settlers, Alfred and Ellen Bussell, left Vasse in 1854 and established themselves near the Margaret River. Alfred learned the local Aboriginal language and employed the Wardandi on Ellensbrook, their sizeable and successful farm. A famous incident involved their sixteen-year-old daughter Grace and one of the Aboriginal stockmen, Sam Isaacs, rescuing passengers from the wrecked coastal steamer *Georgette* in 1876. Both showed great courage, but Grace Bussell was lauded as the hero of the hour. Time, however, has redressed the balance and the role that Isaacs played in the rescue was more adequately acknowledged, when in 1897, he was granted one hundred acres of land at Wallcliffe for his bravery.

Right: Contos Beach.

Whaling

There are reports from 1803 onwards of American whalers travelling from their base in New Bedford, Massachusetts to the south-western coast of Australia to hunt the humpback and the southern right whale as their migratory pattern brought them into these waters. The whalers established a try works (for converting blubber into oil) in Flinders Bay. During the 1830s crews became an important part of the social life of Augusta, Dunsborough and Meelup, where they came ashore for reprovisioning. Items for which they bartered included potatoes, meat, vegetables, butter and cheese. Elijah Dawson's house at Vasse contained a barter room specifically for trade with the whalers. These isolated communities were as keen to welcome the Americans as the sailors were to join in their social life. There were marriages between whalers and the daughters of settlers, and some wives chose to accompany their husbands on whaling ships.

Right: The beach at Moses Rock.
Overleaf: Rocky Point, near Eagle Bay.

The timber industry

Although clearing land for agriculture was made more difficult by the karri and jarrah forests in the South-West, some recognised economic opportunities in the export of timber. The earliest attempts at establishing a timber industry suffered from lack of experience and expertise. The lack of infrastructure, especially railway lines and jetties, meant that heavy timber had to be transported by bullock drays on poorly maintained roads that, in winter, were often little more than quagmires.

The first railway was built in 1871 from Lockeville (near Busselton) to the forests twenty kilometres away. Among the timber mills that helped transform the economy of the region were those of Yelverton at Quindalup and Davies at Coordardup (which was dismantled and rebuilt at Karridale in 1882). Davies built railways to connect his mill to the ports at Hamelin Bay and Flinders Bay. By 1882 jetties, with railway lines running along their entire length, were constructed for both ports. The late 1880s and the 1890s were boom times for the timber industry in the Margaret River region. The mill at Karridale flourished and its employees swelled the population of the local area. Other mills were built at Boranup (1886) and Jarrahdene (1896), and the railway connected Augusta and Margaret River. The

Perth to Bunbury railway line was finished in 1893 and extended to Busselton two years later. The township of Margaret River was gazetted in 1913.

Increased competition from mills which were able to send timber to the ports of Bunbury and Fremantle by rail, along with the depletion of forest reserves in the Karridale area, meant a downturn in the timber industry in this area in the first decade of the twentieth century. The Karridale mill closed in 1906, Boranup in 1910 and Jarrahdene in 1913.

Some view the logging of the South-West as ecologically harmful (even disastrous). It is certainly the case that as much as seventy per cent of Australia's woodlands have been felled at some time since Europeans first settled here and less than twenty per cent of the country's landscape remains as it was in 1788. The timber industry, however, did help increase the population of the area, brought a measure of prosperity and made a significant contribution to the development of infrastructure.

Previous page left: Mulberry Cottage, situated near Rosa Glen, was built in 1927 as part of the Group Settlement Scheme.
Previous page right: Jim House, a logger, in the sawmill he established in 1955 and ran until his death in February 2003.
Right: Poddies (hand-fed calves) on a winter morning off Fifty One Road, Wilyabrup.
Overleaf: Darnell's Trading Post, Witchcliffe.

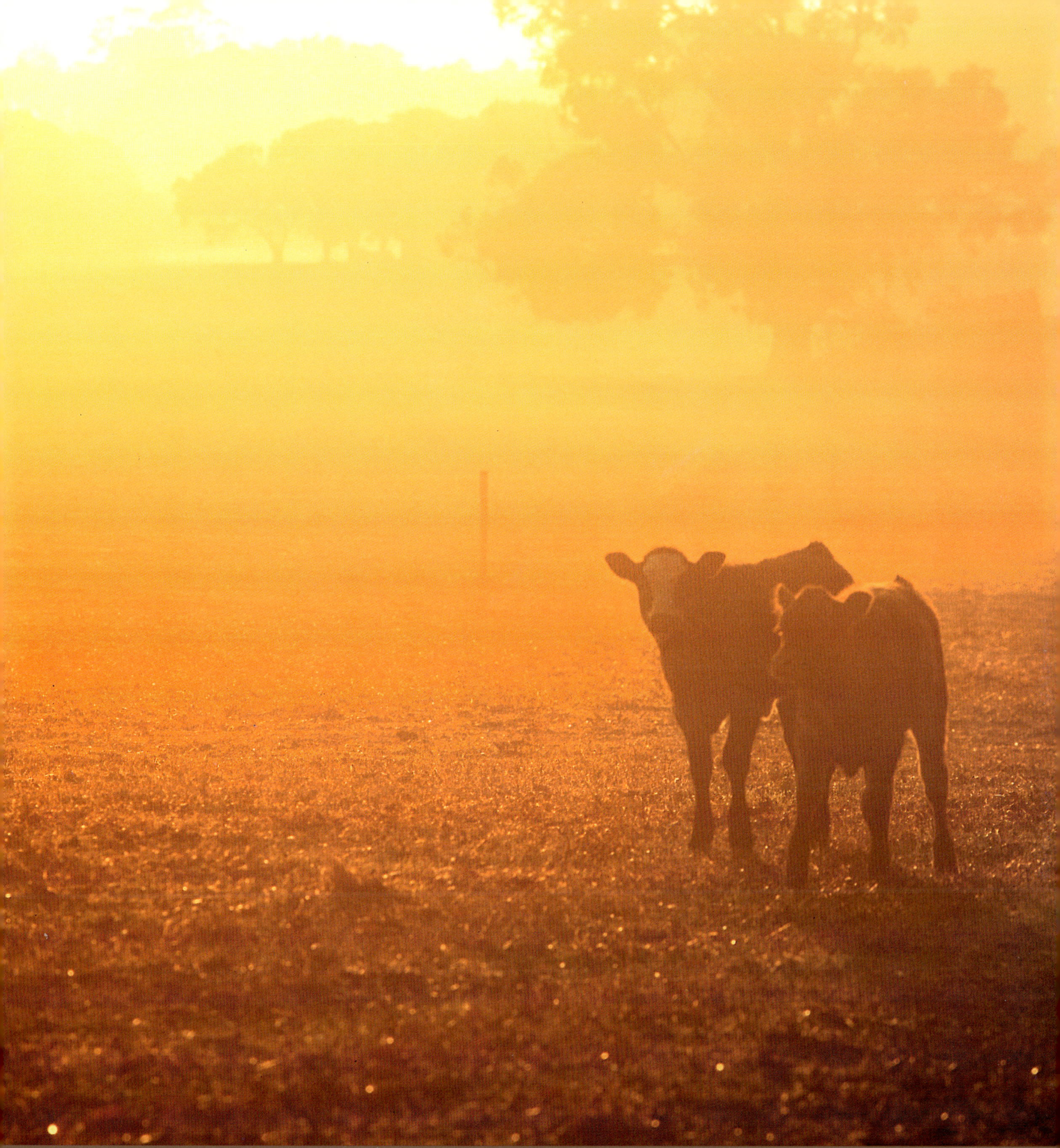

Group settlement

The 1920s was a period of unprecedented prosperity for Western Australia. A key ingredient in this was the successful opening up of the Wheatbelt by the state government with labour from returned servicemen and from British immigrants. Production trebled during the decade.

This success encourage the state government to set up the Group Settlement Scheme (from 1921 to 1930) to establish a dairy industry in the South-West. This would reduce the cost of importing dairy products from the eastern states and at the same time open up the sparsely populated and largely uncleared South-West. Under the Scheme, settlers were to be given training and land in return for clearing and developing their blocks.

The Group Settlement Scheme began with a group of unemployed wharf labourers from Fremantle and miners from the Goldfields being placed on farms in the South-West in 1921 and was extended to six thousand immigrant families from Britain in 1923. A team of twenty men would work under a foreman to cooperatively prepare each of the sixty-five hectare (160 acre) blocks. Part of each block would be completely cleared, some partly cleared, a well would be dug and a small house erected. Workers were paid a living wage while they were helping to establish the group settlement.

The scheme was poorly administered and living conditions for the group settlers were incredibly uncomfortable. Clearing the hardwood forests was much more difficult than anyone had anticipated and the groups simply did not have the manpower, money or machinery to do it effectively. Heartbreaking experimentation was needed to learn how to get the best from the soil and what it was most suitable for. Making a living or even surviving on the land required fortitude, persistence and sustained hard work. By 1924, about thirty per cent of the immigrants and forty-two per cent of the Australian-born group settlers had left their blocks.

Many of the families involved endured terrible hardship, and the cost of settling the South-West was much more substantial than the state government had expected. Nevertheless, the Group Settlement Scheme did make a contribution to the development of Western Australia. By the end of the 1920s, more than forty thousand hectares of the South-West had been cleared and nearly thirty thousand hectares were under pasture. A viable dairy industry had been established and imports of food dropped dramatically.

The infrastructure of the area — especially roads and railway, schools and hospitals — improved during the 1920s as a result of the population increase. Of most importance to the Margaret River region was the railway link between Busselton and Augusta, which was completed by 1925. The opening up of the South-West to settlers also brought builders, tradespeople and storekeepers.

DARNELL'S TRADING POST

A rural community

From the 1930s to the end of the 1970s, the Margaret River region was a typical Western Australian rural community. Its principal industries were dairy and beef farming and timber. Its population and fortunes fluctuated depending on the times: things were tough during the Depression and the war years, and buoyant during the 1950s when primary industries thrived as never before. The economy of the area was sluggish in the 1960s and 1970s, when Margaret River could have been fairly described as 'a stagnant backwater'.

However there were signs of change. Improvements to roads and increased access to motor cars led to the beginnings of a tourism industry. The formation of the Augusta Margaret River Tourist Bureau in 1956 shows that the locals were keen to capitalise on the natural attractions of the region. Tough times in dairy and beef meant that, when possible, the locals looked to diversifying into other areas such as potatoes, pine plantations and, eventually, grape growing.

Above and right: Car wrecks near Cowaramup and Leeuwin Estate.
Overleaf: Hay bales near Voyager Estate.

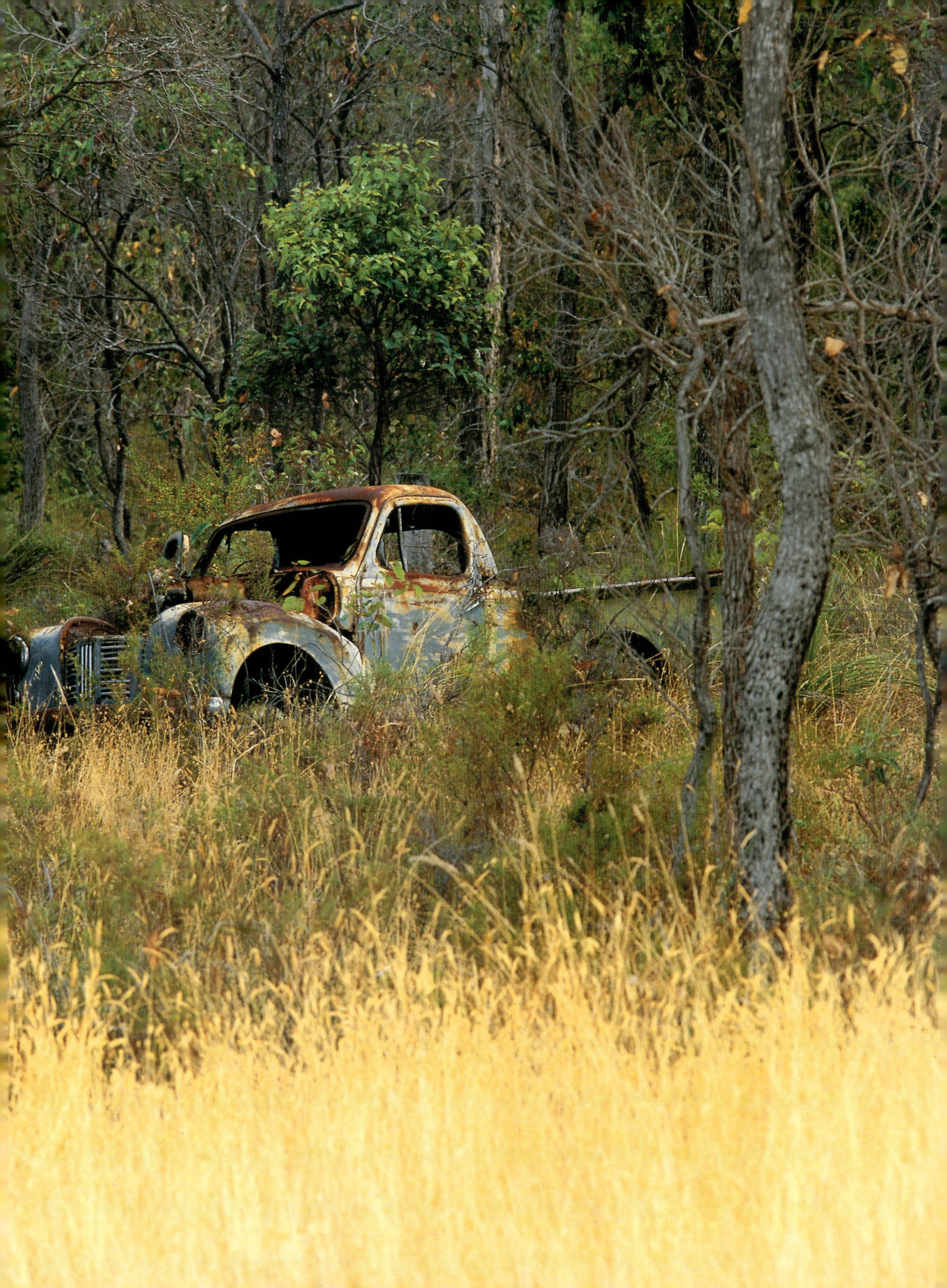

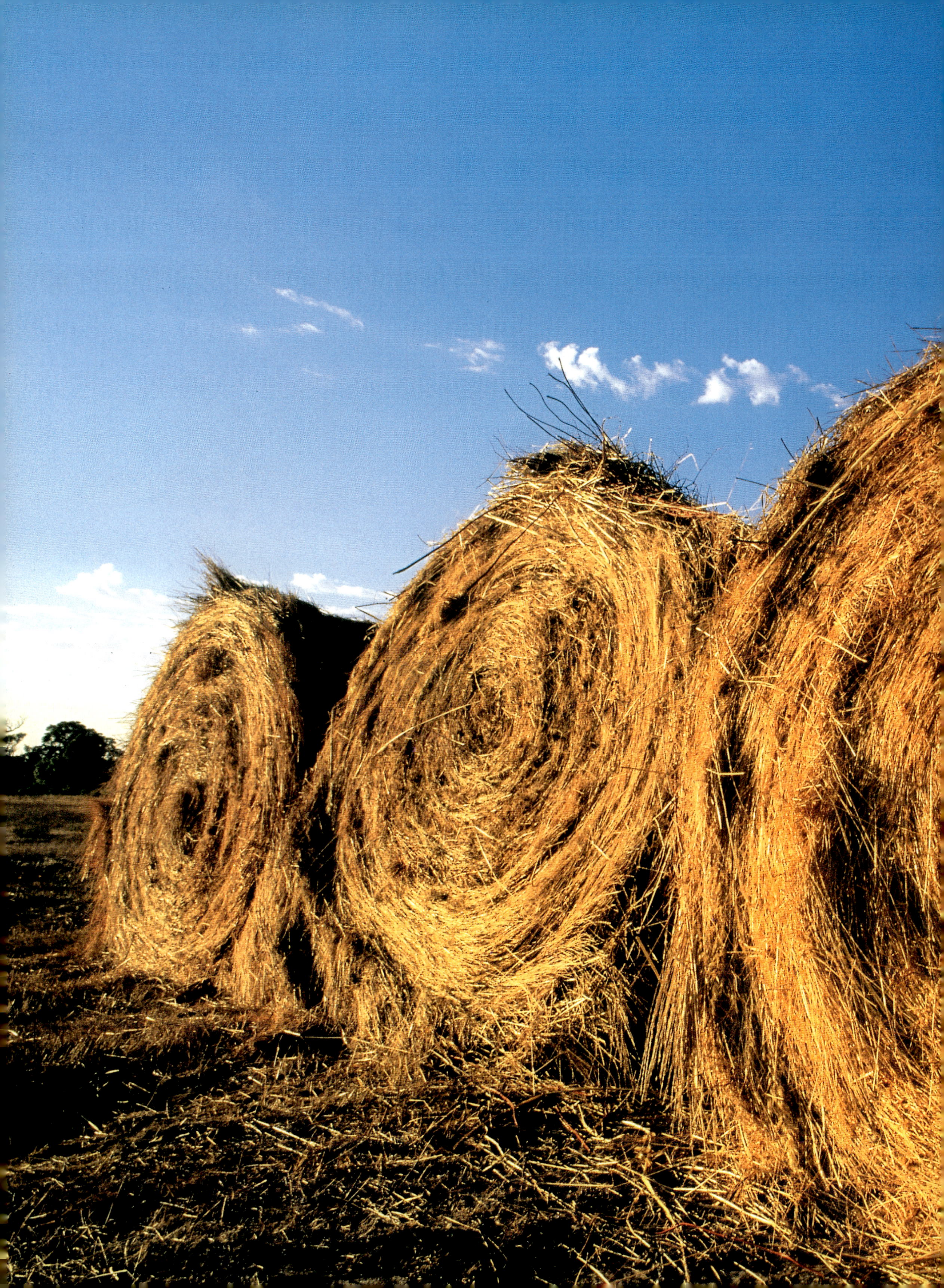

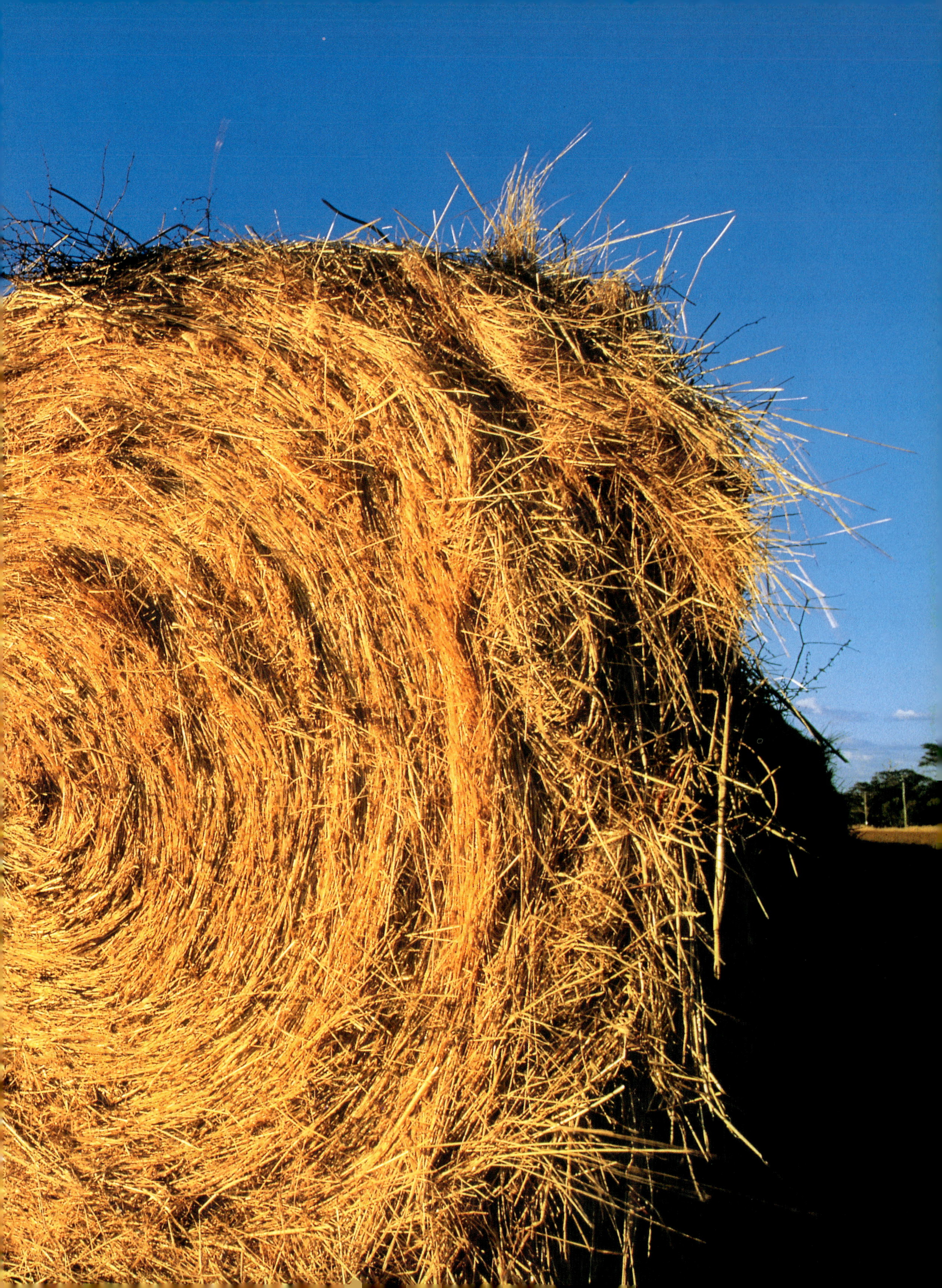

2. The landscape

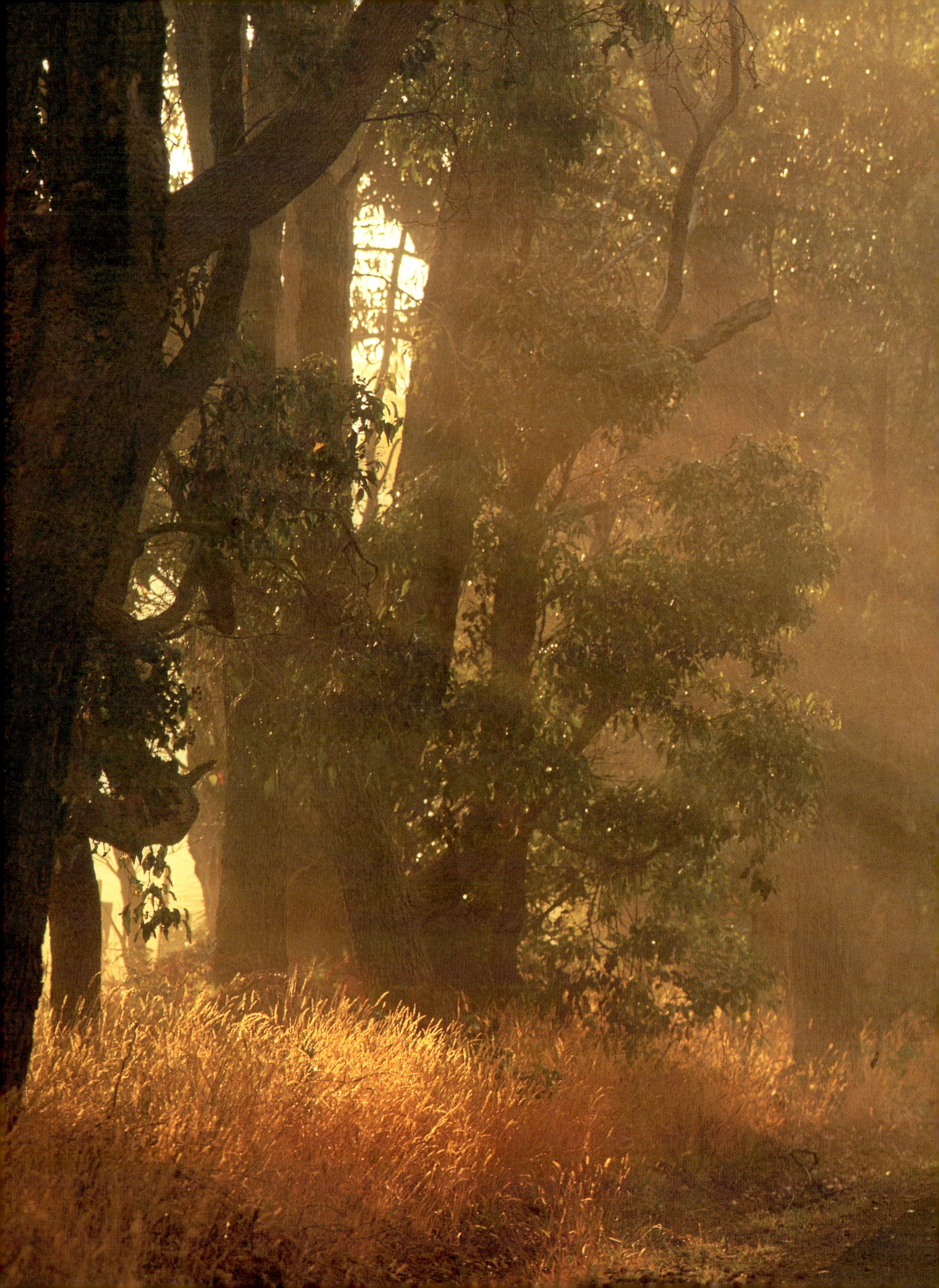

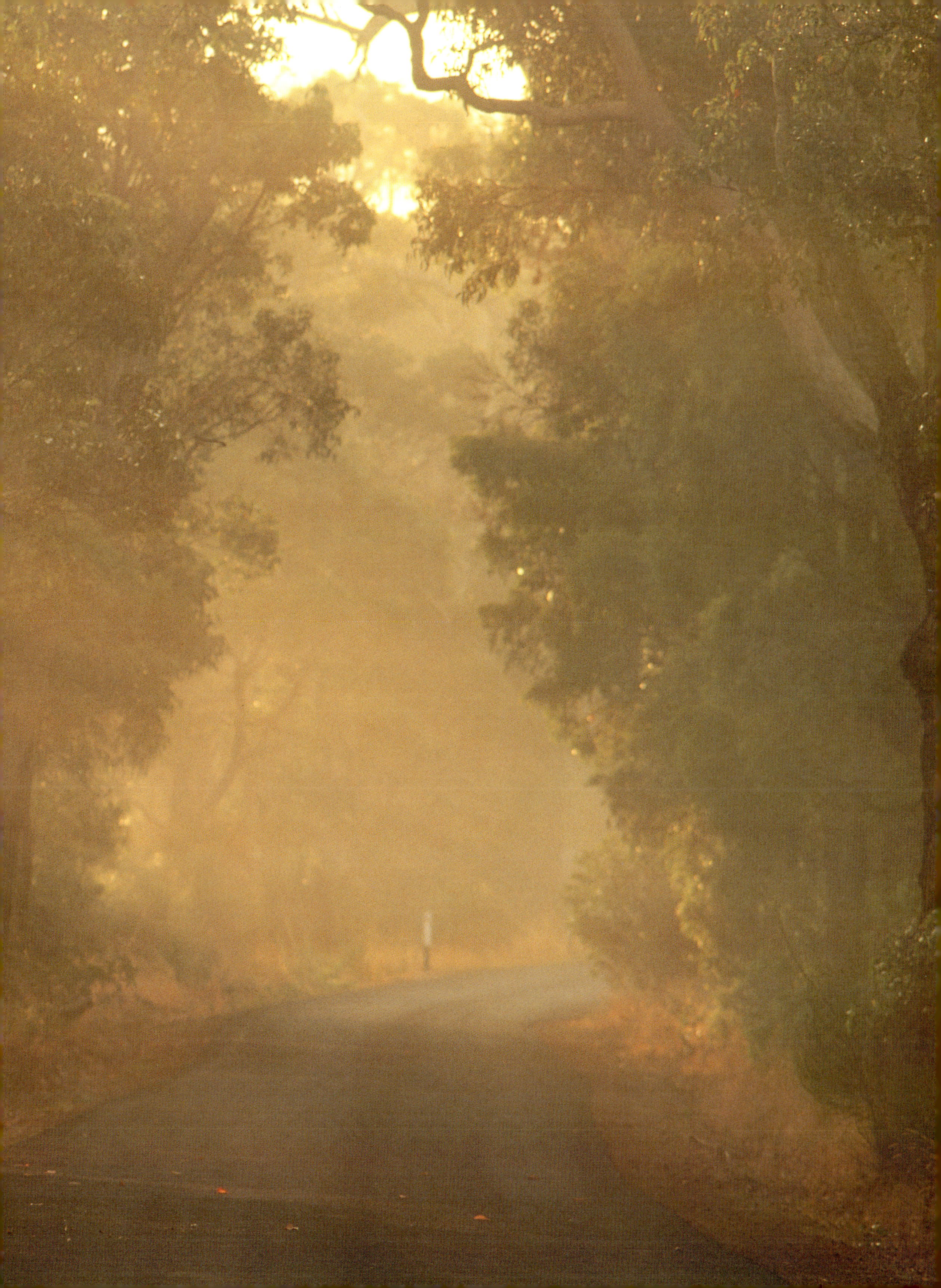

This is an area of contrast, where the relentless surges of two great oceans meet to confront the rugged south-west coast of Australia. The result is constant movement and change on sea and on land. On outcrops of granite and limestone, massive broken boulders crumble and tumble to the sea. Wide, gently rolling slopes covered in shrubs and grassy heath sweep to the coast, broken suddenly by soaring cliffs that rise from the shore below.

There is a constant battle between the ocean and the land. At first the land fortress resists, but eventually it yields. Over thousands of years, the wind and waves have shaped this distinctive part of the coast. Fresh chunks of granite and limestone that have fallen and lie broken and exposed are evidence that the process continues today.

Near the coast, low shrubs and heath are kept in neat trim by buffeting winds blowing straight off the sea, contrasting with the forests and dense bush on richer soils further inland. But even inland there is constant change and contrast. The impact of the prevailing winds that rip in from the west is clearly visible. Towering karri trees somehow manage to withstand them and stand tall in great forest clusters, but nuggetty shrubs, bushes and smaller trees, including marri and casuarina, are often bent twisted and crooked by the merciless winds.

When Europeans arrived dense bush and deep forests covered the district. As settlers pushed into the region the forests were gradually cleared to establish pasture, or logged to provide timber for export. In more recent times the landscape has changed once more as much of the pasture that once grazed livestock has become vineyards, and a lot of open pasture has been replanted with trees, both as a source of income and for windbreaks to protect the precious and sometimes fragile vines.

Page 43: Margaret River close to the river mouth at Prevelly.
Previous page: Fifty One Road, Wilyabrup.
Above: Wyadup Rocks overlooking Injidup Beach.
Overleaf: Near the mouth of Wilyabrup Brook.

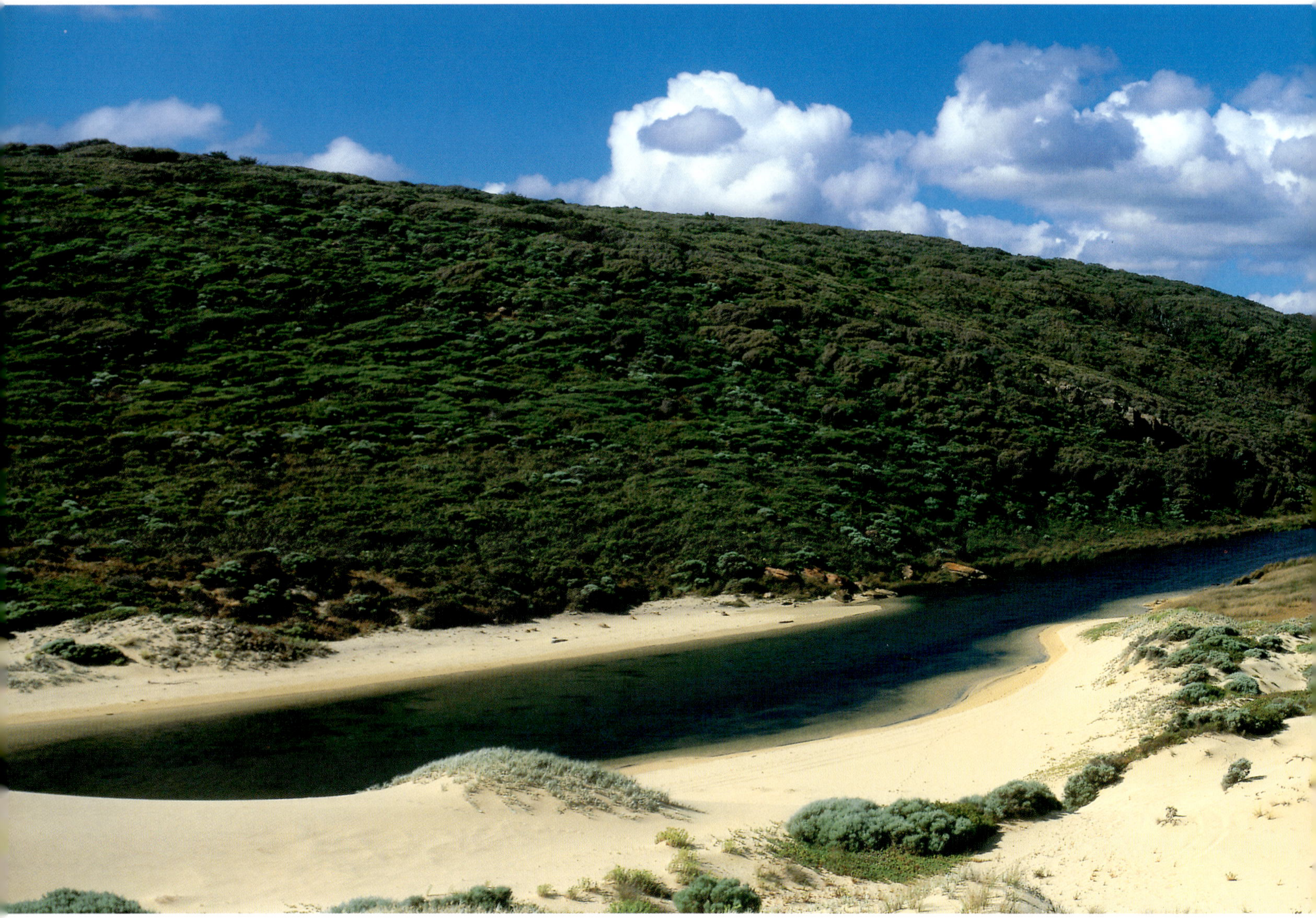

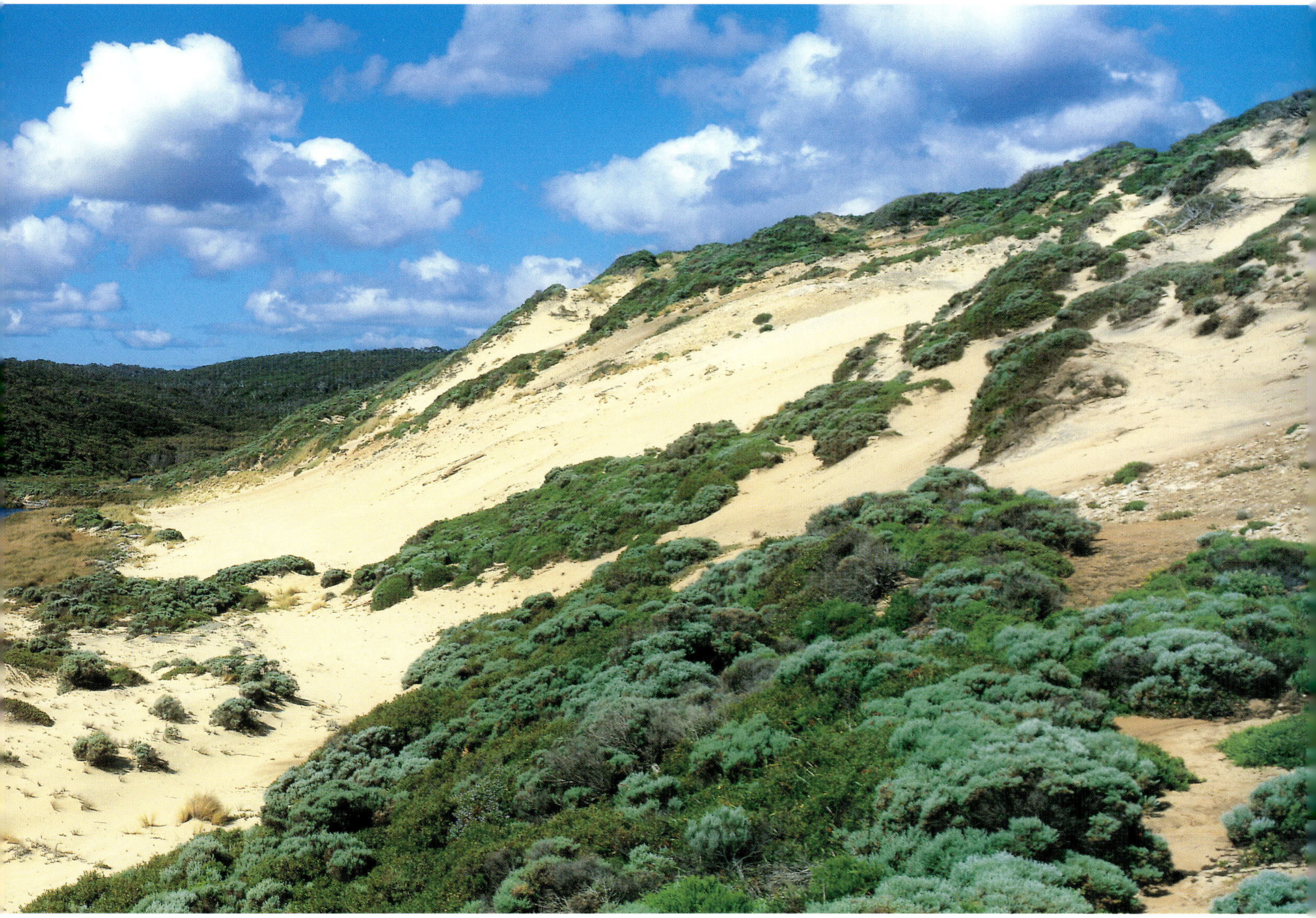

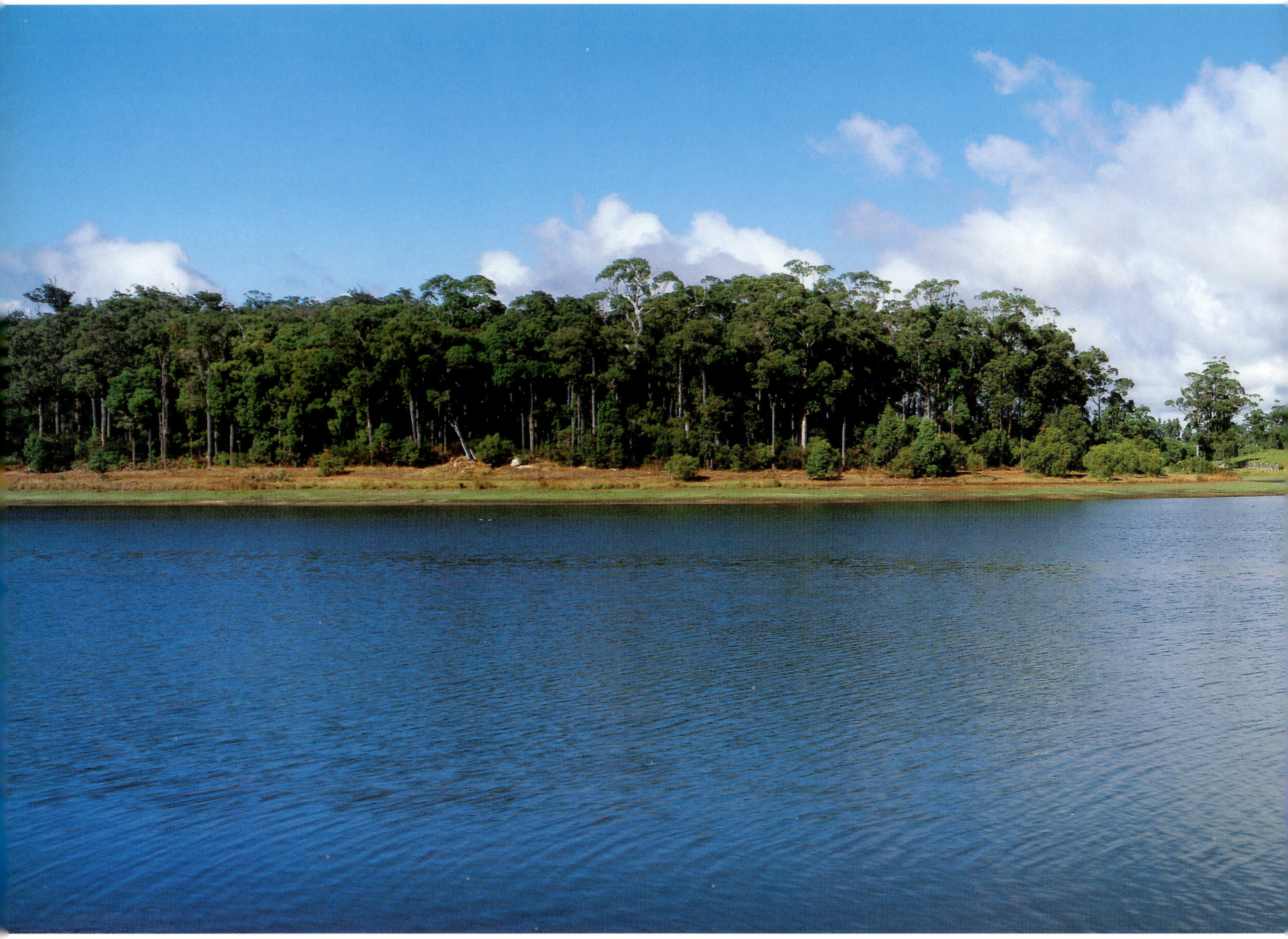

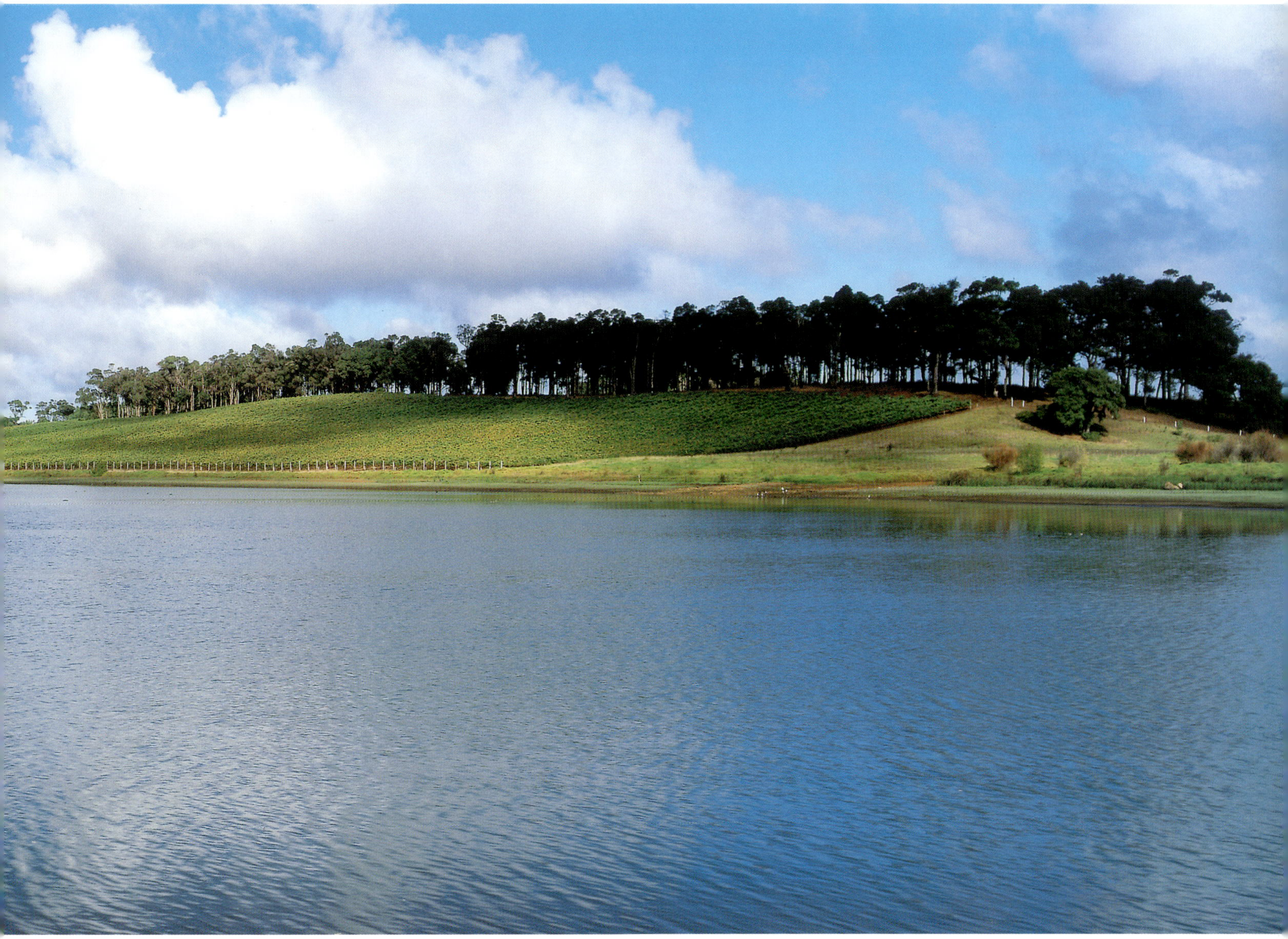

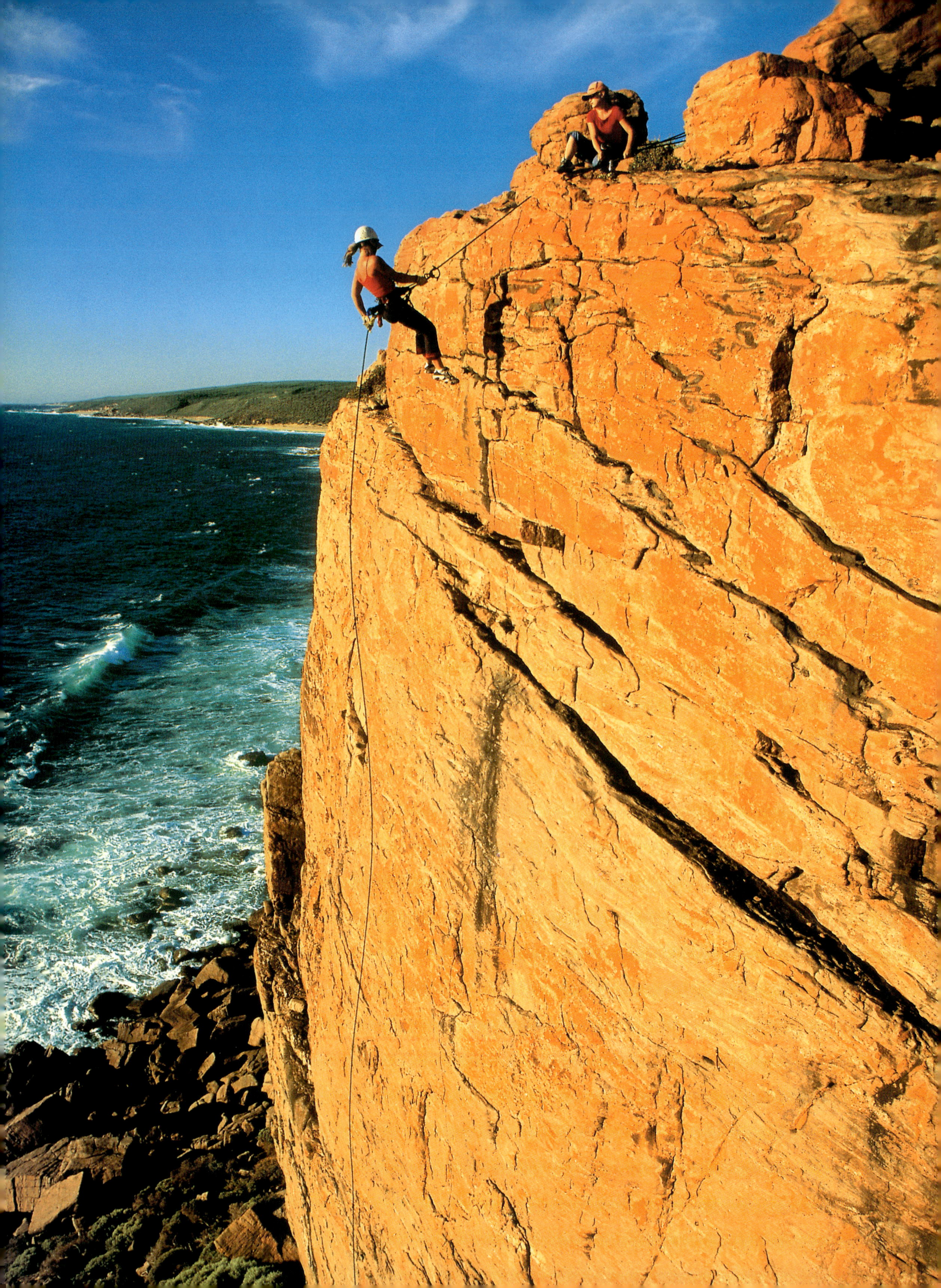

Previous page: Looking across the dam to the Devil's Lair vineyard.
Left: Abseiling down the Wilyabrup Cliffs (Claire Finucaine on the rope
supported by Karolina Puchalka at top).
Above: Aboriginal children, Loch and Maitland Scrimgeour, playing among the
sand dunes on Wilyabrup Beach. This area near the mouth of Wilyabrup
Brook is a place of cultural significance for the Wardandi.
Overleaf: Bunker Bay.

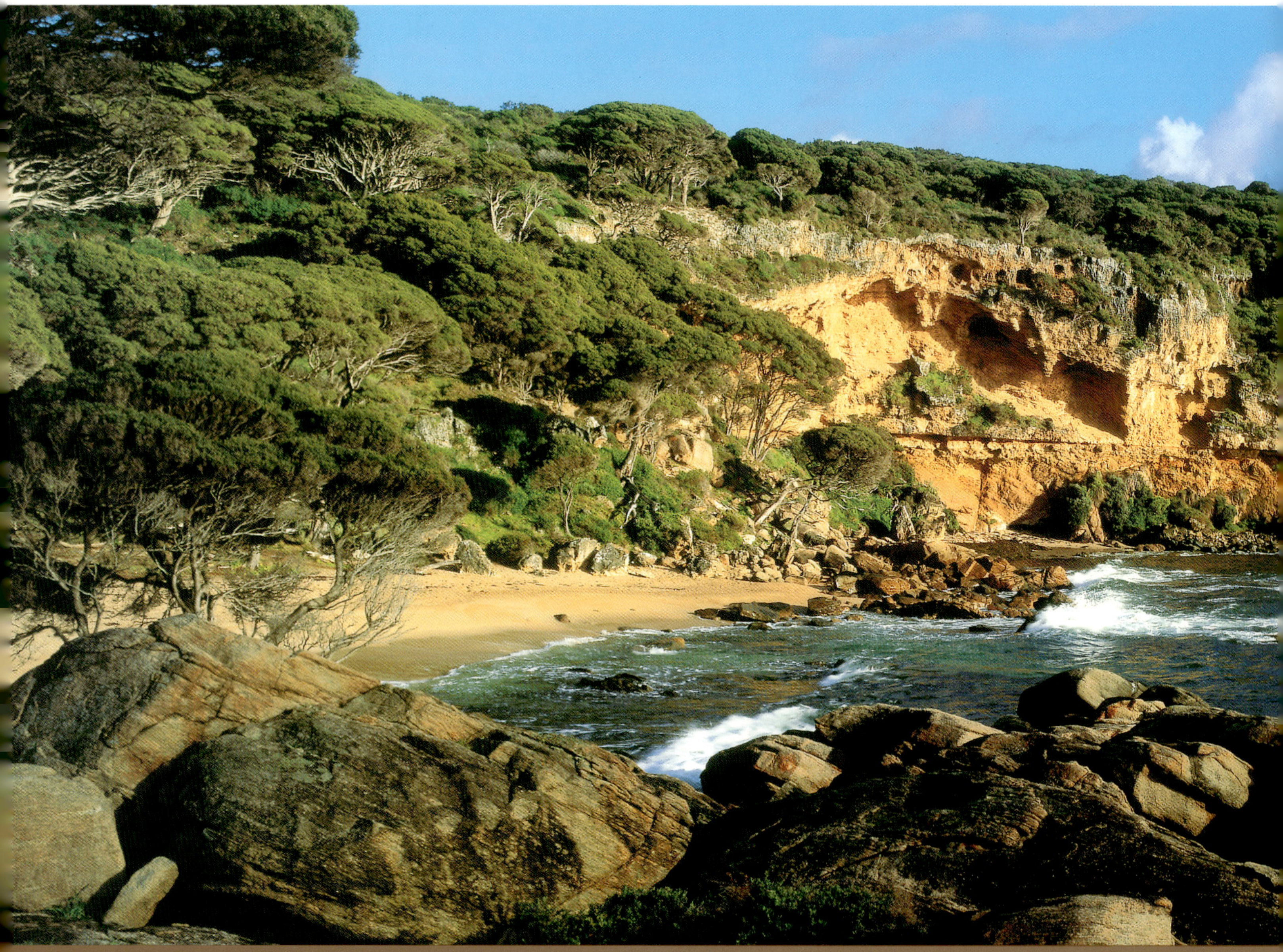

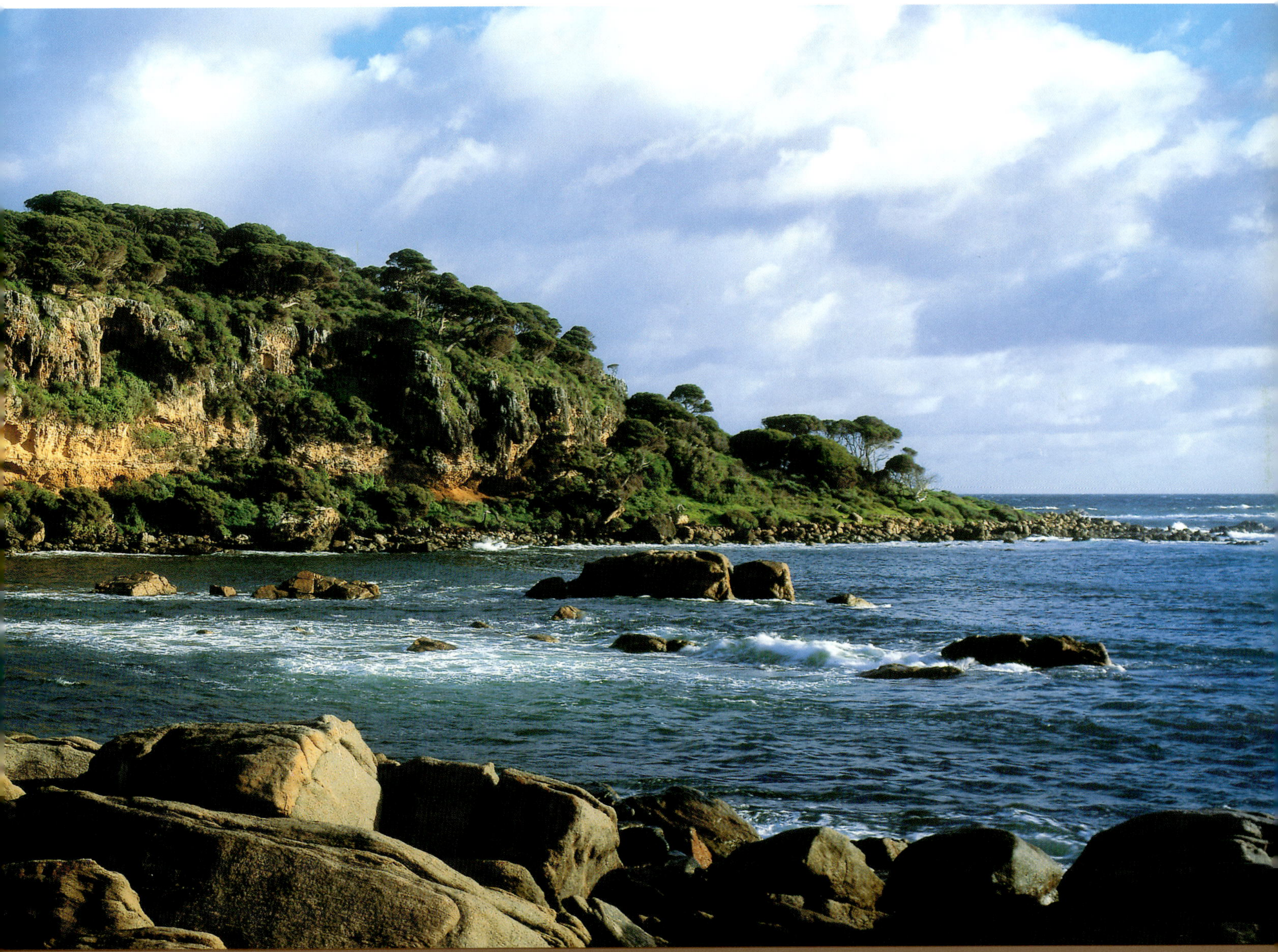

Caves

Beneath the surface of this region is another world — serene, dark and quiet. There is mystery and rare beauty here in the twisting honeycomb of caves and startling rock formations threading through the limestone. There are more than three hundred and fifty known caves, and probably many more, holding secrets revealed only to a few people.

The limestone and granite rock has provided the perfect raw material for nature to express itself as a sculptor, carving a labyrinth of caves over the centuries with the constant movement of water through rock and earth.

Some caves are easily accessible and provide experienced and novice cavers alike with the opportunity to see unique crystalline formations that are thousands of years old. Equally exciting, embedded in cave walls and ceilings are fossil remains that provide clues to some of the animals that once roamed this area. The most popular and accessible caves are Lake, Jewell, Mammoth, Yallingup and Moondyne. Many others can only be explored with experienced guides.

Mammoth Cave, which was first seen by Europeans in 1850, is only a few kilometres from the town of Margaret River. Within its massive cavern, and easily seen by visitors, are the remains of extinct animals, including the Tasmanian tiger (thylacine), huge wombat-like creatures and giant kangaroos. These prehistoric remains are more than thirty-five thousand years old.

Just a few kilometres south of Margaret River is Lake Cave. The first European record of it was made in 1867 by Fanny Bussell, a member of one of the district's prominent pioneering families. Apparently the sixteen-year-old Fanny stumbled on the crater entrance while out looking for stray cattle. A series of stairways and paths descend through the crater, where giant karri trees grow, and into a setting of immense beauty. The central feature is the lake, which never dries and is surrounded by delicate straw and shawl formations of stalagmites and stalactites. However, the most remarkable feature of Lake Cave is the suspended table which hangs just above the lake from two big columns. There is a sense of peace and calm within this quiet dome, with the eerie stillness of the lake reflecting the glittering formations that surround it.

Just north of Augusta is Jewell Cave, which has the longest straw stalactite in a tourist cave in the world. The Organ Pipes Cavern and Jewell Basket formations look spectacular under floodlights. The huge cavernous halls of Jewell Cave were not known to Europeans until 1957. However, when the fossil remains of a Tasmanian tiger dated to about 25,000 BC were discovered, Jewell Cave became a significant research site.

Near Jewell Cave is Moondyne Cave, named after Western Australia's only bushranger of the nineteenth century, Moondyne Joe, who is believed to have hidden in the cave. This cave provides a more

Above: Karri tress growing in the crater at the entrance to Lake Cave.
Overleaf: Stalactites form the Organ Pipes, one of the highlights of Jewell Cave.

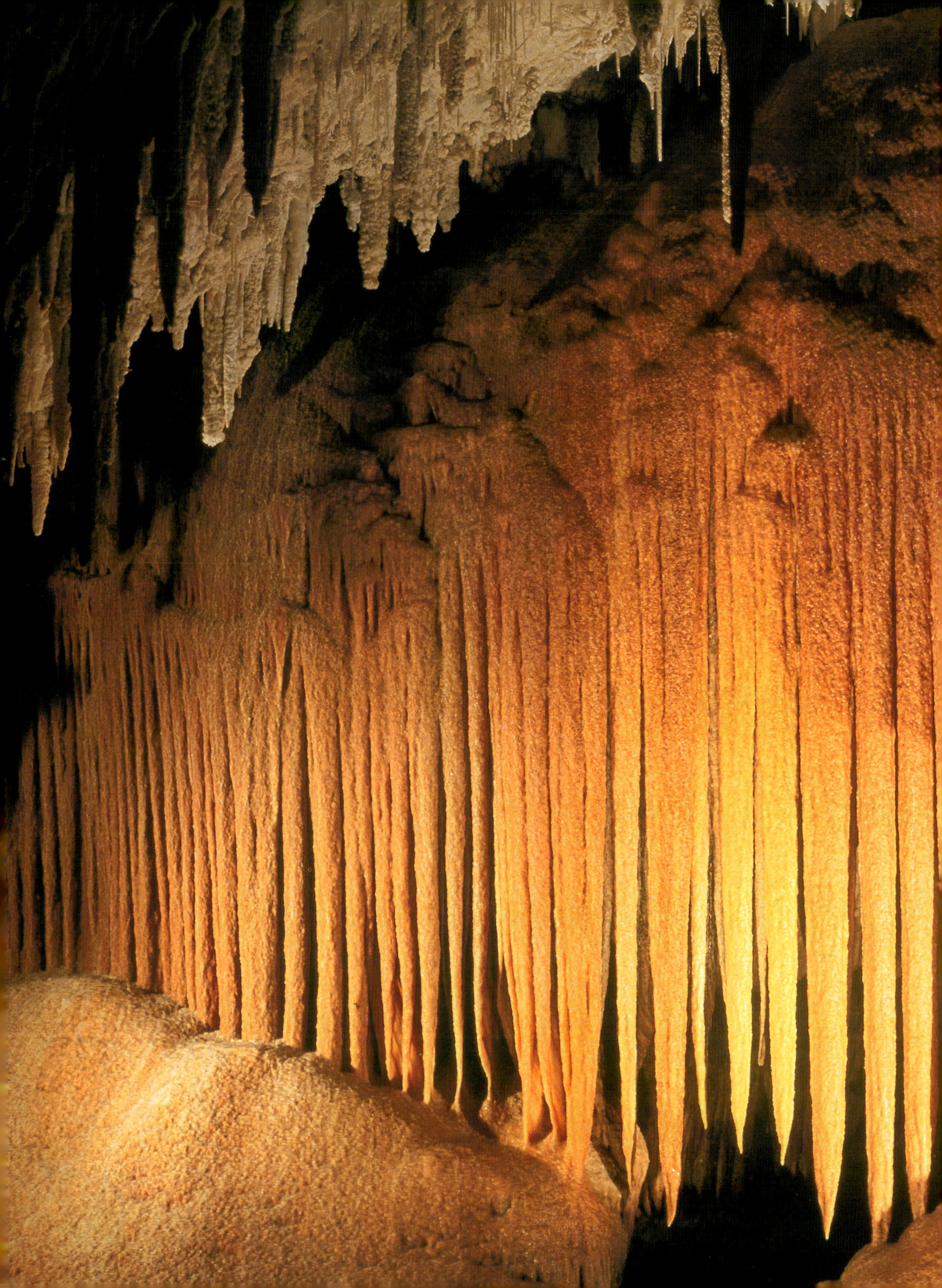

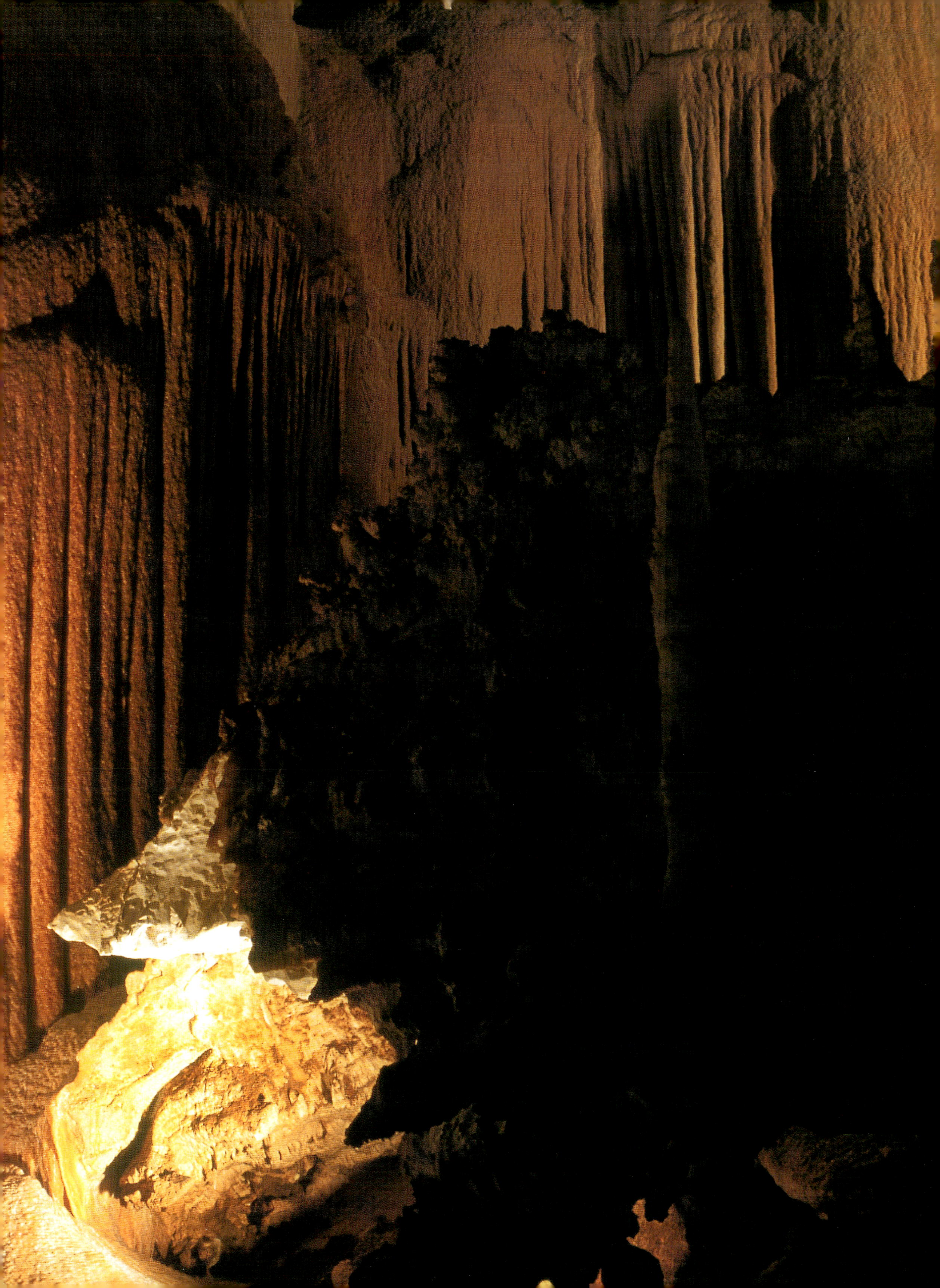

Above: The Suspended Table formation in Lake Cave.
Right: Stalactites hang from the ceiling of Jewell Cave in a spectacular formation known as the Karri Forest.

challenging experience for the adventurous caver. After donning overalls, helmet and miner's light, visitors can feel the exhilaration of exploring this hidden world.

Yallingup Cave is also known as Ngilgi's Cave. This Aboriginal name has its origin in the legend of the battles between Ngilgi, the good spirit of the sea, and Wolgine, the bad spirit of the cave. According to legend Ngilgi fought Wolgine and eventually won the cave. Ngilgi Cave was discovered by Europeans in 1899 and tours began in 1900. So popular did the tours become that nearby Caves House was opened to cater for visitors.

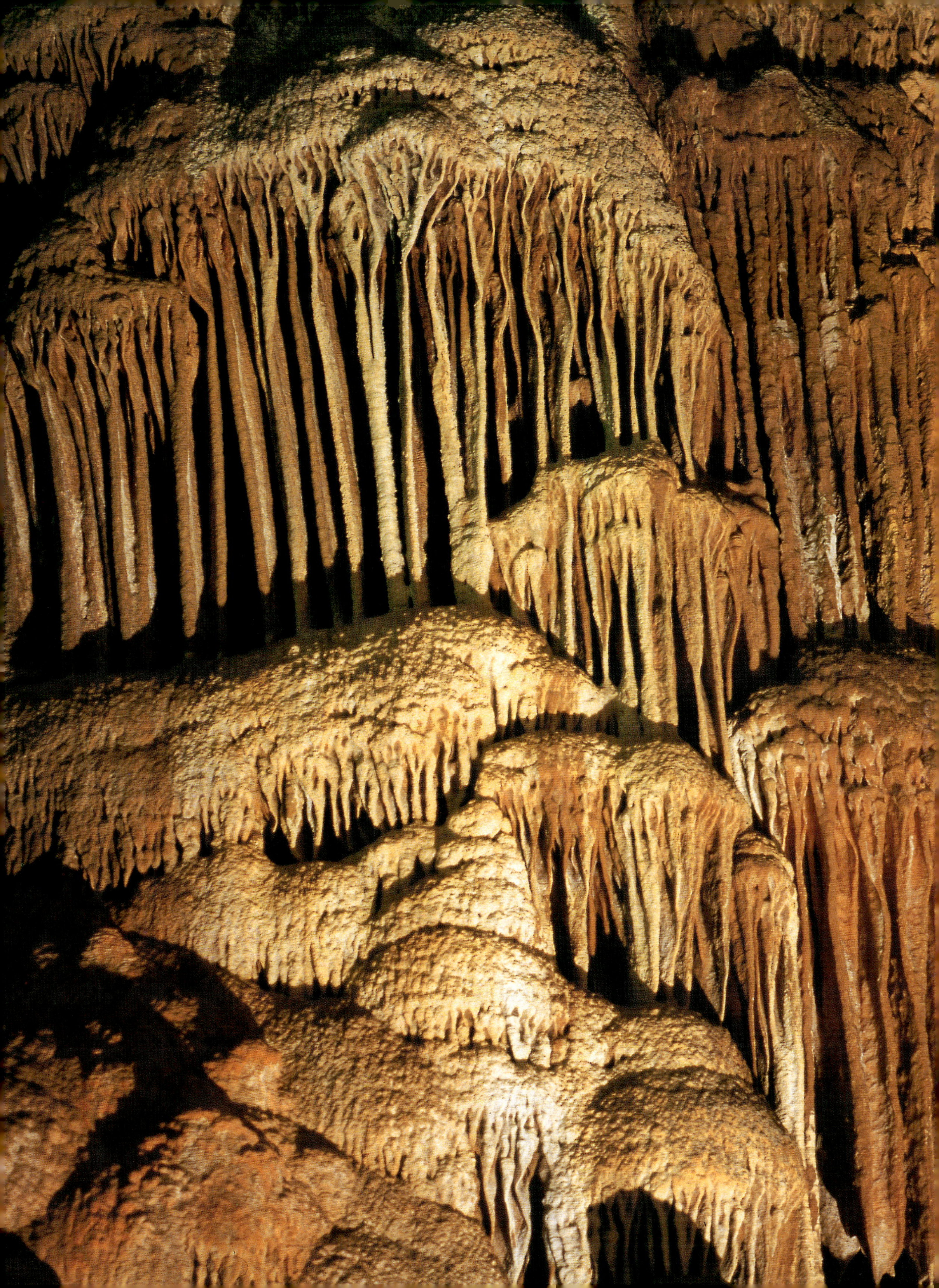

Boranup Forest

Today Boranup Forest is popular for camping and picnics, and for bushwalks along its winding gravel roads and paths. The karri trees rise tall and straight from the dense forest floor, towering to nearly seventy metres to form a canopy over this special place. There are even taller trees in some of the more inaccessible parts of the forest.

It is hard to imagine now that about a hundred years ago this tranquil and serenely beautiful environment was a place of frenetic activity as the rich source of timber was logged, supporting the nearby town of Karridale and its eight hundred or so men, women and children. Today's still, quiet air was filled with the gnawing sound of saws and thud of axes, punctuated by the crackle and crash of falling giants that made the ground tremble and shake. The puff of the steam trains that took the huge logs to the nearby Karridale timber mill blew a trail of smoke as the shrill of the whistle announced its passing.

The Karridale mill, which was the most modern and efficient in the state, operated for nearly thirty years until 1913, providing timber for the waiting ships on the six-hundred-metre long Hamelin Jetty nearby.

Sadly, raging fires whipped through Boranup Forest in 1961, destroying what remained of the town of Karridale, and with it an important link to a piece of history.

Boranup is a place of paradox. Its very name, which is an Aboriginal word for 'place of the male dingo', takes on a perverse character when you realise that dingoes were systematically exterminated in the South-West many years ago because they were seen as sheep killers. Even the majestic karri trees are not where they would normally be. This is the westernmost spot on the Australian mainland for karris, which prefer deep rich red loamy soils or the less fertile grey sands. Here they grow in limestone soils.

And the forest, which appears unspoiled, a preserved piece of natural flora, is in fact a regrowth forest, long since recovered and thriving after the logging and milling.

Above: Boranup Forest in autumn.
Overleaf: Boranup Forest in spring.

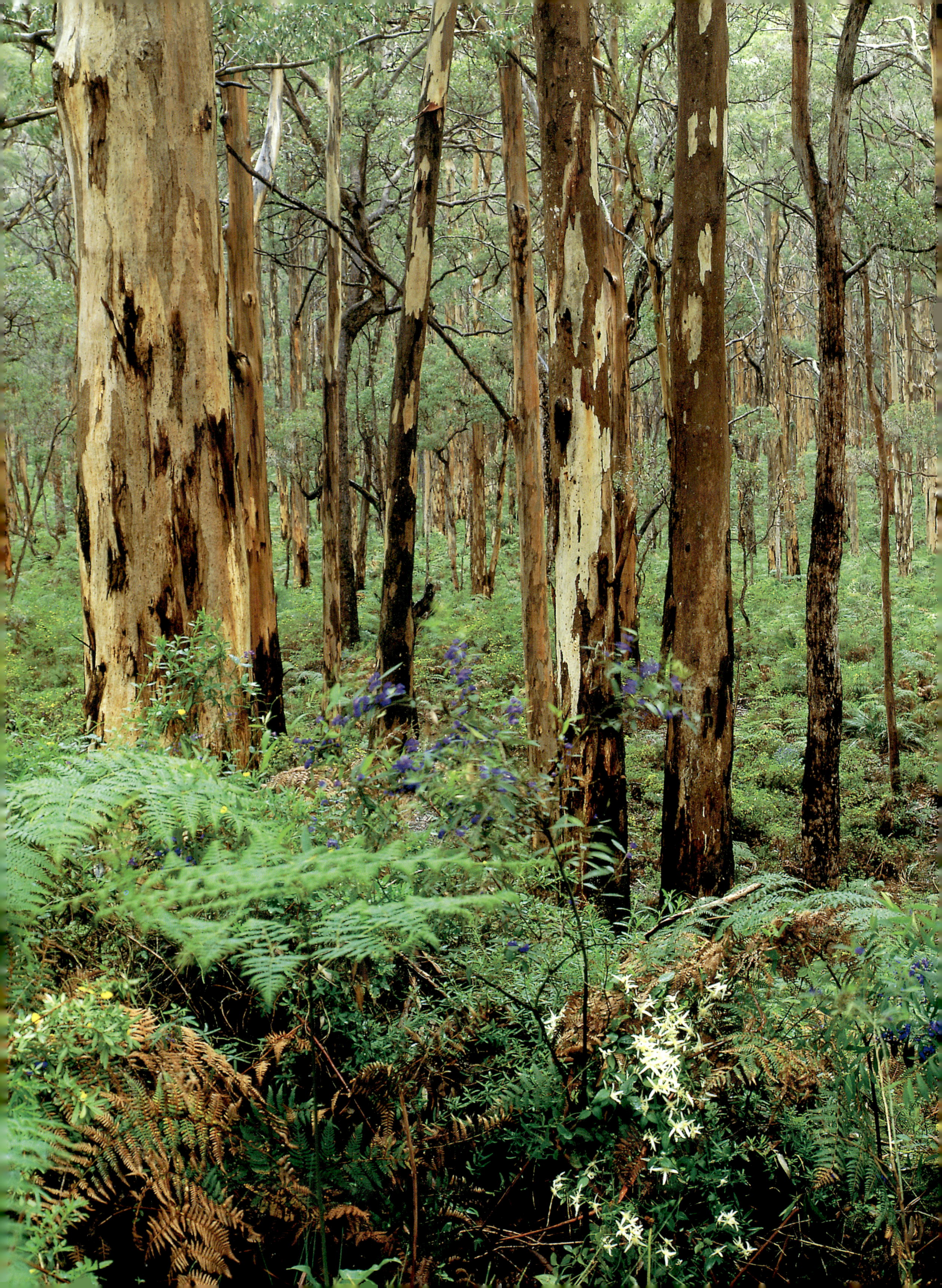

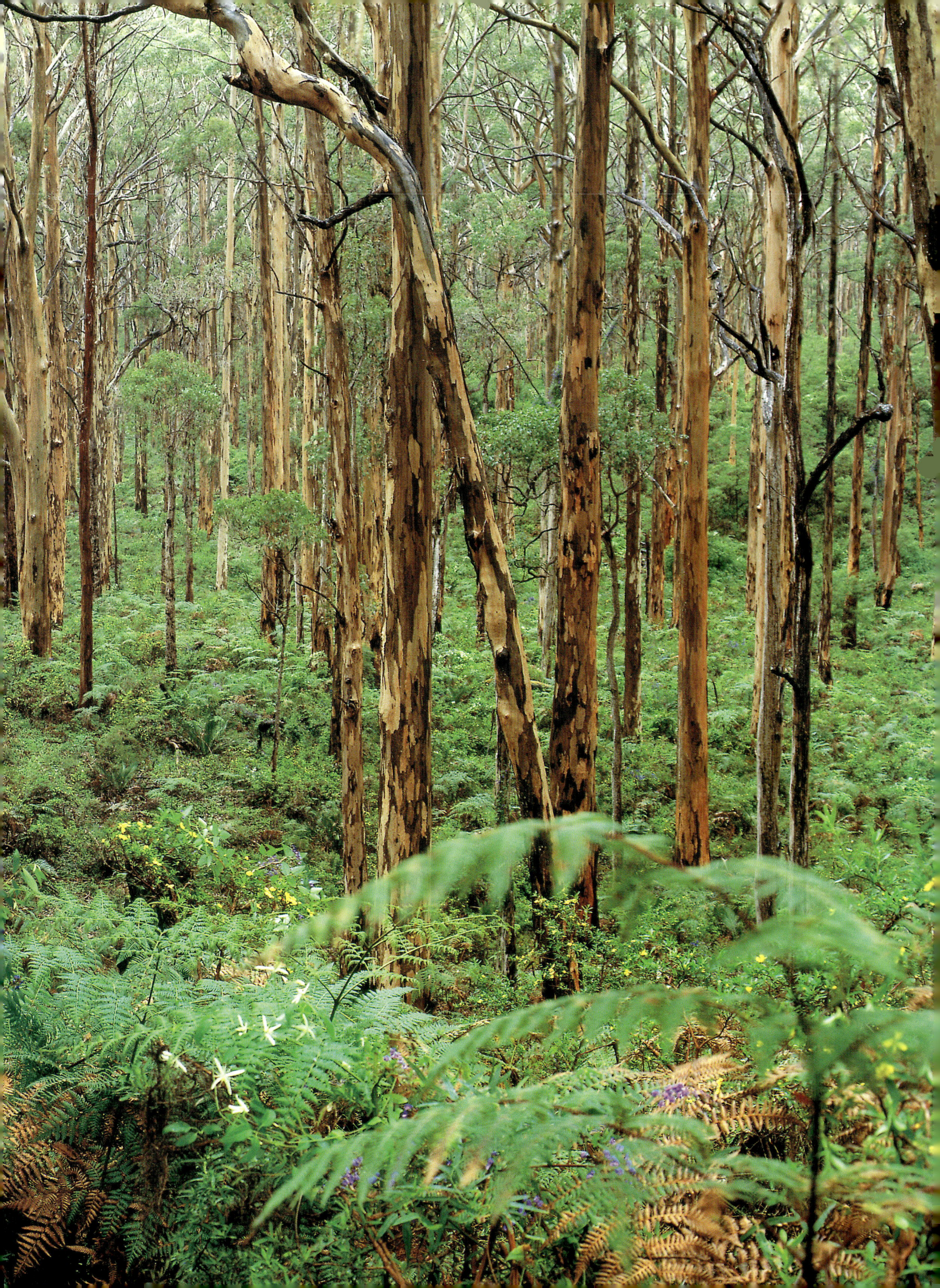

3. The flora and fauna

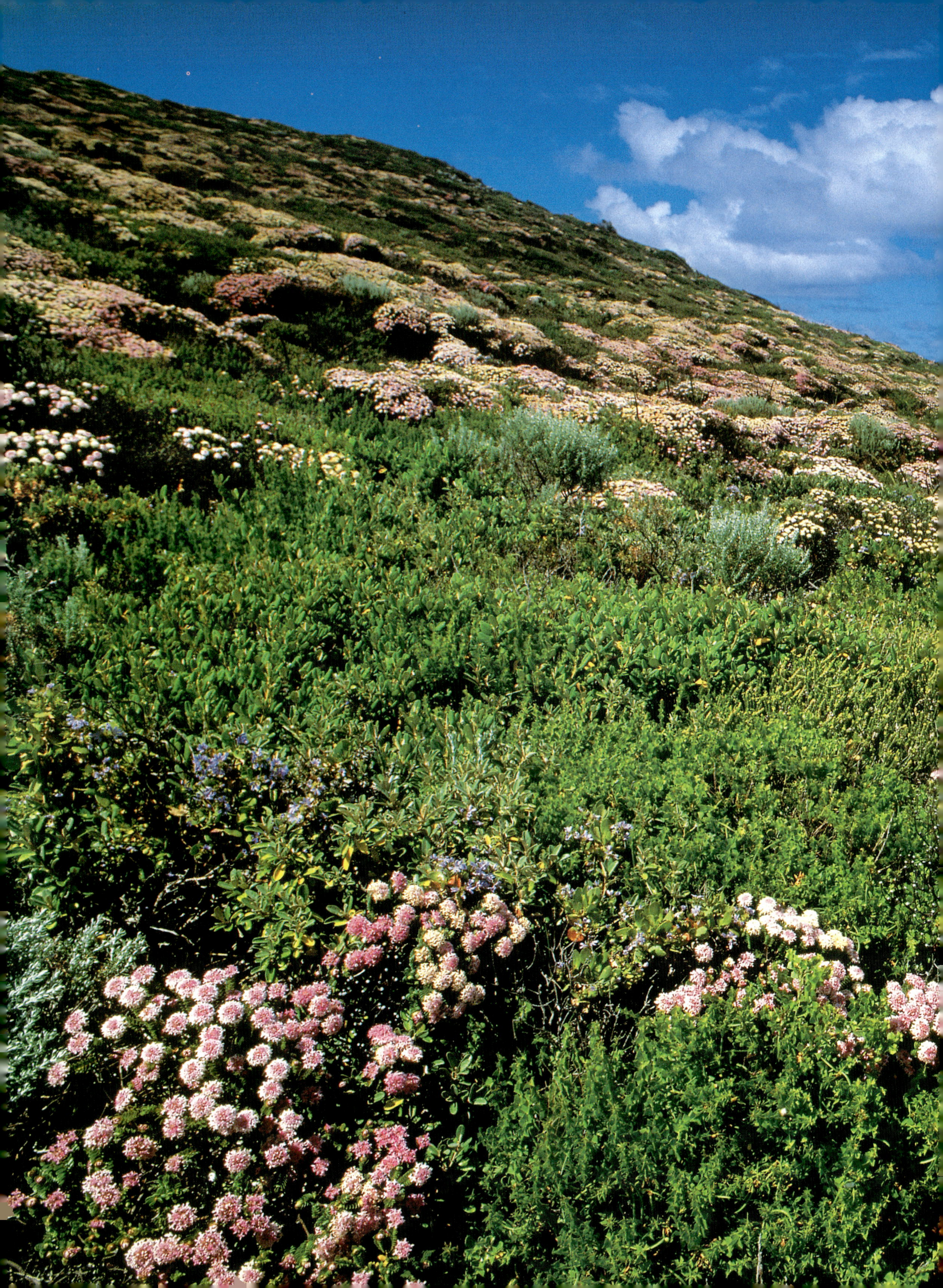

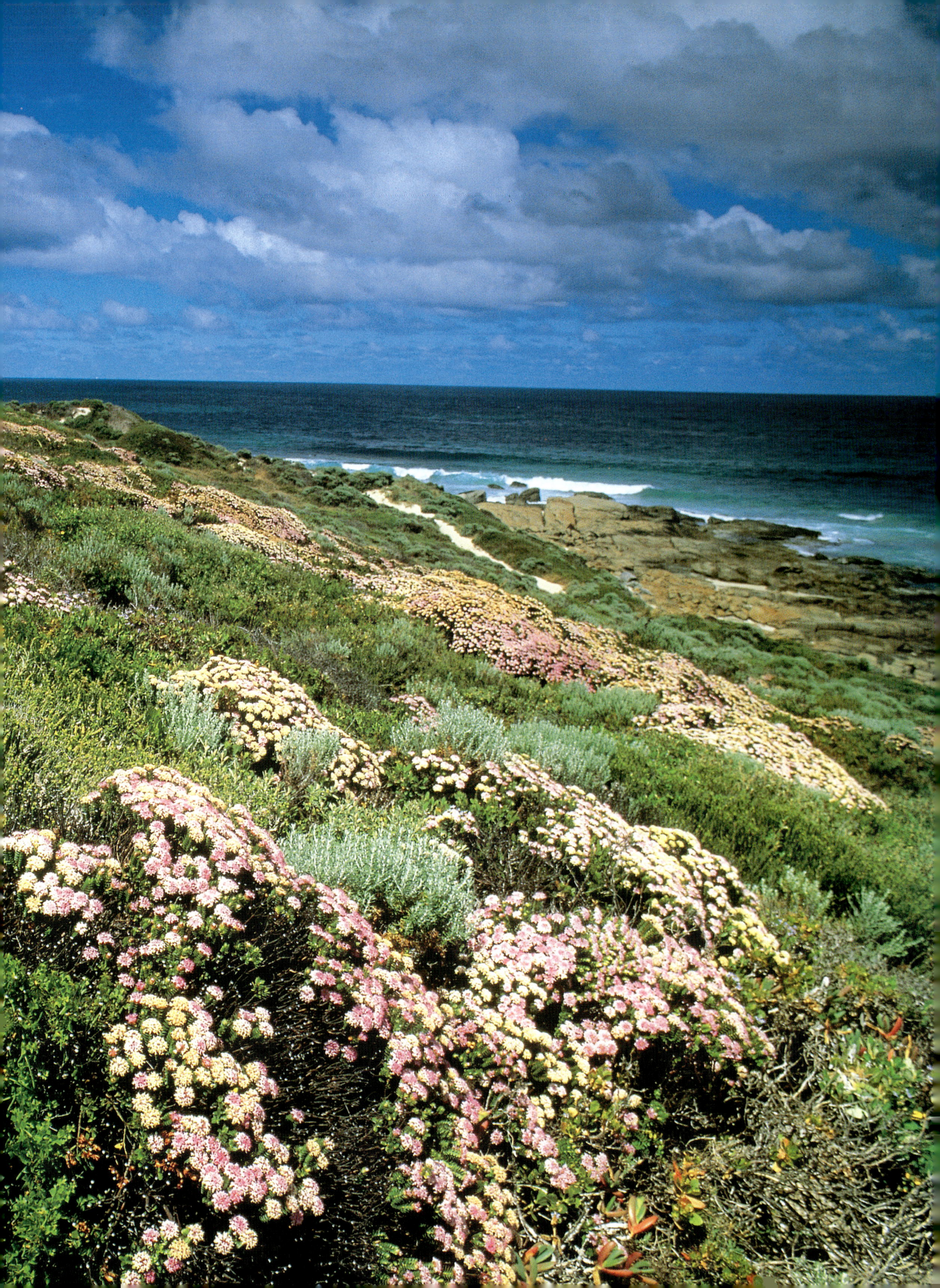

The Cape region is rich in Australia's unique and varied flora and fauna, and contains one of the most diverse ranges of flora found anywhere in the world. Some species are found only in specific sites within this very small part of the continent.

Page 67: Wildflowers in the Leeuwin-Naturaliste National Park with the Augusta Lighthouse in the background.
Previous page: Spring wildflowers at Gas Bay, south of Prevelly.
Above: A summer shot of the Augusta Lighthouse, built by timber magnate M C Davies in 1896.
Right: Sunset over Augusta Lighthouse on Cape Leeuwin.

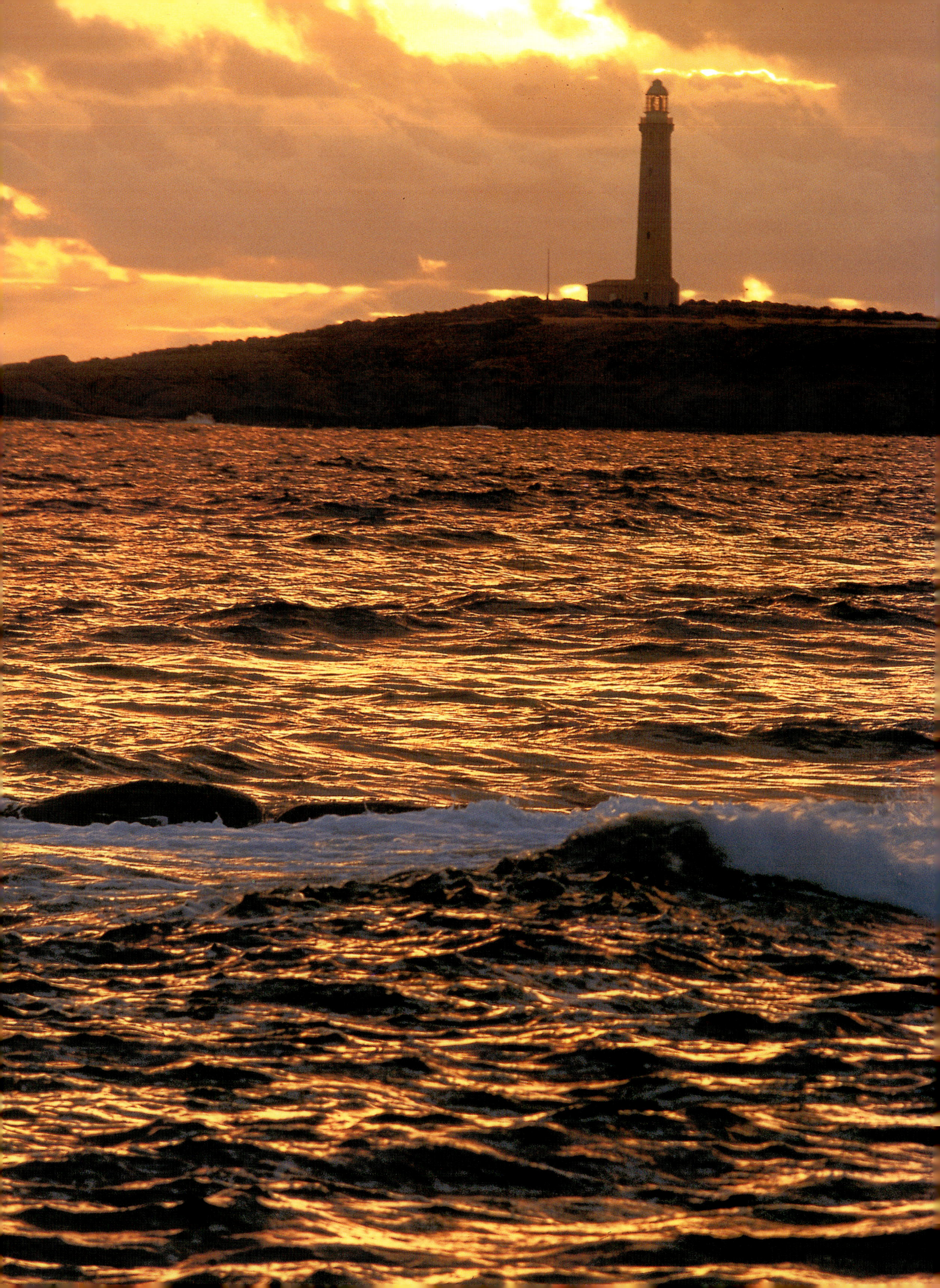

Flora

Of the eleven thousand species of flora known in Western Australia, more than seventy-five per cent grow in the South-West. Many are found nowhere else in the world.

The region is probably most famous for its trees: karri, jarrah and marri. Standing above the rest is the karri, one of the world's tallest trees, which can grow to ninety metres. It is also one of the most distinctive with its straight light grey and reddish-brown trunk. Jarrah is renowned for its use in furniture and floorboards, where the deep dark red grain can be polished to a high finish. Its gnarled surface and twisting trunk set it apart from its taller neighbour.

Marri is distinctive for its rough bark and large nuts. It can vary in height quite considerably, depending on the vagaries of the wind. Its abundant white flowers provide a considerable source of food for birds. Casuarinas and peppermint trees are also found throughout the region in good numbers.

From late August, small splashes of bright colour start to appear among the dominant greens, browns and grey of winter forest and coastal heath. The warmer weather of spring then brings out the full spectrum of the paintbox as the state's famous wildflowers reveal their extraordinary range and diversity against a backdrop of different shades of green.

Among the most brilliant and varied are the orchids. There are more than a hundred different species of orchids in the Cape region, most commonly flowering in spring, although some can be found throughout the year. These extraordinary plants have adapted to a variety of terrain, from the exposed coastal areas to sheltered spots deep within the forest and bush.

Some of the better known and most distinctive include the purple enamel orchid with its striking shiny flowers; the soft muted yellow donkey orchid with its distinctive large twin leaves; and the brilliant yellow cowslip orchid, the most recognisable and common of the spider orchids, often seen in clumps of thousands of bright yellow plants.

There are also many other species, including the world famous kangaroo paws, wattles, banksias, grevilleas, hakeas and hoveas.

Right: Orchids at Quindalup.

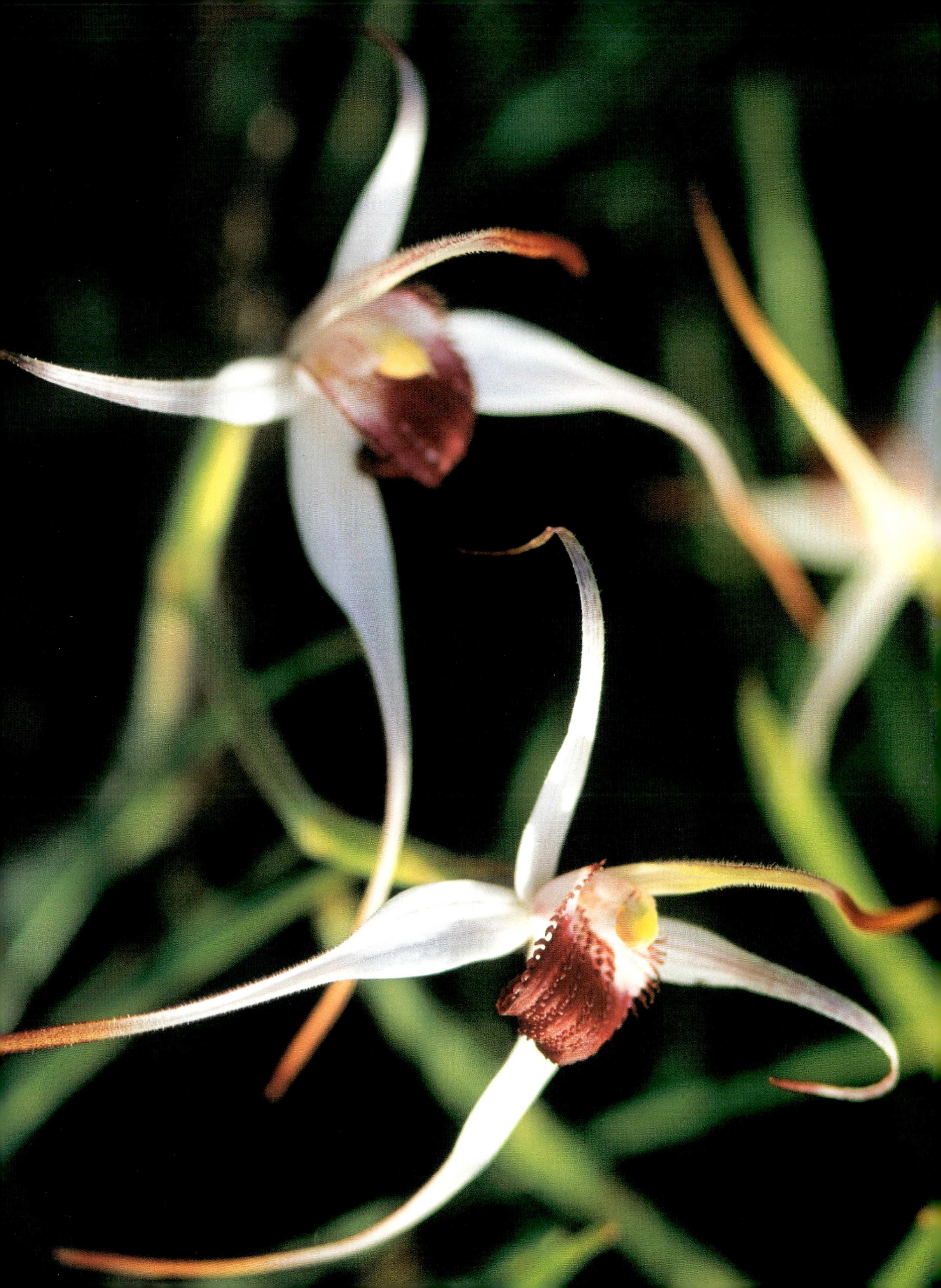

Above: Sunset near the outskirts of Margaret River.
Right: Statuesque karris spotlit at Karriview Lodge.

74

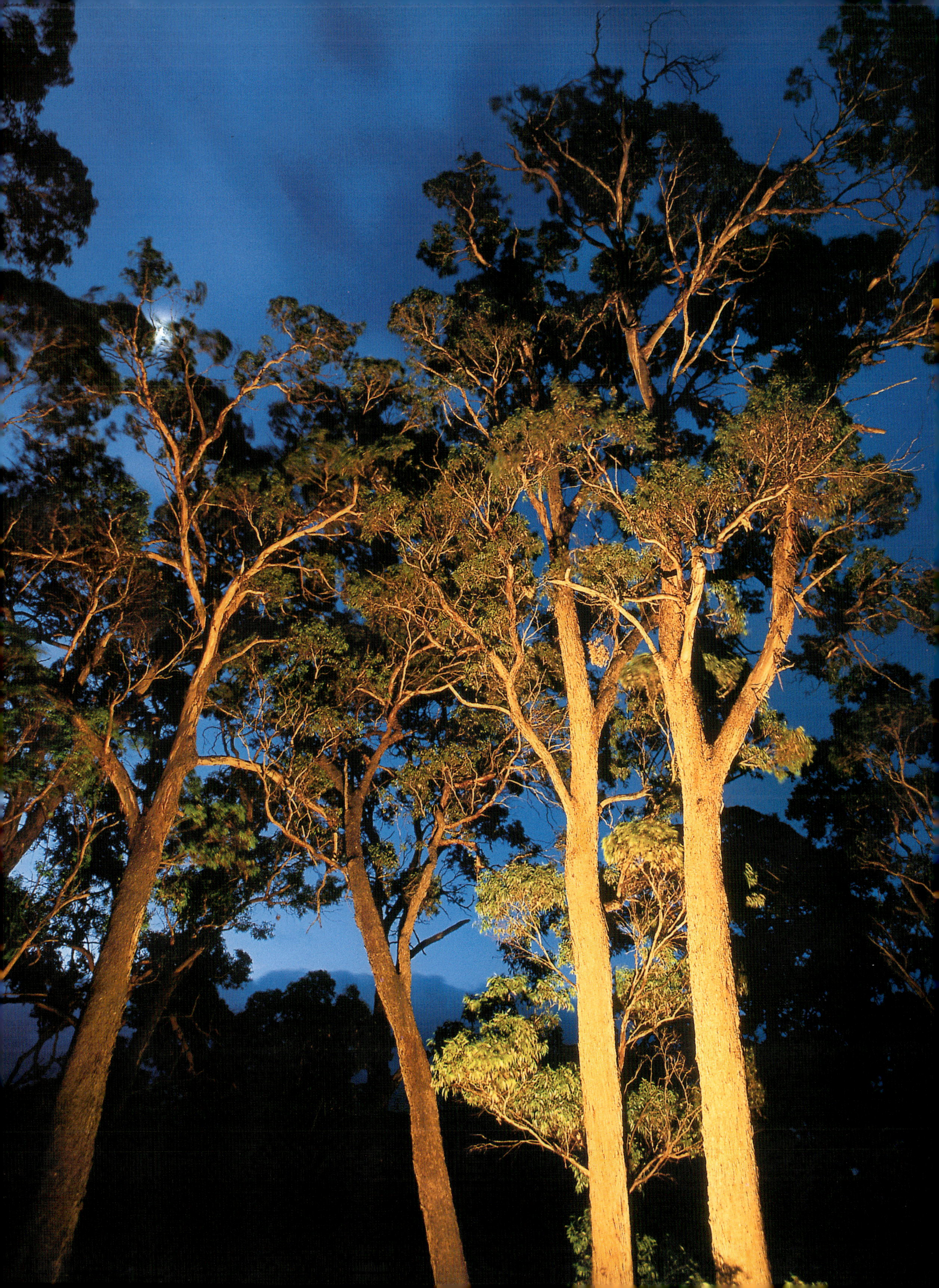

The birds

From coast to forests, across open heath and farmland areas, the region is both a permanent and temporary home to many species of birds. Some are migratory and visit only briefly to nest, or perhaps stay a little longer, but for most this is their home.

Among those found near the coast, often on rocky outcrops, are cormorants, herons, petrels and albatross. On the beaches, exposed reefs and cliffs are plovers and egrets which nest and feed on the coast. There are vast numbers of the common silver gull, while the pied cormorant, Caspian tern and crested tern are in healthy numbers and feed on the abundant marine life in these rich waters. The Pacific gull is less common.

Further from the sea, on the open heath with its low coastal shrubs, are wrens, kites and falcons; in the pastoral areas are eagles, ducks and parrots; and among the forests are cockatoos, fairy wrens, purple-crowned lorikeets, the common white-naped honeyeater, robins such as the white-breasted robin, the tawny frogmouth and the red-eared firetail.

No discussion of the birds of the region would be complete without mention of the silver-eye, the scourge of winemakers. It is one of Australia's most common birds, with a distinctive silvery white rim around its eyes, an olive-green back and a white belly. Its fondness for ripe fruit has made it an enemy of orchardists and grape growers throughout the South-West. When the marris don't blossom silver-eyes descend onto the vines and gorge their way through the precious fruit.

Right: A juvenile gull at Cosy Corner near Augusta.

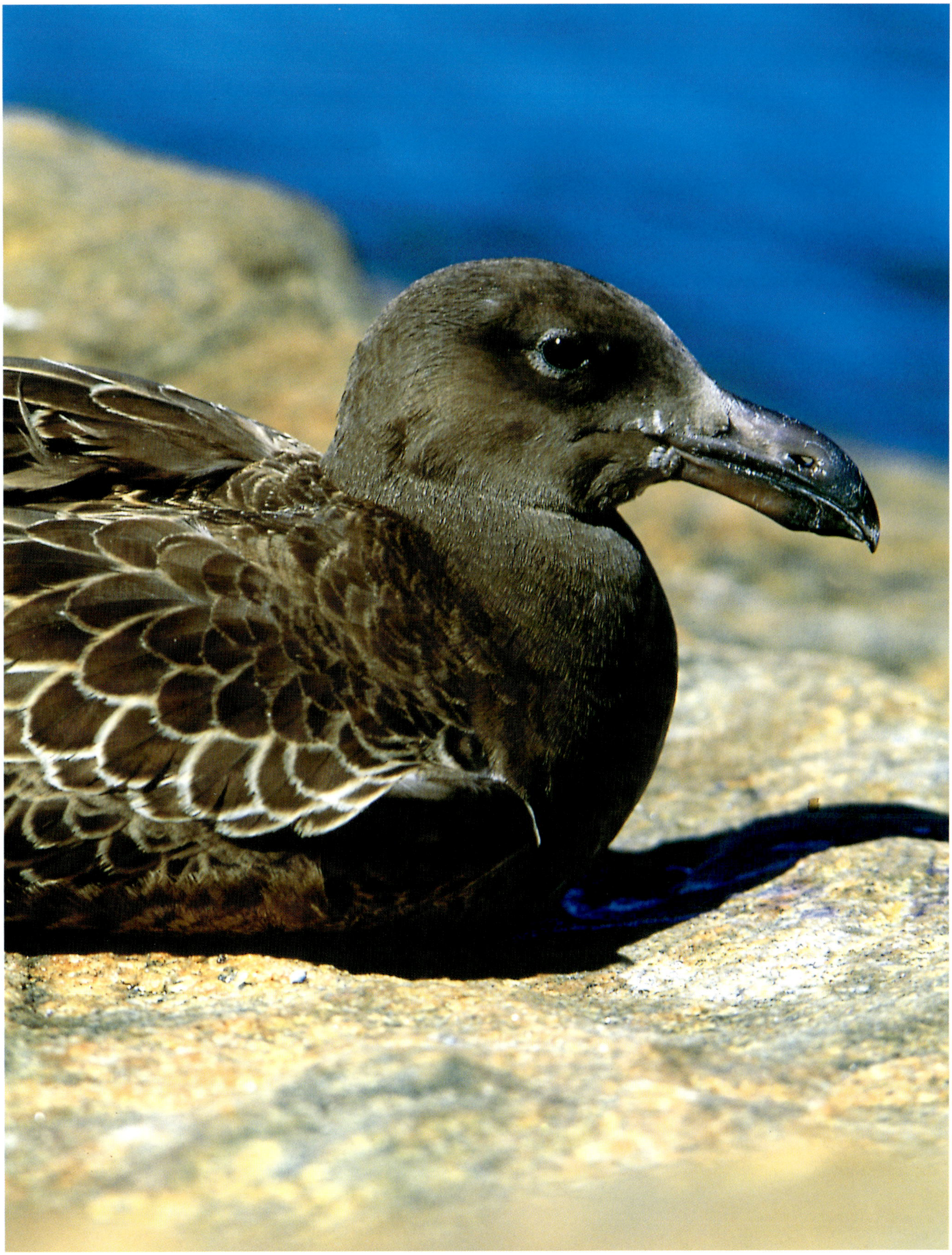

Fauna

From the timid and appealing kangaroo and possum to the feared and highly venomous tiger snake and dugite, the theme of extreme contrast in this region is reiterated. Not all the reptiles are dangerous however; one of the most common is the bobtail goanna, a short and sluggish animal often seen crawling slowly across roads. Beware its powerful jaws!

Native animals are usually in more danger from humans than the other way around. Increasing numbers of people, with their dogs and cats, contribute to the significant threat to the native fauna of the Cape where natural habitats have been logged or cleared to make way for pasture, vineyards and housing developments. Increased traffic in the region claims frequent road casualties. Kangaroos are the most affected, but many other native animals are killed under the glare of car and truck lights.

Domestic dogs and cats are a major problem. Cats, in particular, are responsible for killing huge numbers of native animals, and have brought some species to the point of extinction. Foxes, too, which were introduced many years ago, are still widespread and pose a continuing threat to native fauna.

Right: Kangaroo amongst the vines at Sandalford.
Overleaf: Kangaroos on the cliff tops at Moses Rock.

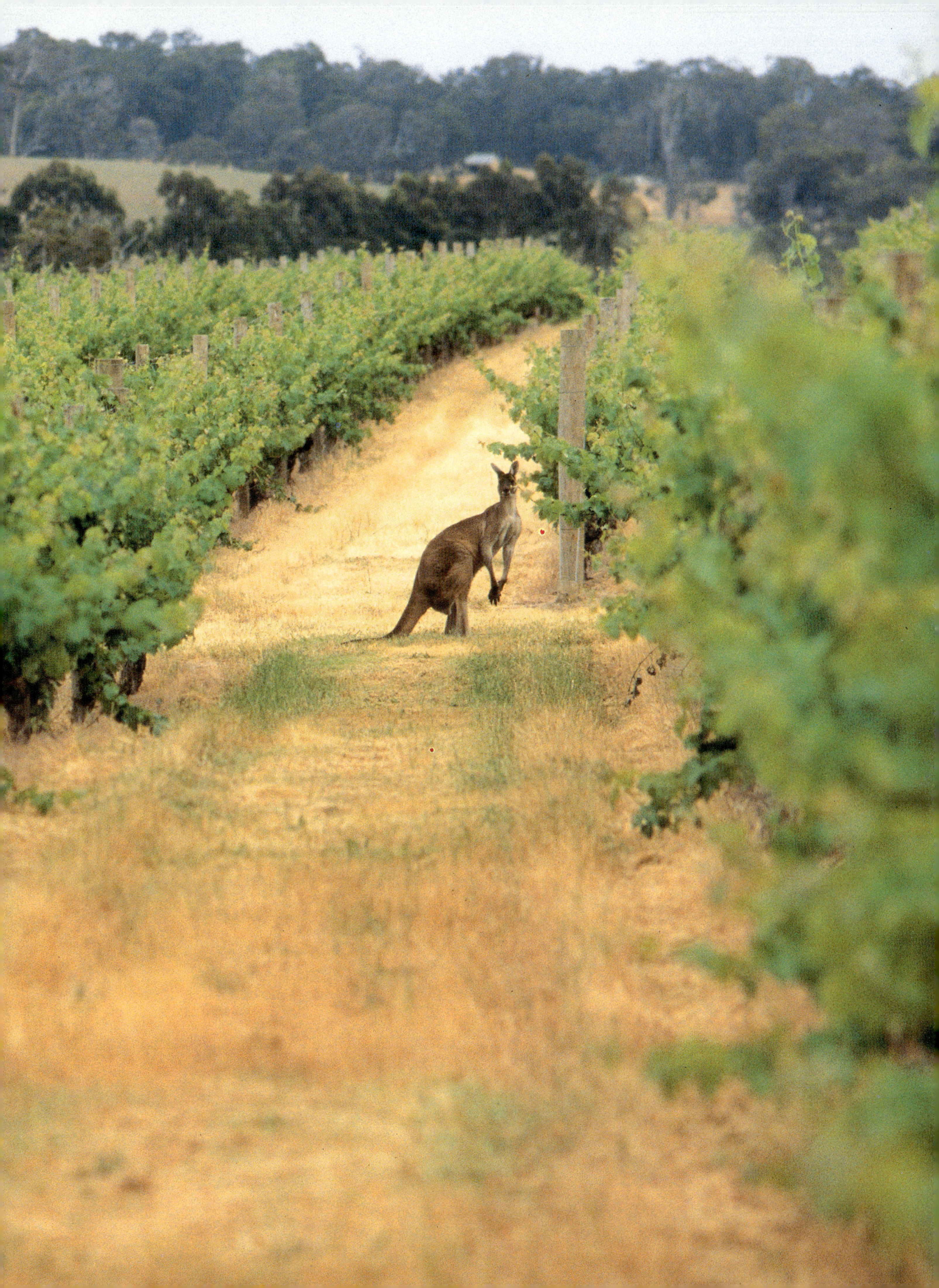

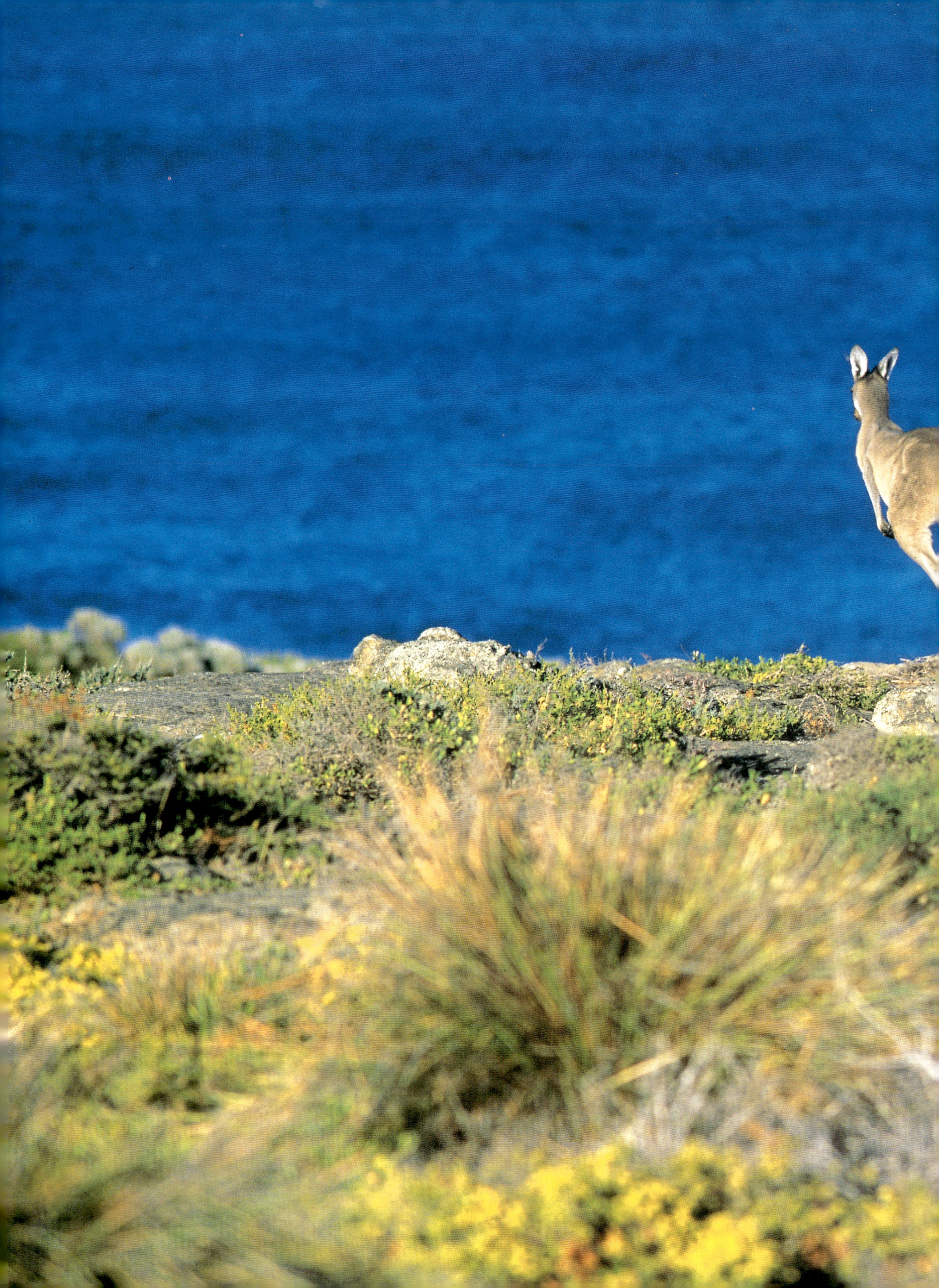

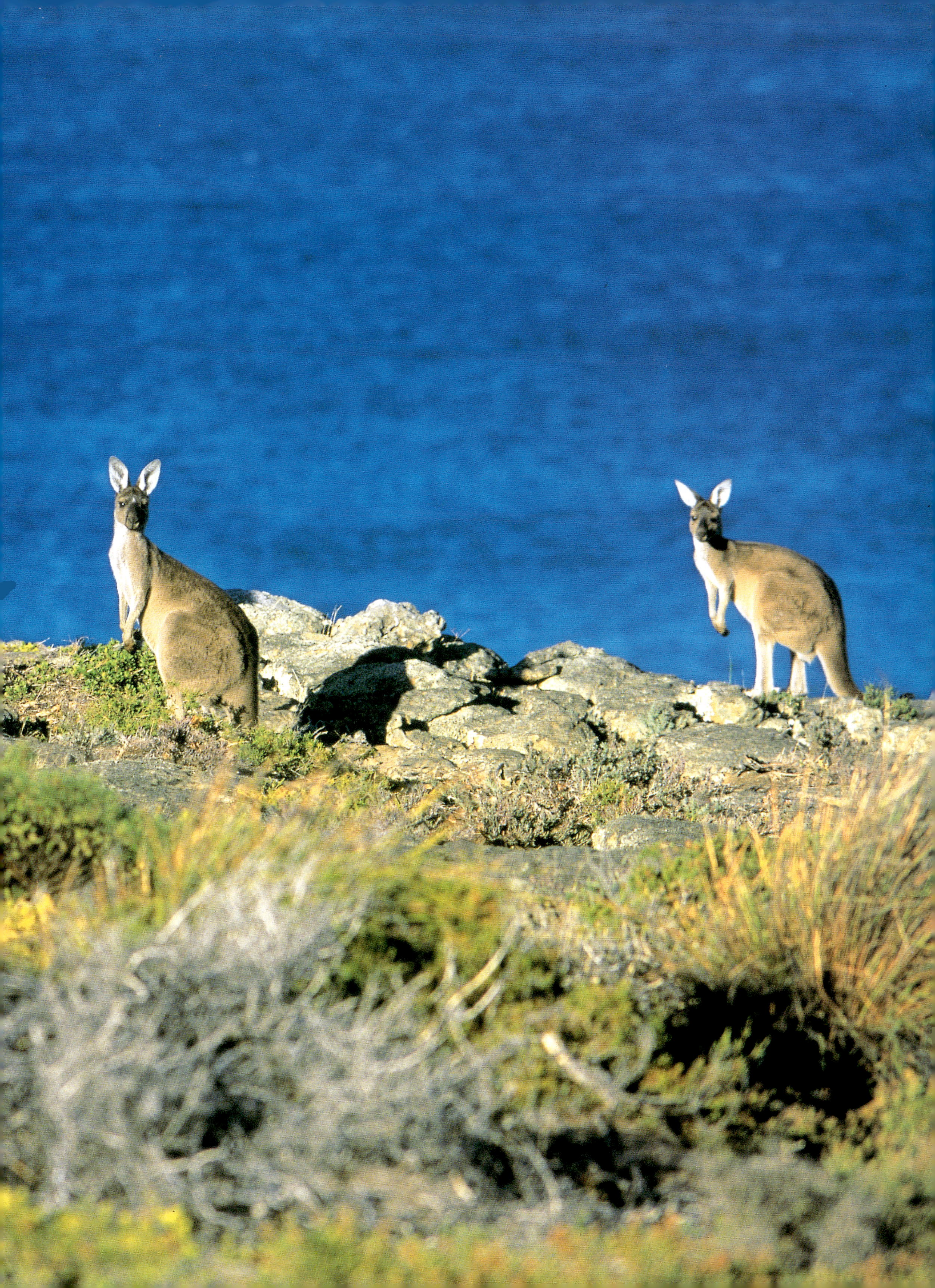

4. The sea

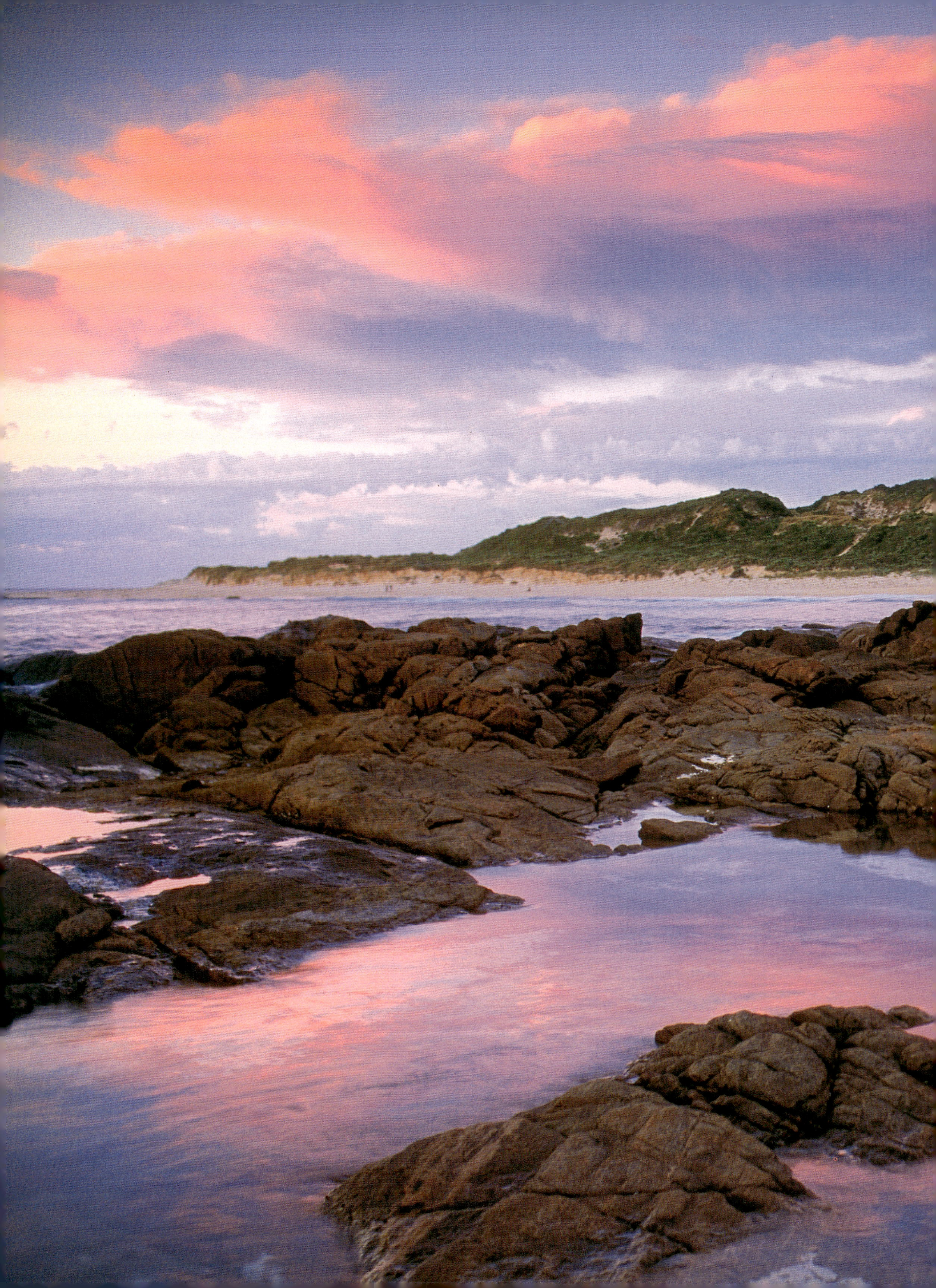

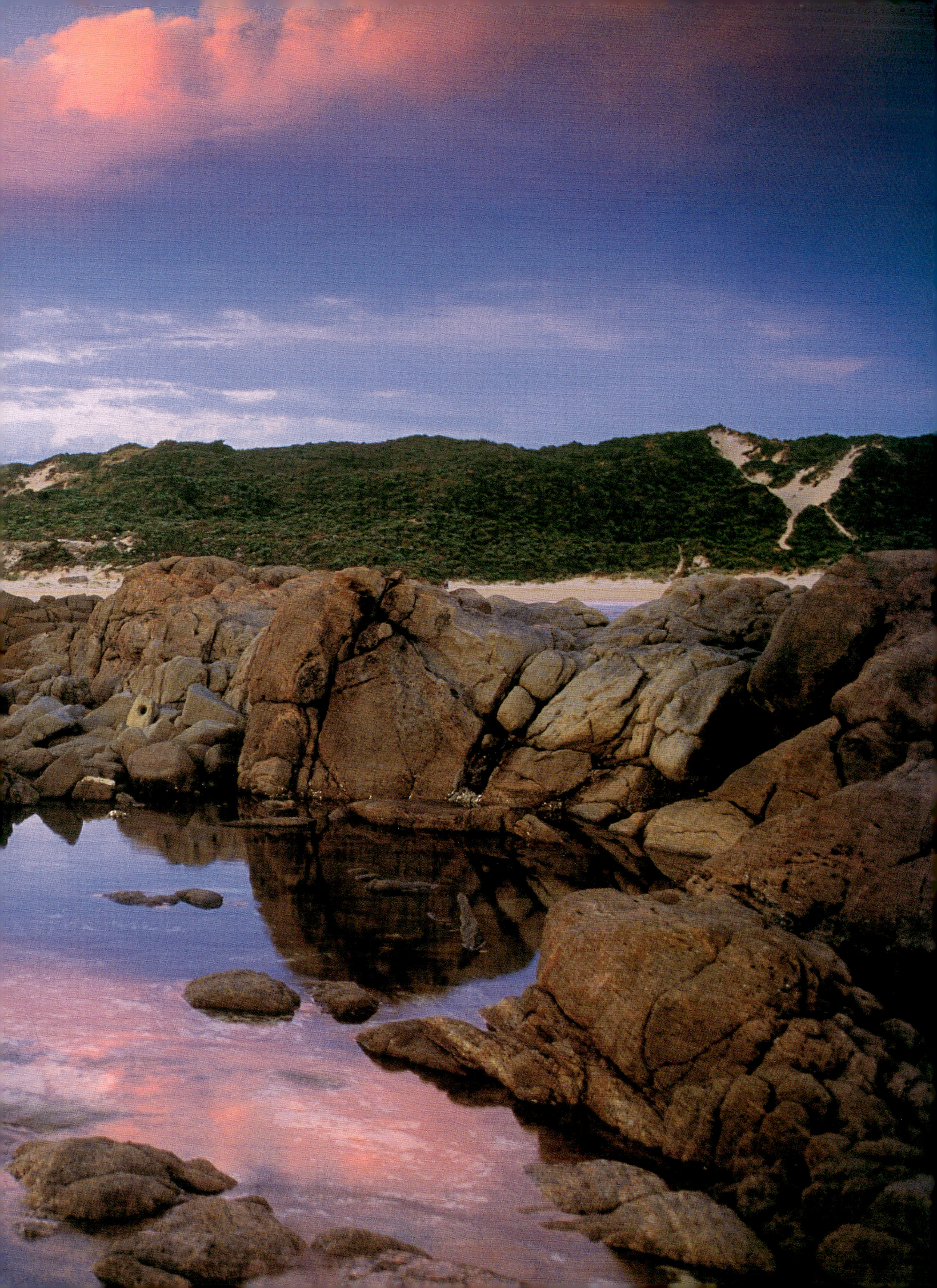

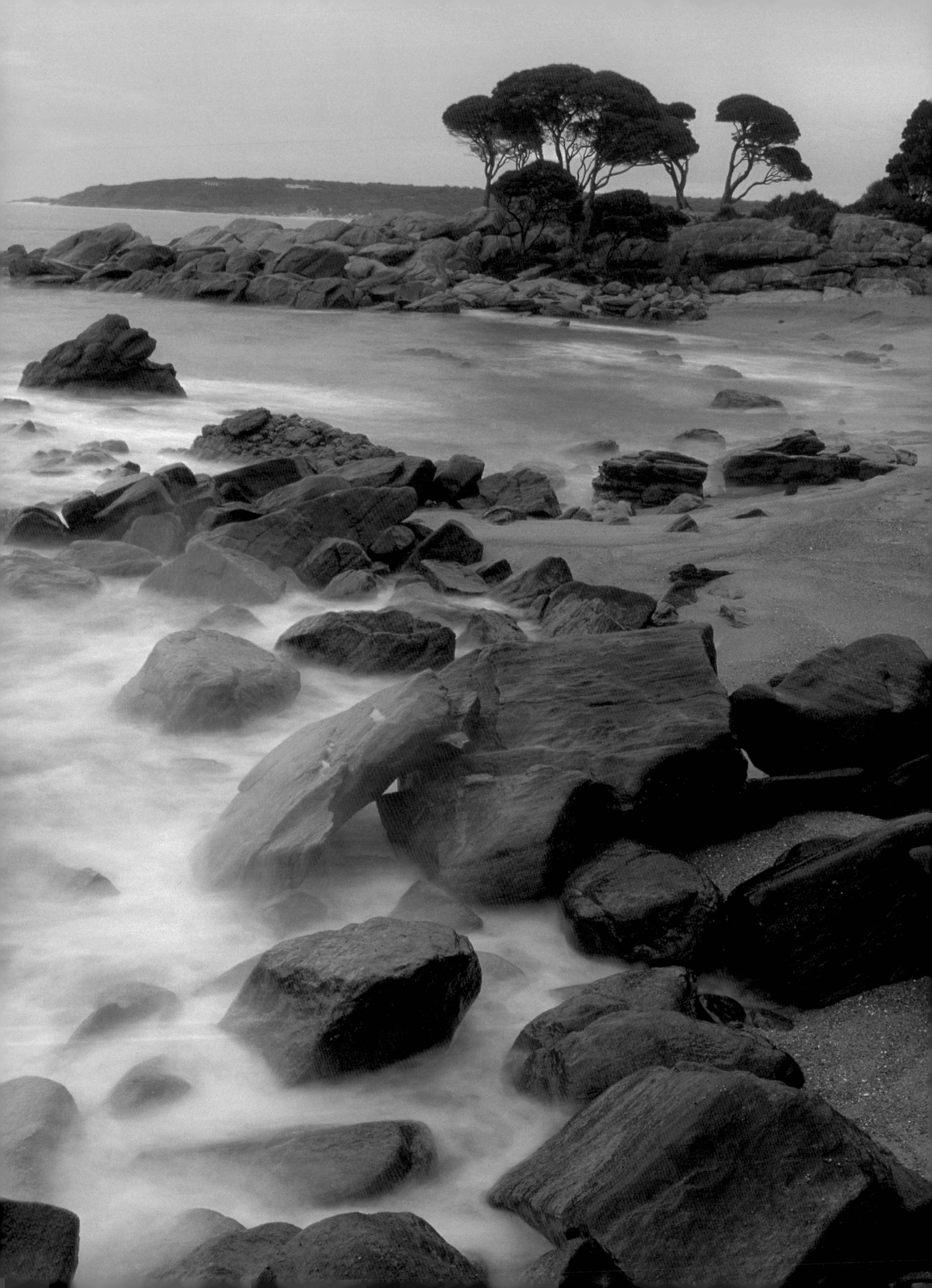

It is just a hundred and thirty kilometres from Cape Naturaliste to Cape Leeuwin as this small corner of the Australian coast sweeps south towards the Southern Ocean. Along its journey, the coast changes regularly from cliff to reef to sandy beaches. This is where the Indian Ocean meets the Southern Ocean and where the huge swells that began more than a thousand kilometres away, somewhere off in the roaring forties to the south-west, crash onto cliffs and reefs. From high on the cliffs, the views are breathtaking. From reefs and ledges closer to the sea, the sense is of awesome power — spectacular and frightening.

Page 83: Sunset at Hamelin Bay.
Previous page: Sunset at the mouth of the Margaret River near Prevelly.
Left: A chilly winter's morning at Bunker Bay.
Above: The schooner *Willie* at anchor in Geographe Bay.

Above: Matthew Chaffer swims with his dog Lucy at Injidup Point.
Right: Fishing at Cosy Corner, near Augusta.

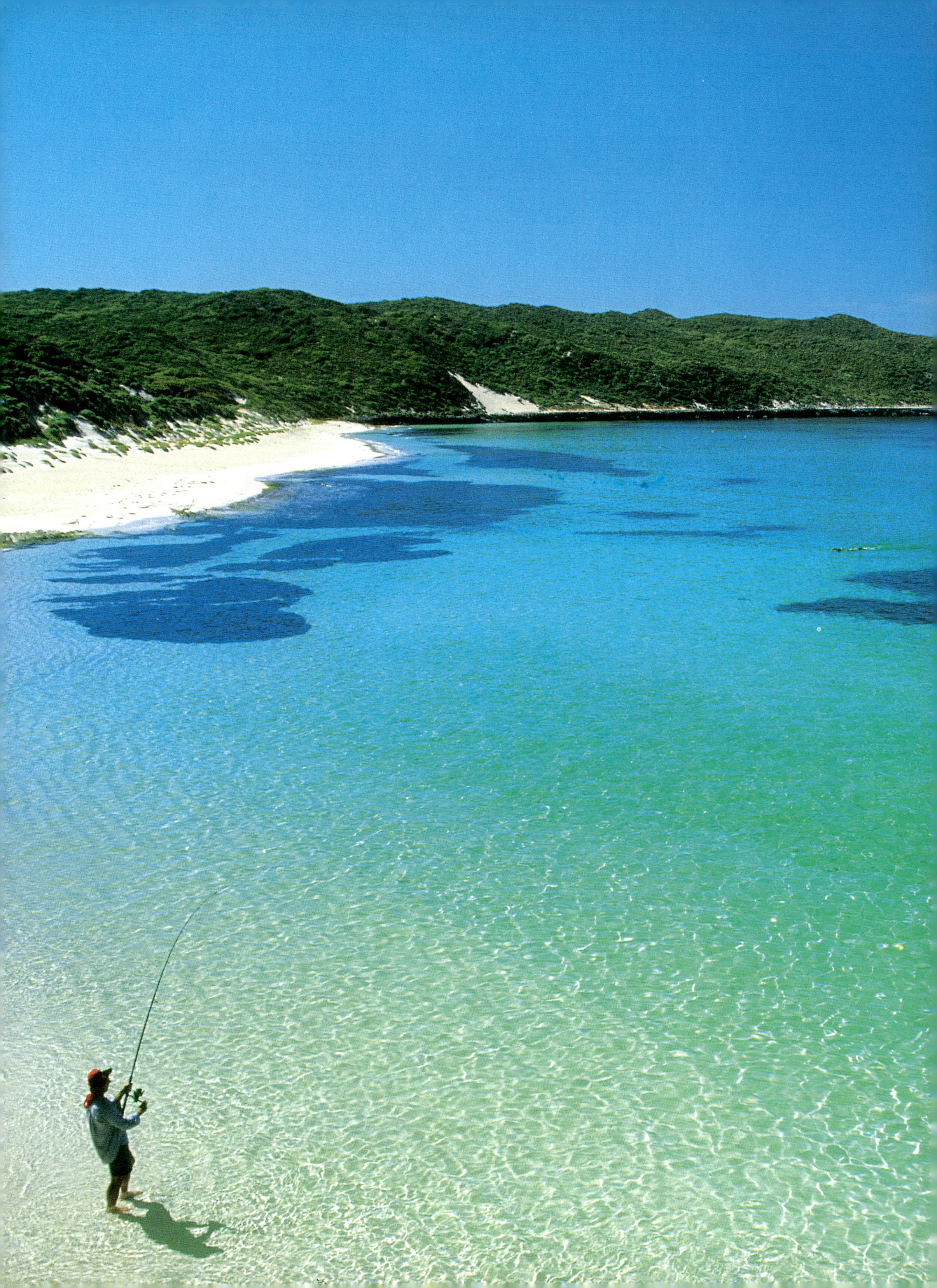

Above: Round Rock, near Contos Beach.
Right: The beach at Wilyabrup.
Overleaf: Canal Rocks, near Yallingup.

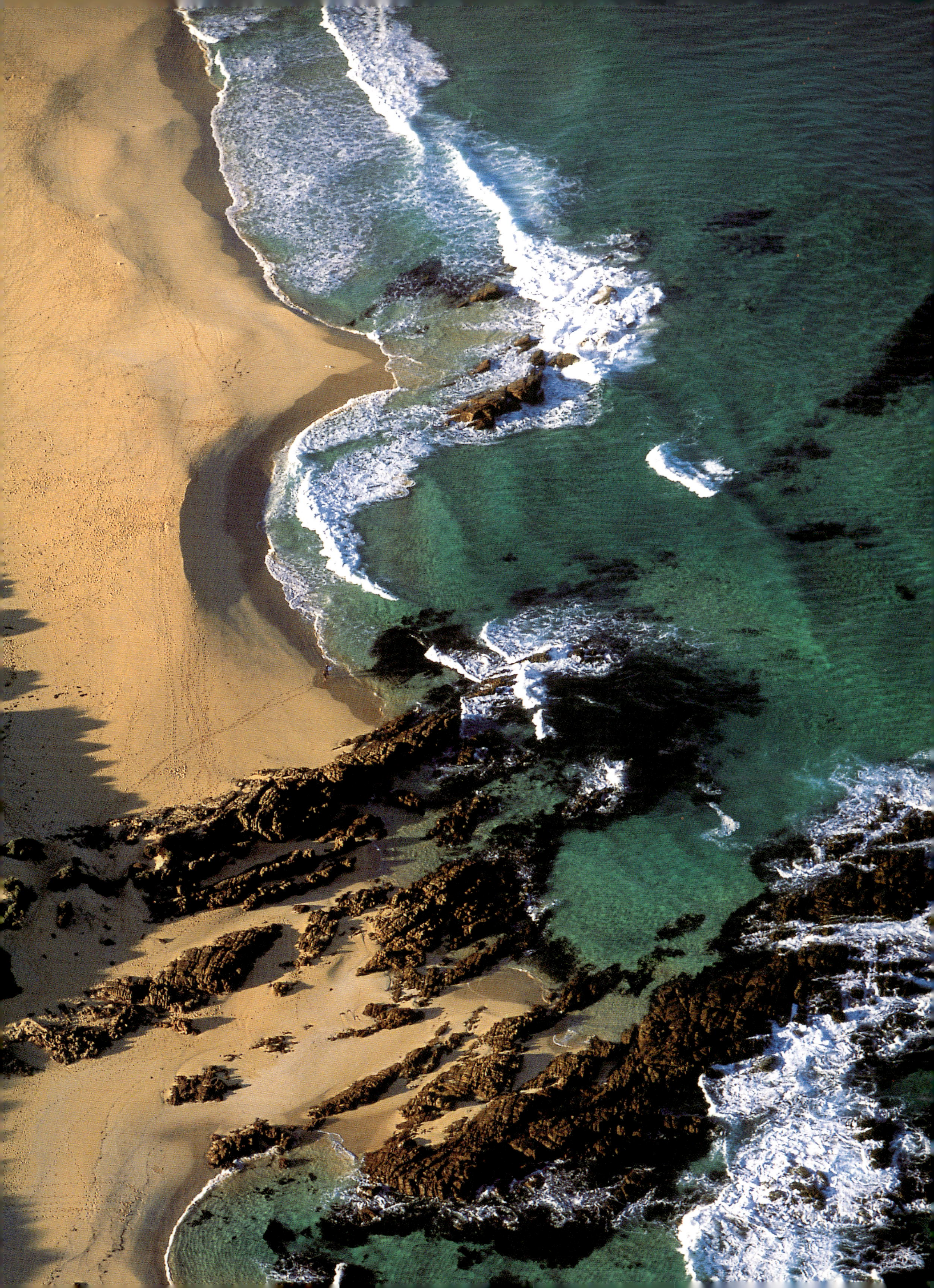

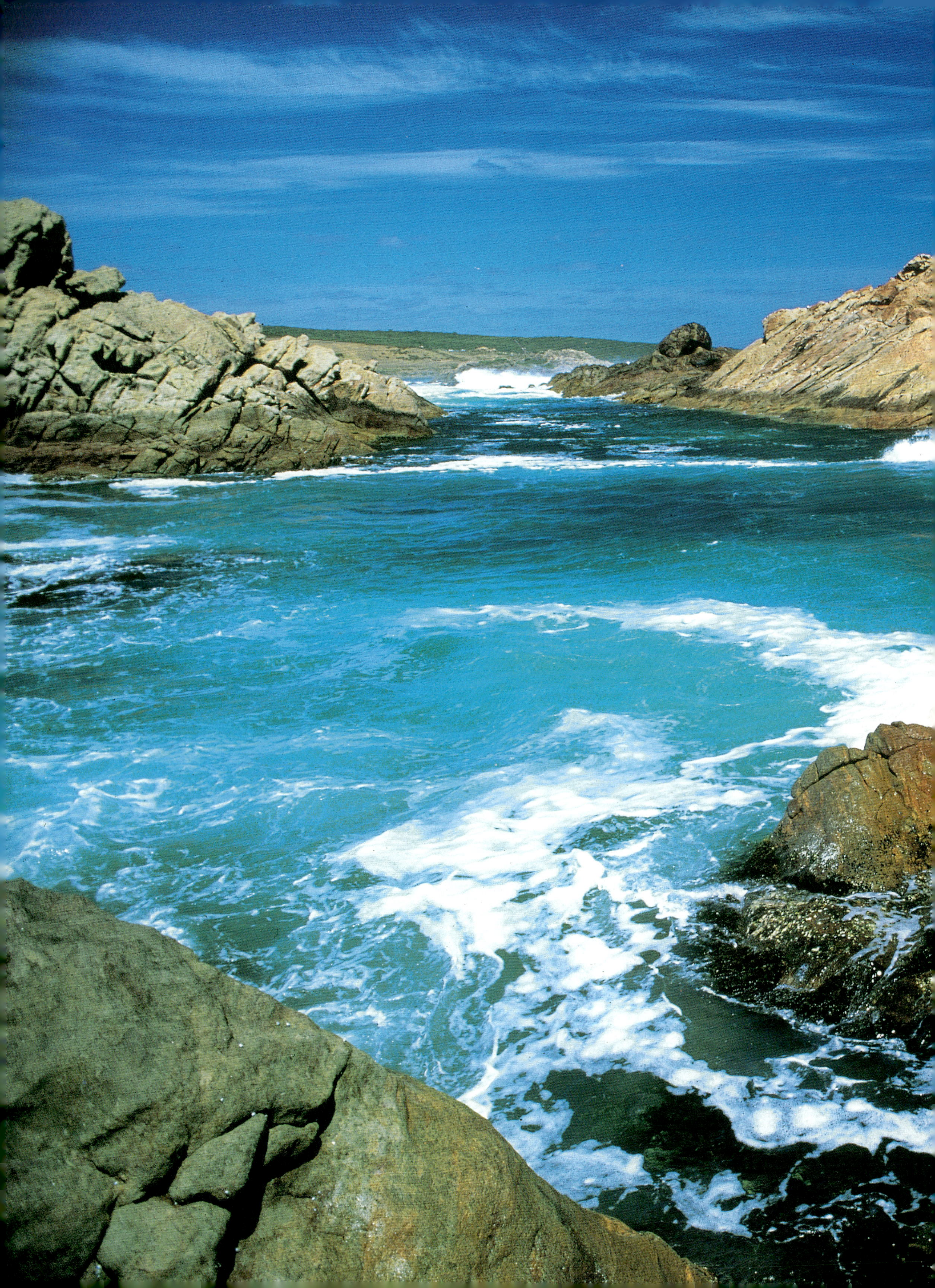

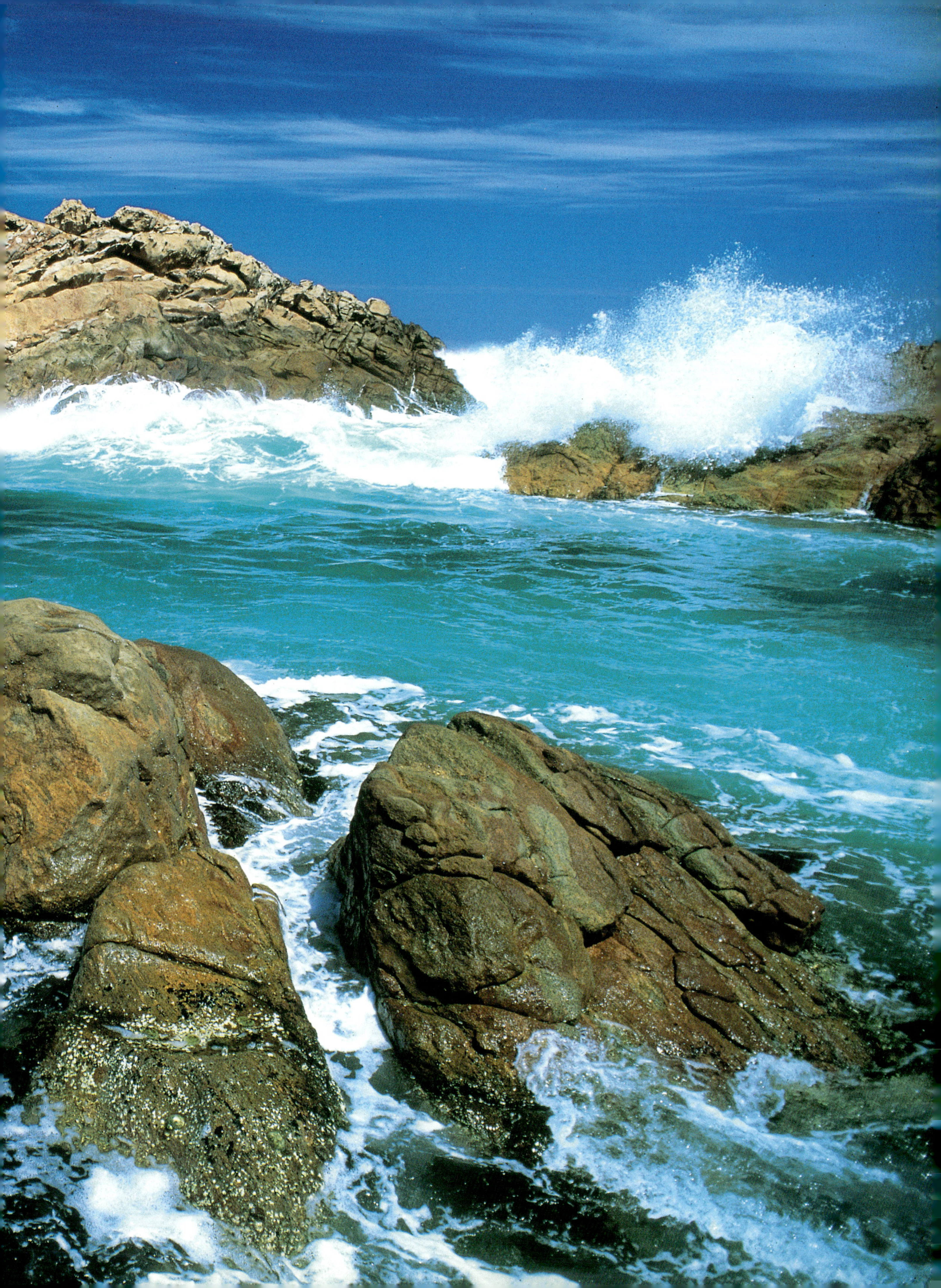

Above: Rocks at Gas Bay, near Prevelly.
Right: The derelict Hamelin Bay jetty, built for the timber industry in 1882.
Overleaf left: Chelsea Sutherland, Claire Ridley and Paula Arthur enjoy the Margaret River Masters.
Overleaf right: Vanessa Lamb paddles out through the Keyhole, Main Break, Margaret River.

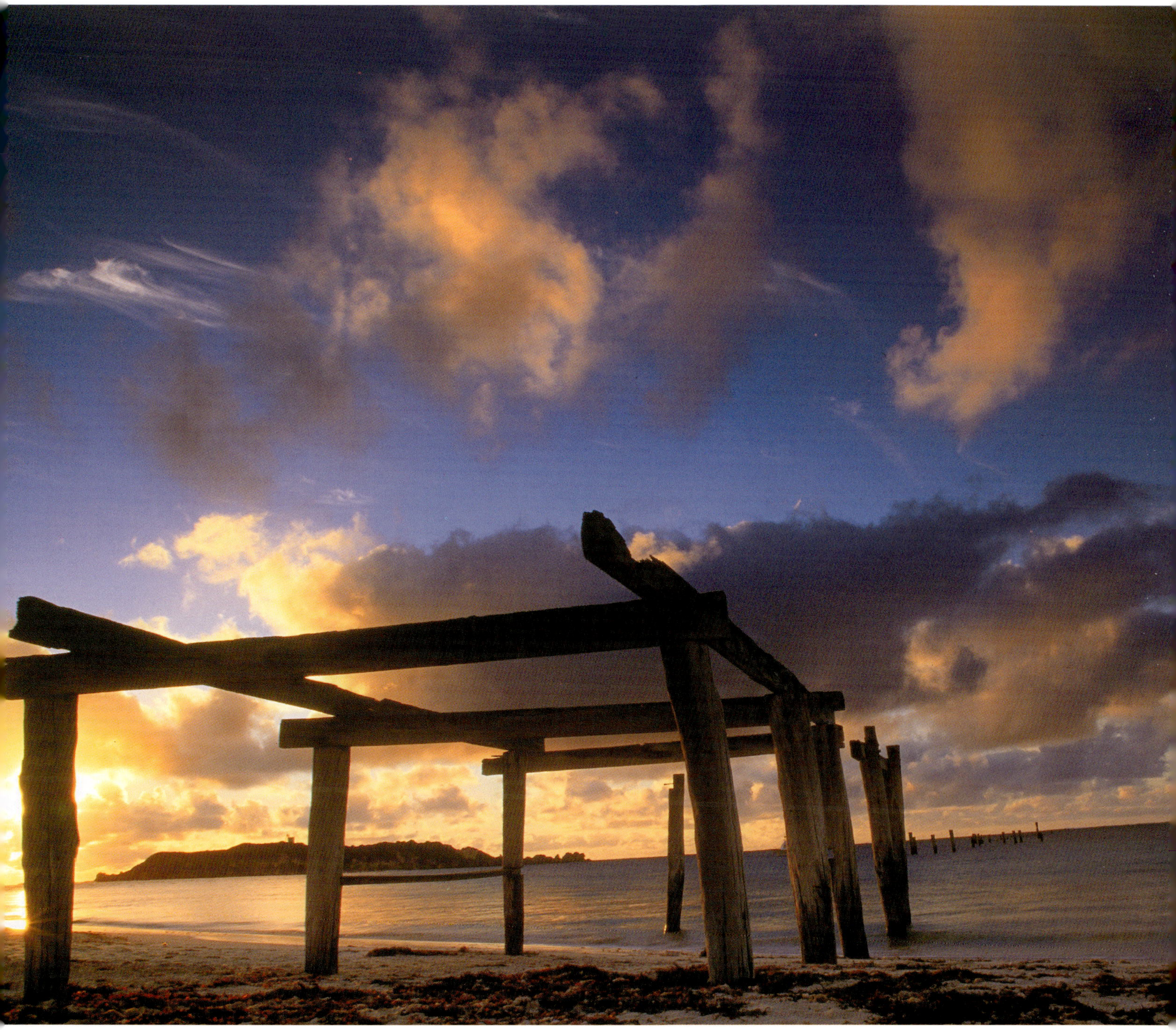

Surfing

Along this stretch of coastline are more than seventy-five surfing breaks. The swells which pound the reefs and beaches produce some of the world's best and most powerful surf. And the most dangerous. Winter and spring are the best seasons but there are not too many days when there is not a decent break working.

The world's finest surfers come here to compete, and at any time you are likely to see professional surfers sharing breaks with amateurs of all ages. Many are in their fifties and sixties, and high-profile wine personalities such as Denis Horgan, David Hohnen and Vanya Cullen are well known for their skill on a board.

With names like Suicides, Gallows, Guillotine, Grunters, the Boneyard and the Box, this is not a place for the timid, faint-hearted or the unwary. The huge swells can drive surfers deep onto a reef and almost before a breath can be taken, drive them down again.

For raw power, size and consistency, Margaret River Main Break, at the mouth of Margaret River itself, stands supreme. It is here that the best of the best put themselves to the test, but even the most experienced treat Main Break with respect. From the car park at Surfers' Point, a hundred or more metres away, it can look benign and friendly, but up close, it is an altogether different and more imposing reality. A plaque dedicated to the memory of a young surfer who lost his life surfing the break is testament to its power and danger.

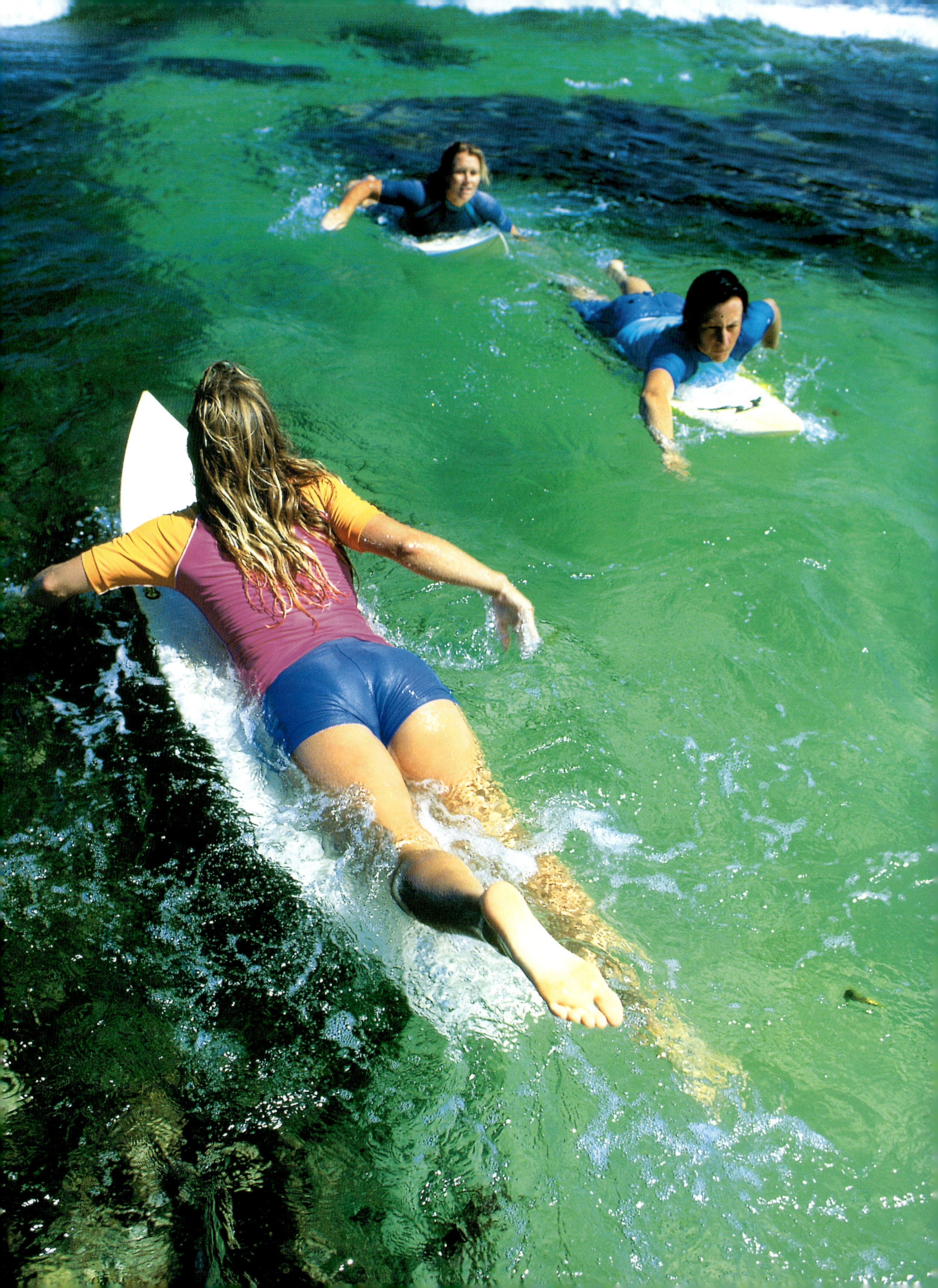

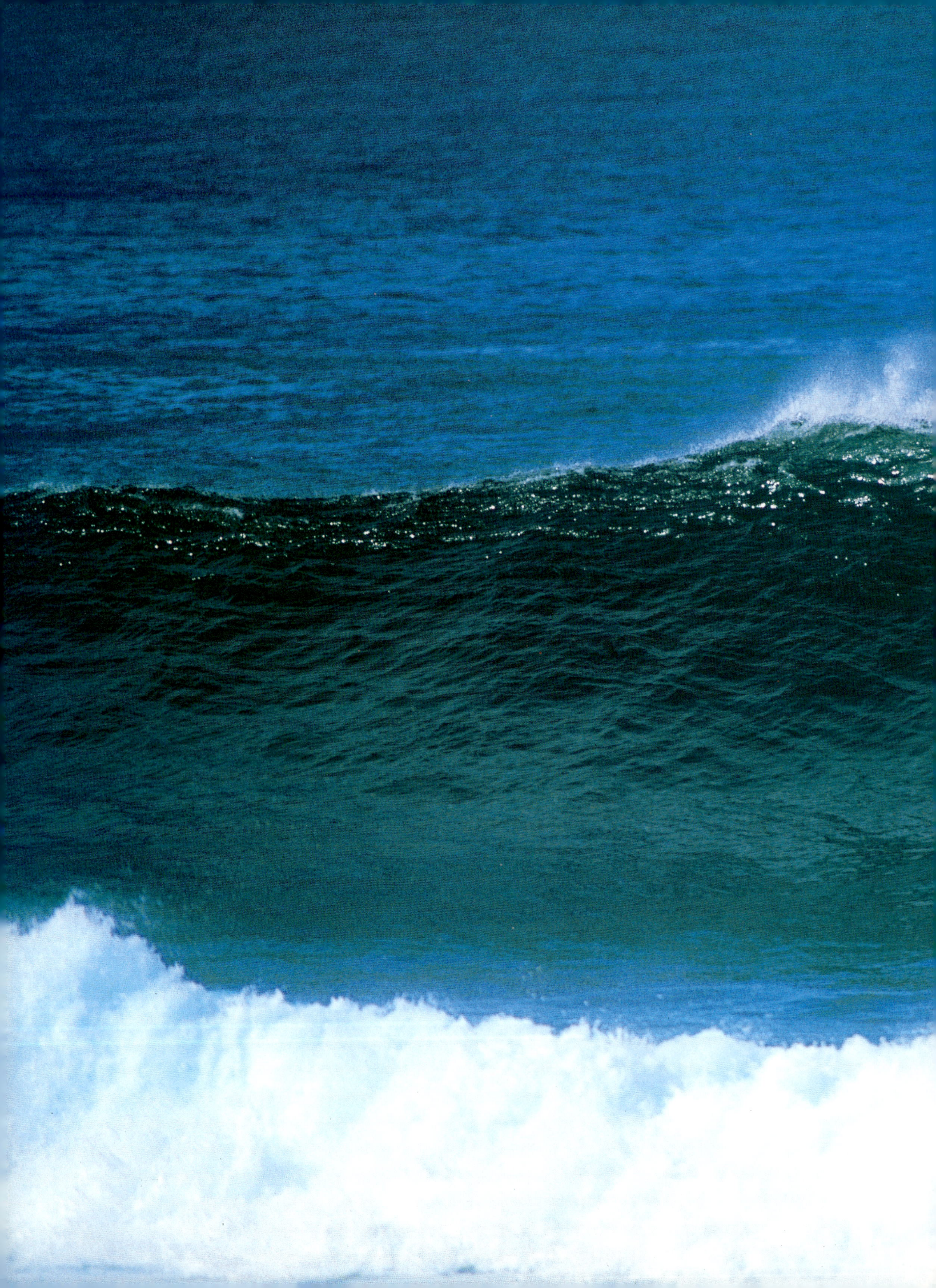

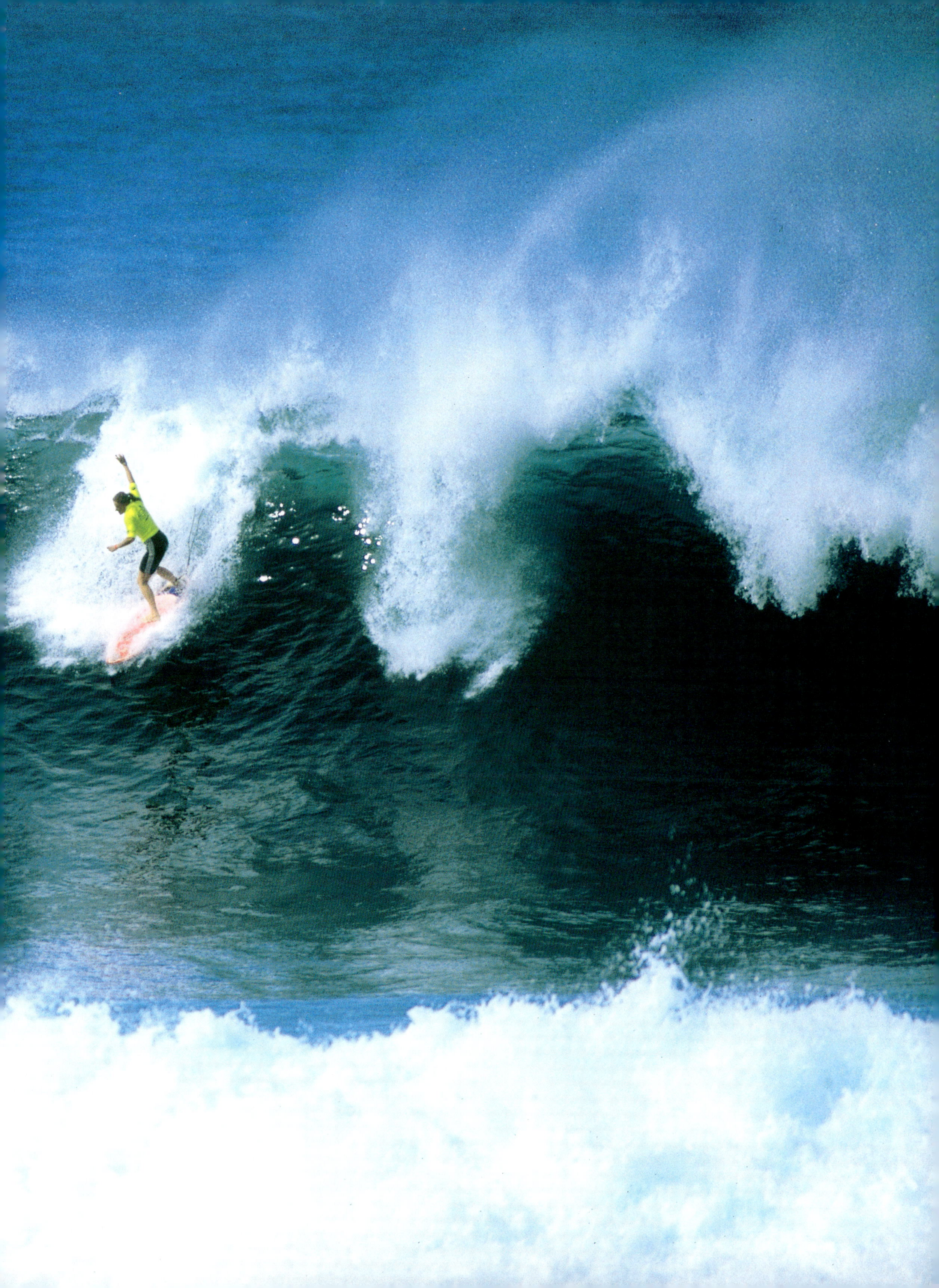

Closer in from Main Break, towards the river mouth, is the Box, a gnarly, ugly little break over shallow reef and popular with brave bodyboarders. Slightly to the south is the appropriately named Suicides, another break reserved for experienced surfers.

A little further north is the coastal township of Gracetown on Cowaramup Bay, one of the prettiest places on the coast. There are three excellent surf breaks in this bay. North Point with its steep, fast and powerful surge provides spectacular viewing from the rocks that seem to be almost under the lip. Swells here can get very big and very dangerous. A rocky ledge just below the surface can trap the unwary. South Point is often awesome, with the power and size of a big swell intimidating even from the safety of the beach a few hundred metres away. This break is thick and driving with a very steep take-off and is definitely not for the inexperienced. Inside South Point is the relative friendliness of Huzzawooee that bubbles up regularly on the southern end of the bay and is ideal for younger and less experienced surfers.

When all is quiet in Cowaramup Bay, a short drive to the southern side and a five-hundred-metre walk along the beach takes you to Lefthanders, a fast steep snappy break regularly frequented by the hottest surfers on the coast.

Further north, towards Cape Naturaliste, is Yallingup. This was one of the first places to attract surfers to the area and is still one of the most popular and consistent breaks. However, it can be very dangerous and on some days even the best and most fearless stay on shore.

Previous page: Competing in the Margaret River Masters.
Right: Dotty, Charger, Harry and Ben
— they call themselves the 'ferals'.

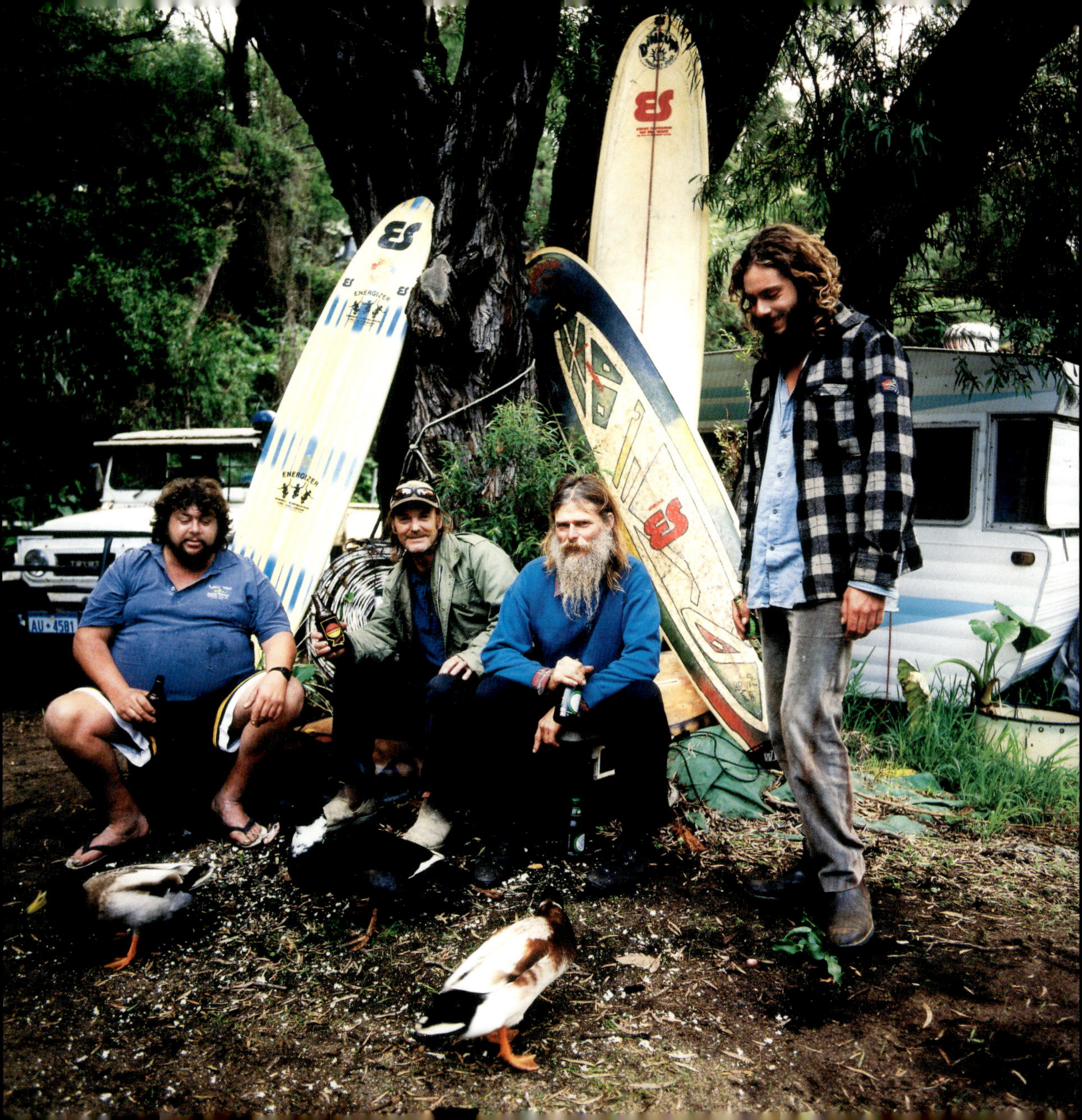
ES
ENERGIZER
ES
ES
AU·4581

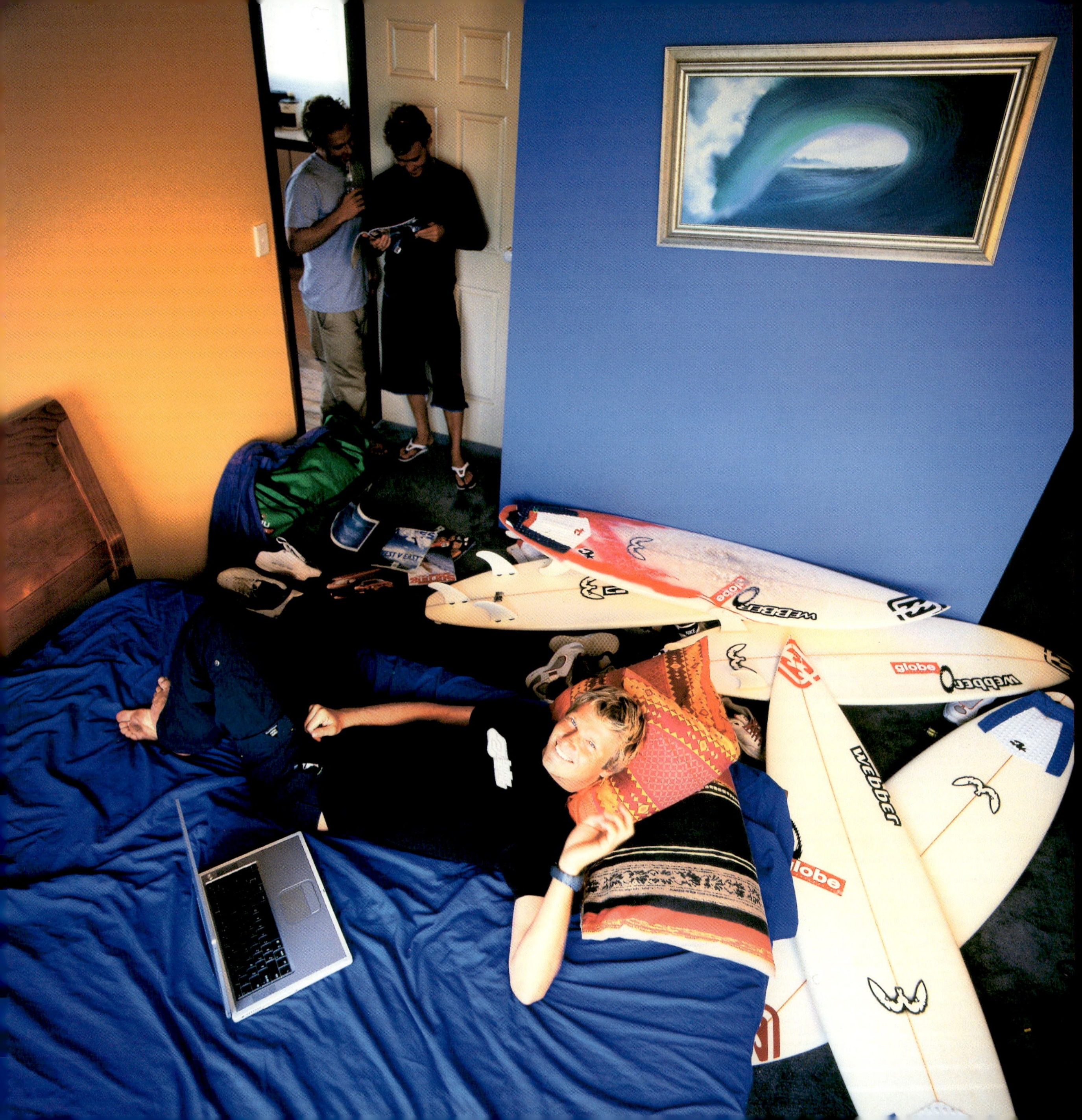
globe
webber

Left: Champion surfer Taj Burrow chills out in his bedroom.
Above: Working the waves at the Margaret River Masters.
Overleaf: The Box, just north of Prevelly.

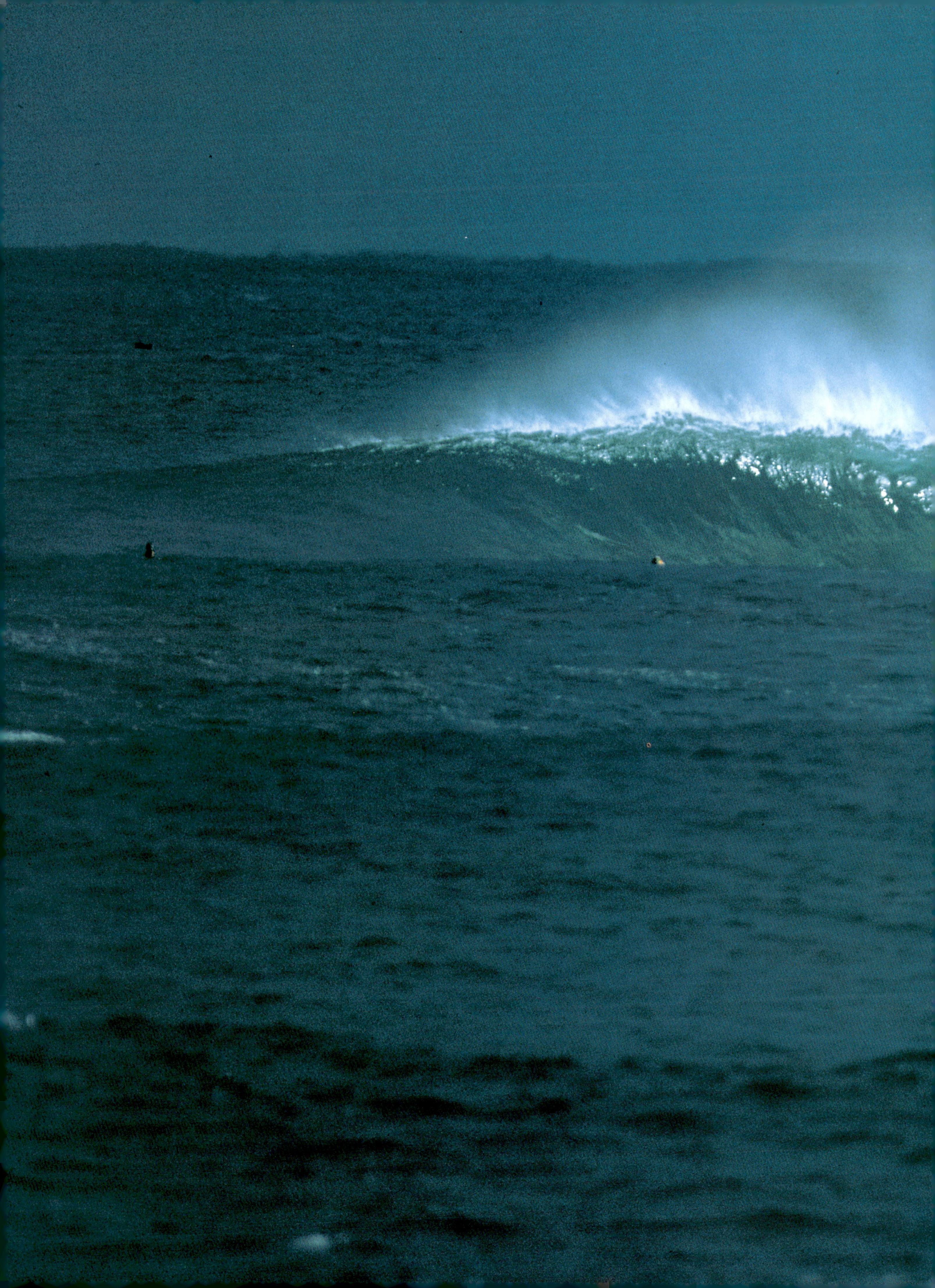

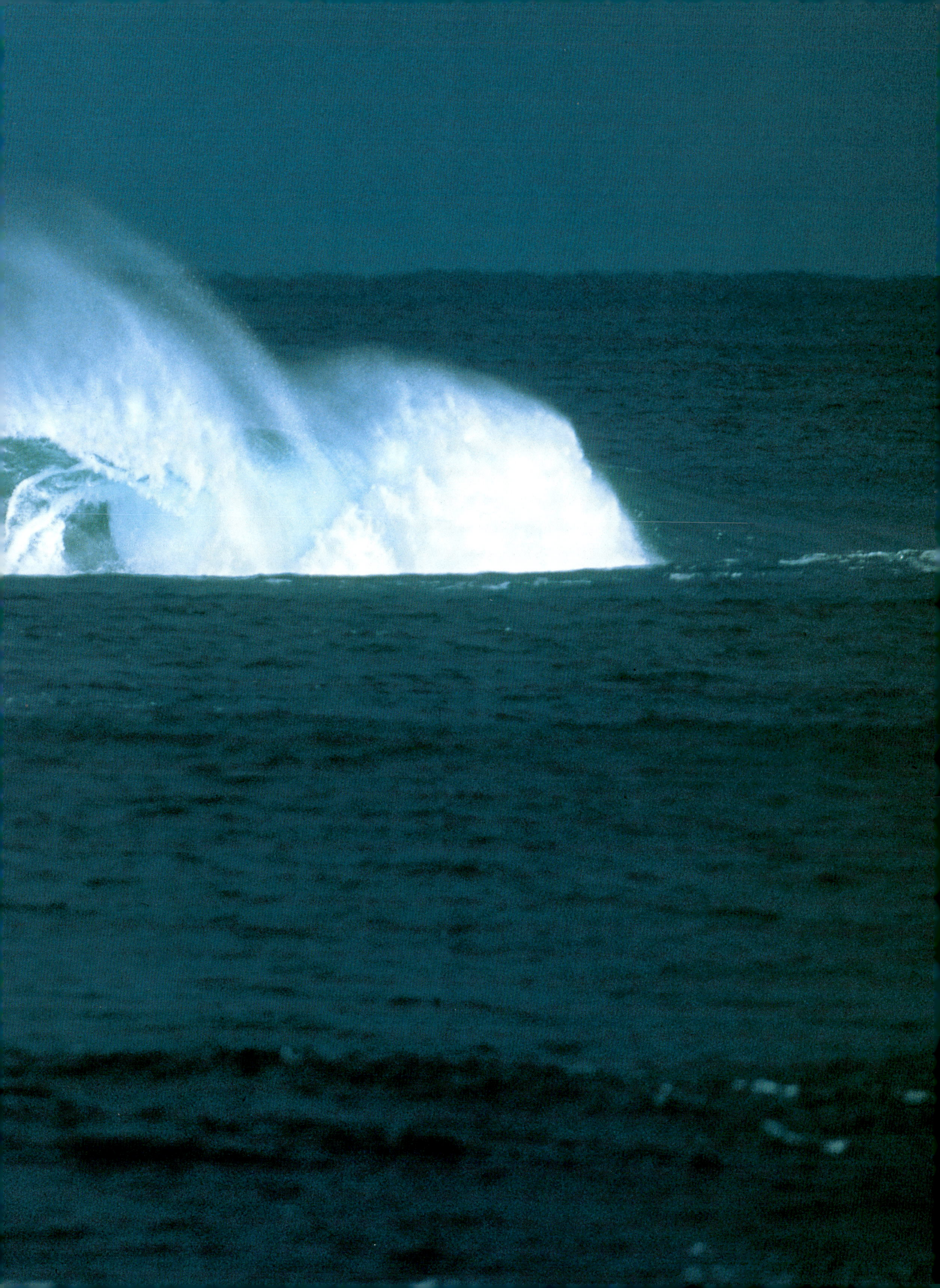

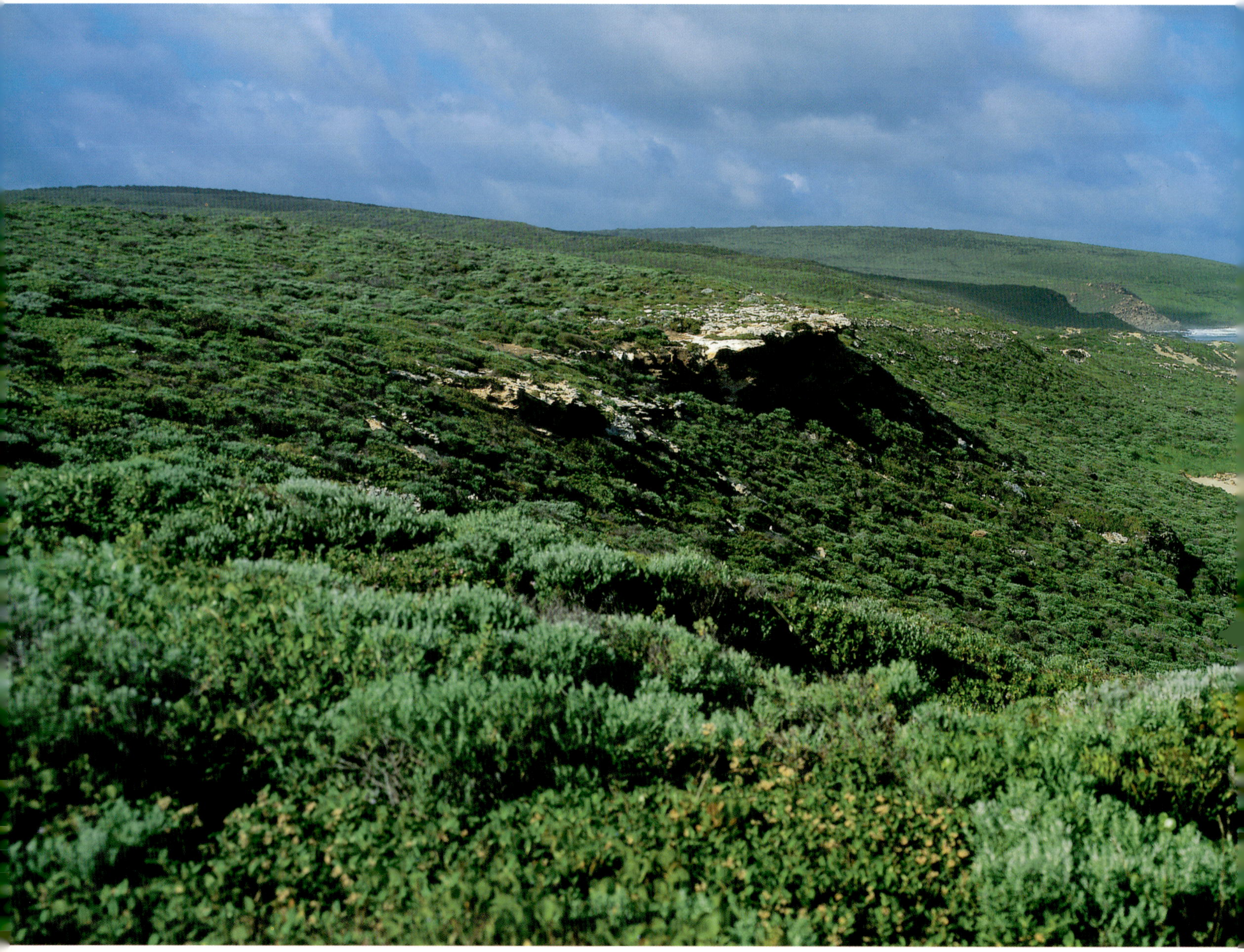

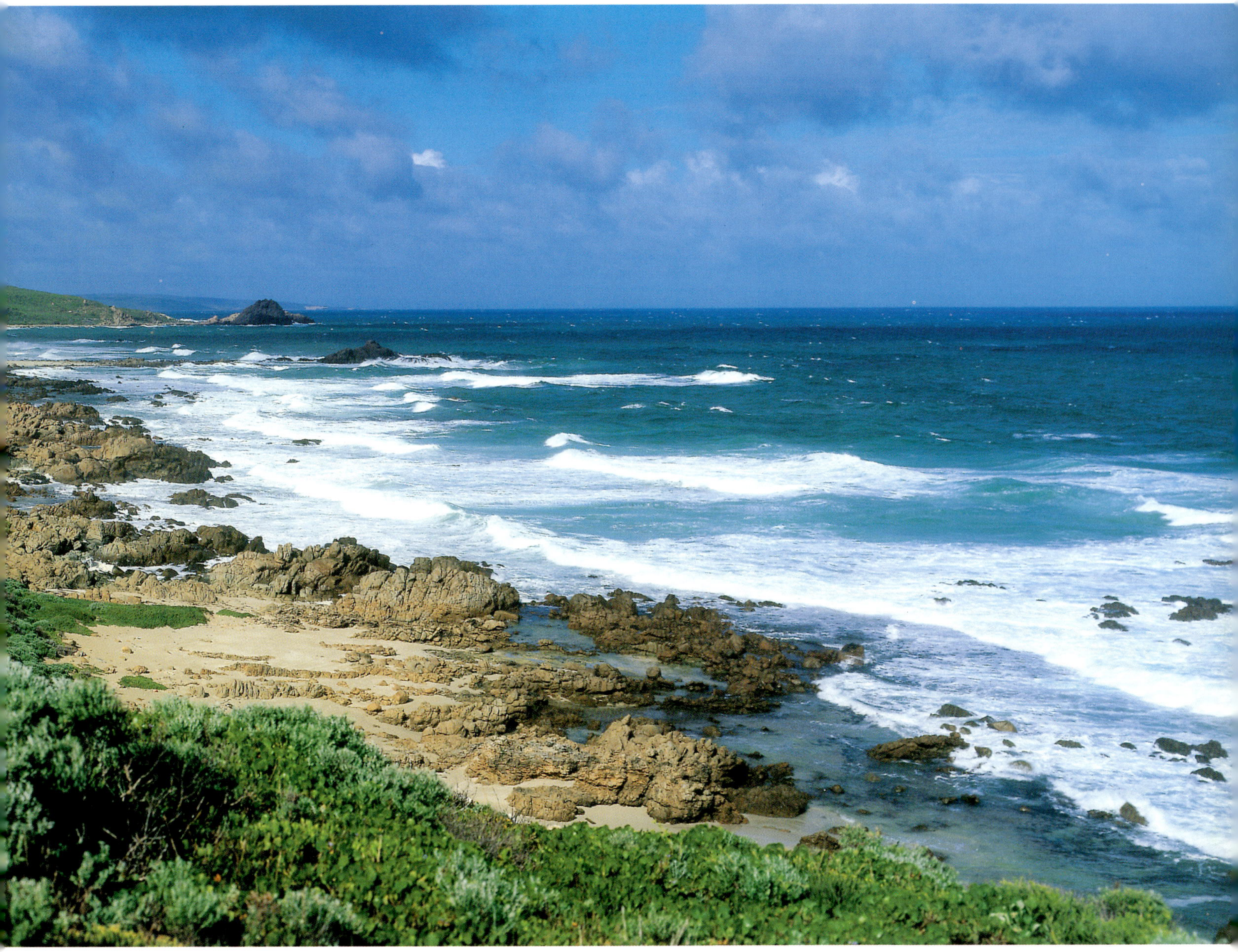

The whales

Humpbacks, like most other whales, were once hunted almost to the point of extinction. However the hunting of humpbacks ended in 1963 and since then their numbers have increased significantly. There are now estimated to be between two thousand and three thousand humpbacks off the Western Australian coast, making this one of the best places to see these magnificent animals.

The slightly smaller southern right whale was also hunted ruthlessly. Although whaling of the southern right officially ended in the 1930s, illegal operations continued until the 1970s, preventing them from recovering in good numbers. Encouraging numbers have started to appear and it is estimated that about two hundred visit the south and west coasts of Australia each year. To the delight of shore-based whale watchers as well as those in charter boats, these whales often come in very close to shore, particularly the adult females when they are about to give birth. Charter operators must follow a very strict code when approaching whales to ensure they do not upset them but, in fact, whales are generally quite inquisitive, and a younger calf will come surprisingly close to a boat before a protective mother shepherds it away.

Previous page: Looking towards Gull Rock from Cape Naturaliste.
Right: Blue whale at play in Geographe Bay.
Overleaf: Humpback whale diving off Dunsborough.

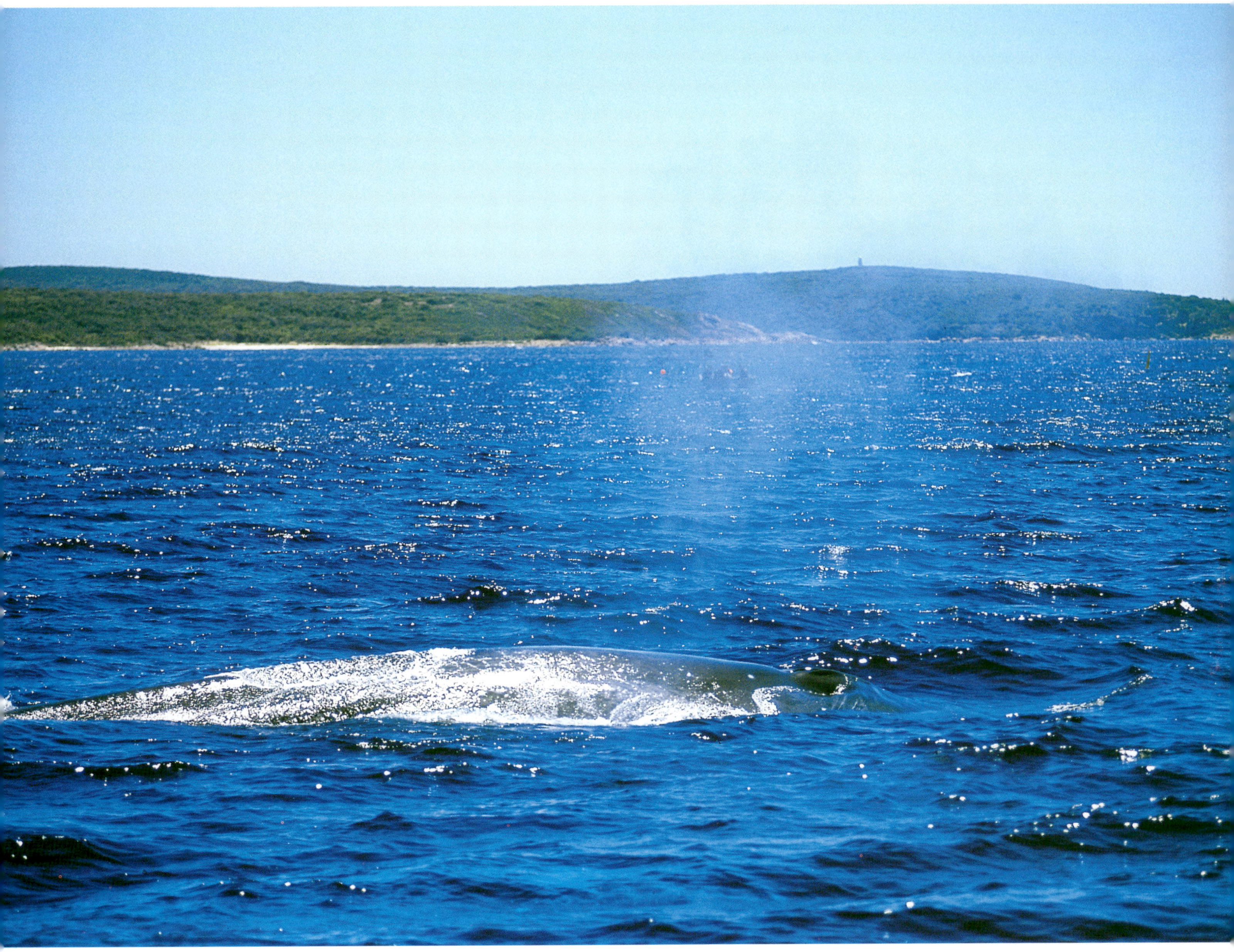

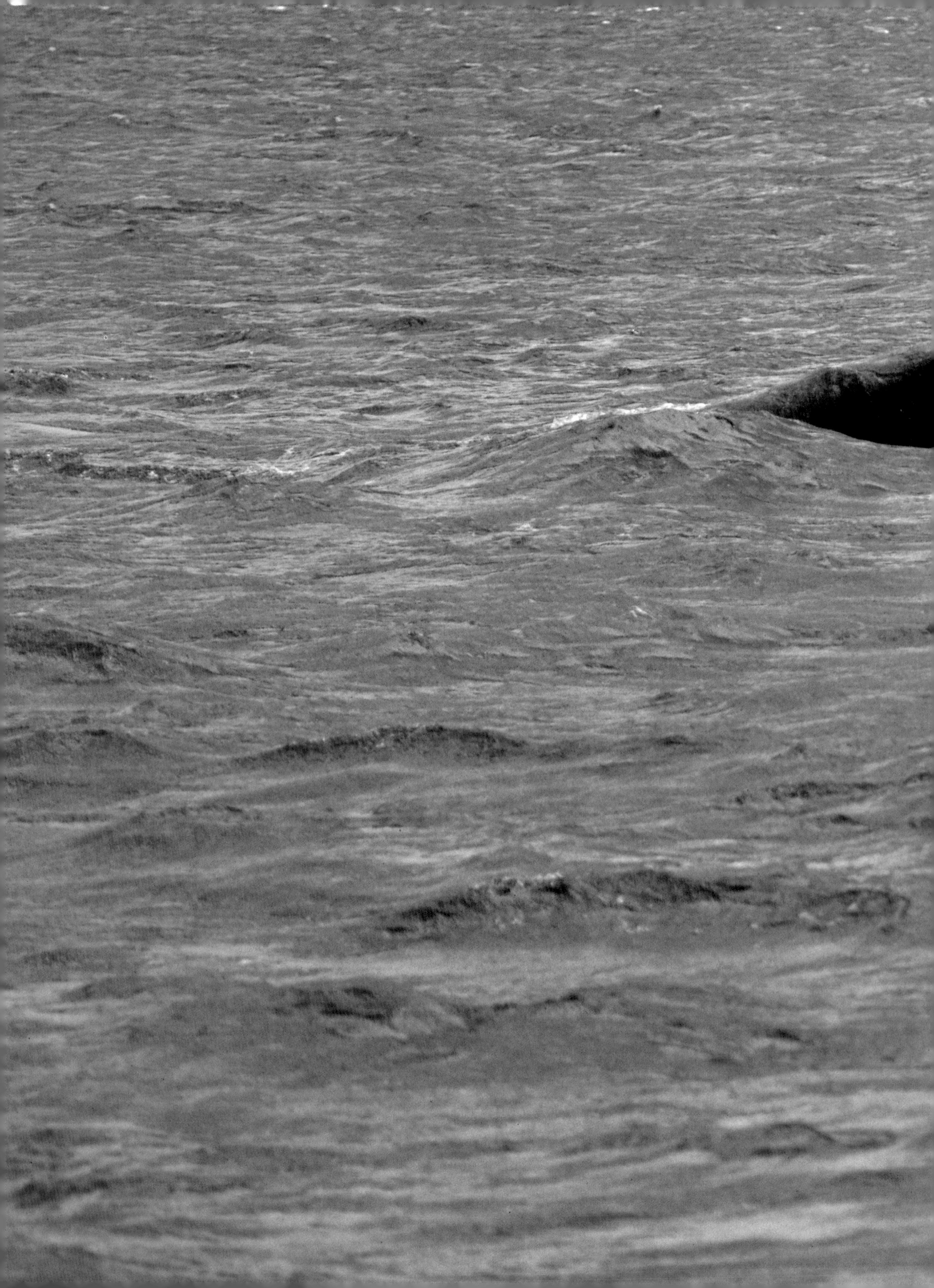

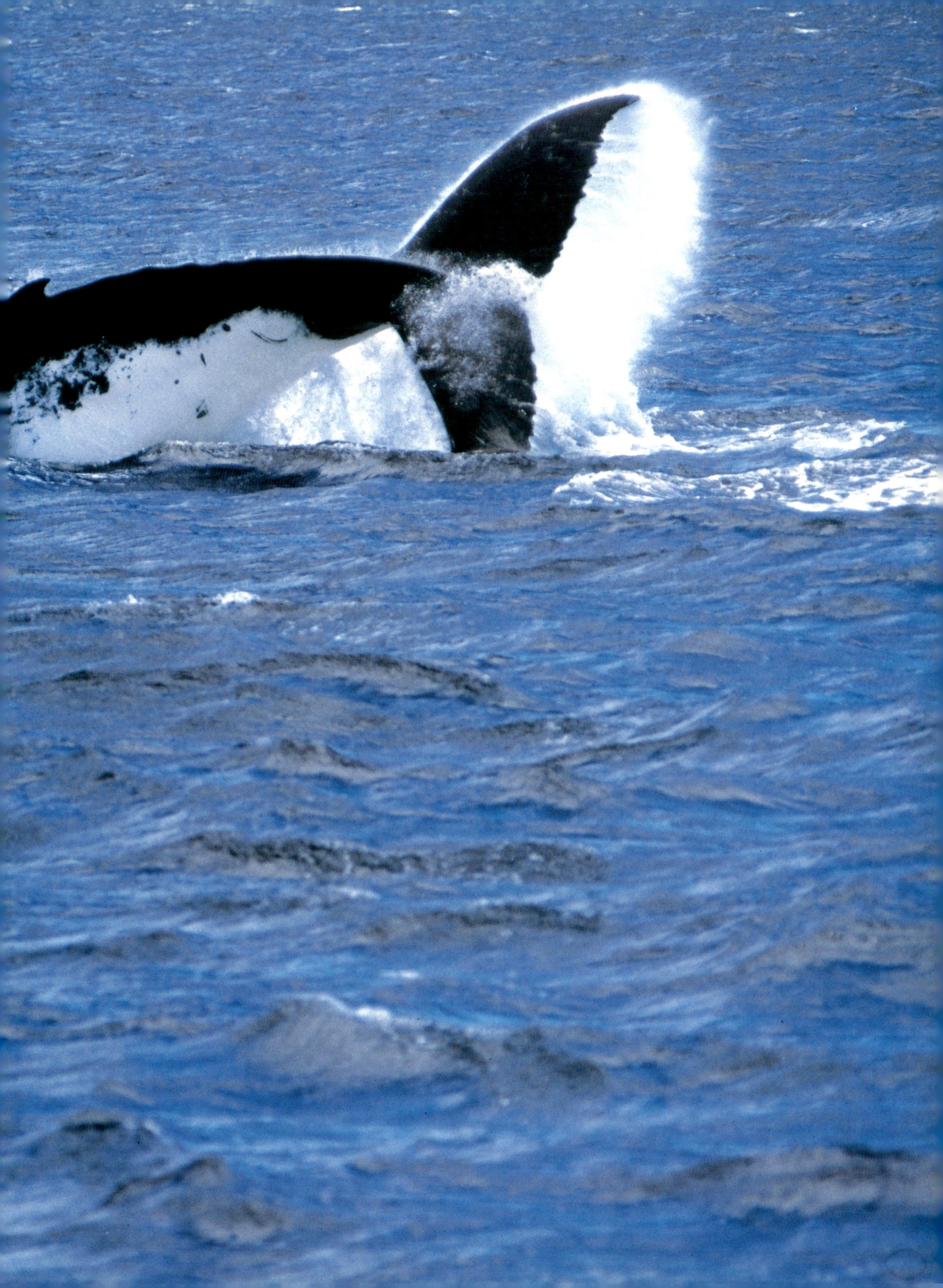

5. The architecture

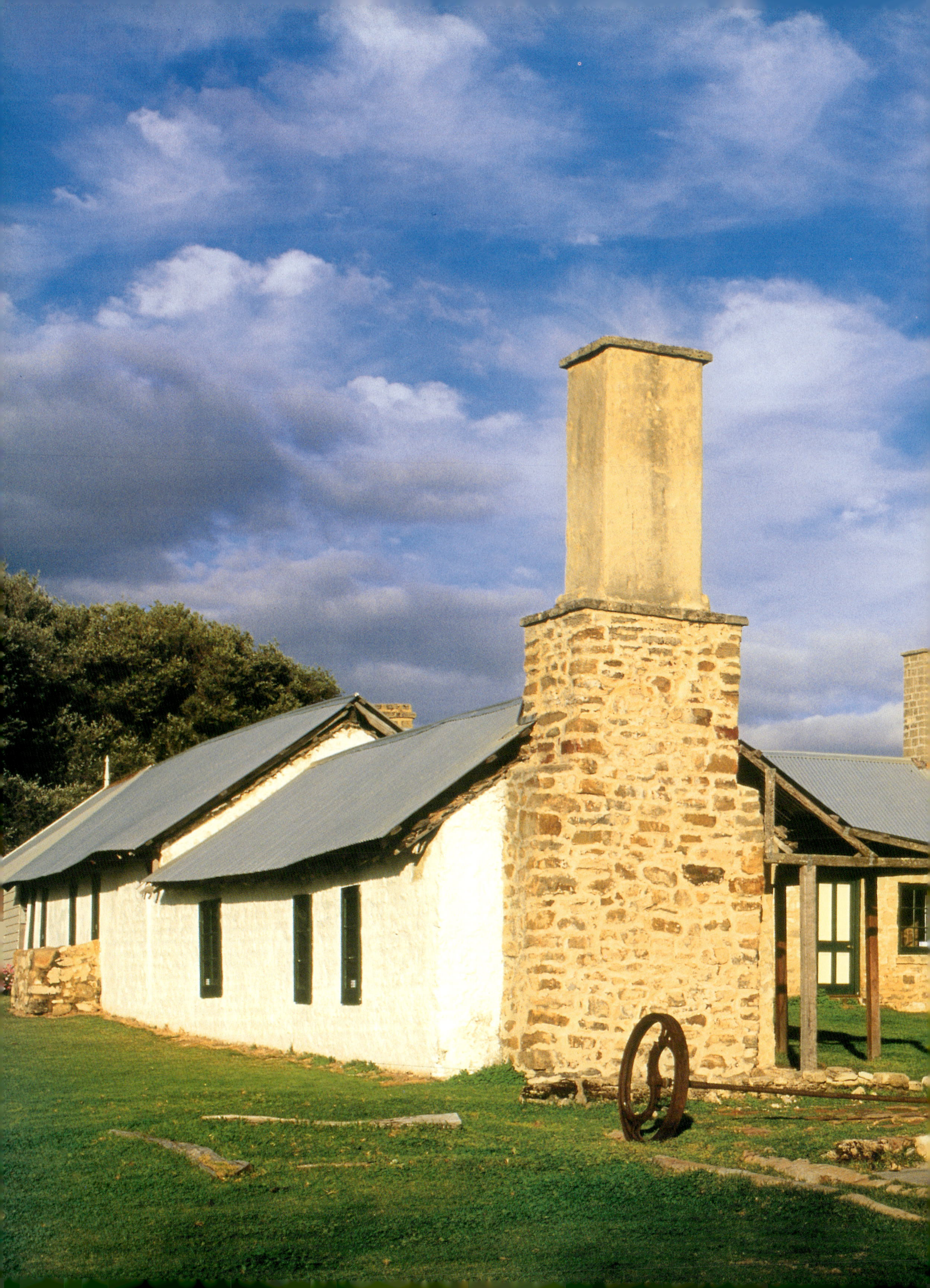

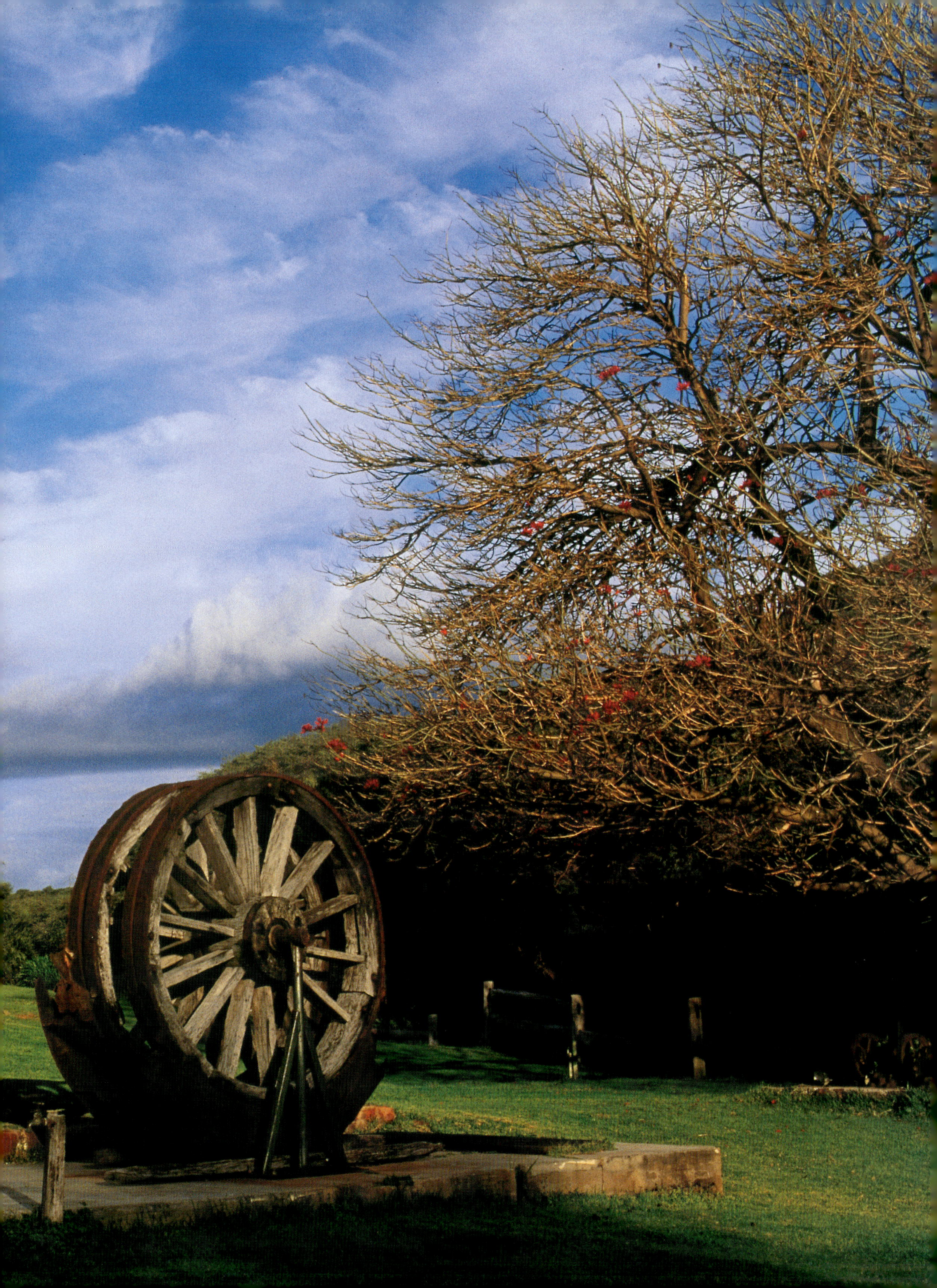

More than any other building, Ellensbrook House represents the coming of European settlement. Its history reflects the struggles, the optimism and the sadness of one of the district's most well-known pioneering families. The Ellensbrook dwellings have been largely restored to their original state and are now vested in the National Trust.

Alfred and Ellen Bussell started building the house in 1855. They had thirteen children, and the graves of three of their children, who died in infancy, lie beneath a nearby cluster of peppermint trees. Even now the house stands quite isolated from the rest of the area's population, and you can only wonder at what it was that enabled the Bussells to survive and prosper a hundred and fifty years ago.

Ellensbrook provides some excellent examples of innovative pioneering building methods, for instance, the boat mast used as a ridge beam in one of the first rooms built in the house. To create a framework for the house, rough bush poles and paperbark, brought from the banks of the Margaret River with the help of local Nyungars, was sealed with a type of plaster created by burning limestone from nearby dunes. A little later in its history, hand-cut slabs were used for weatherboard additions.

The site was ideally located, close to the sea and to a permanent stream. The Wardandi knew the area as Mokidup, a traditional summer camping site for thousands of years. The site is steeped in legend. You can almost feel the eerie presence of spirits beneath the cool and slightly humid leafy canopy. Close by is the waterfall, known by the Wardandi as Meekadarribee, which means 'bathing place of the moon'. According to Aboriginal legend this is where the moon came for privacy to bathe and find her lost silver gleam. The waterfall is said to echo the sounds of laughter of the spirits of Aboriginal lovers Mitanne and Nobel, finally reunited after death.

Ellensbrook is significant as a place of early contact between Europeans and Aborigines. The relationship with the local Aborigines from the early expeditions into the area by Captain John Molloy was generally good. It was the policy of Molloy and John Bussell, who had joined Molloy on his journey after arriving in the colony in 1830, to establish good relations with the Aborigines. The Bussells at Ellensbrook received assistance in many of their day-to-day activities from the local Aboriginal community, apparently sharing a peaceful relationship.

Page 113: Former cattle yards of Elders, near Cowaramup.
Previous page: Ellensbrook House, built by Ellen and Alfred Bussell from 1855.
Right: Quindalup waterfall.
Overleaf: Meekadarribee Falls, an Aboriginal sacred site close to Ellensbrook House.

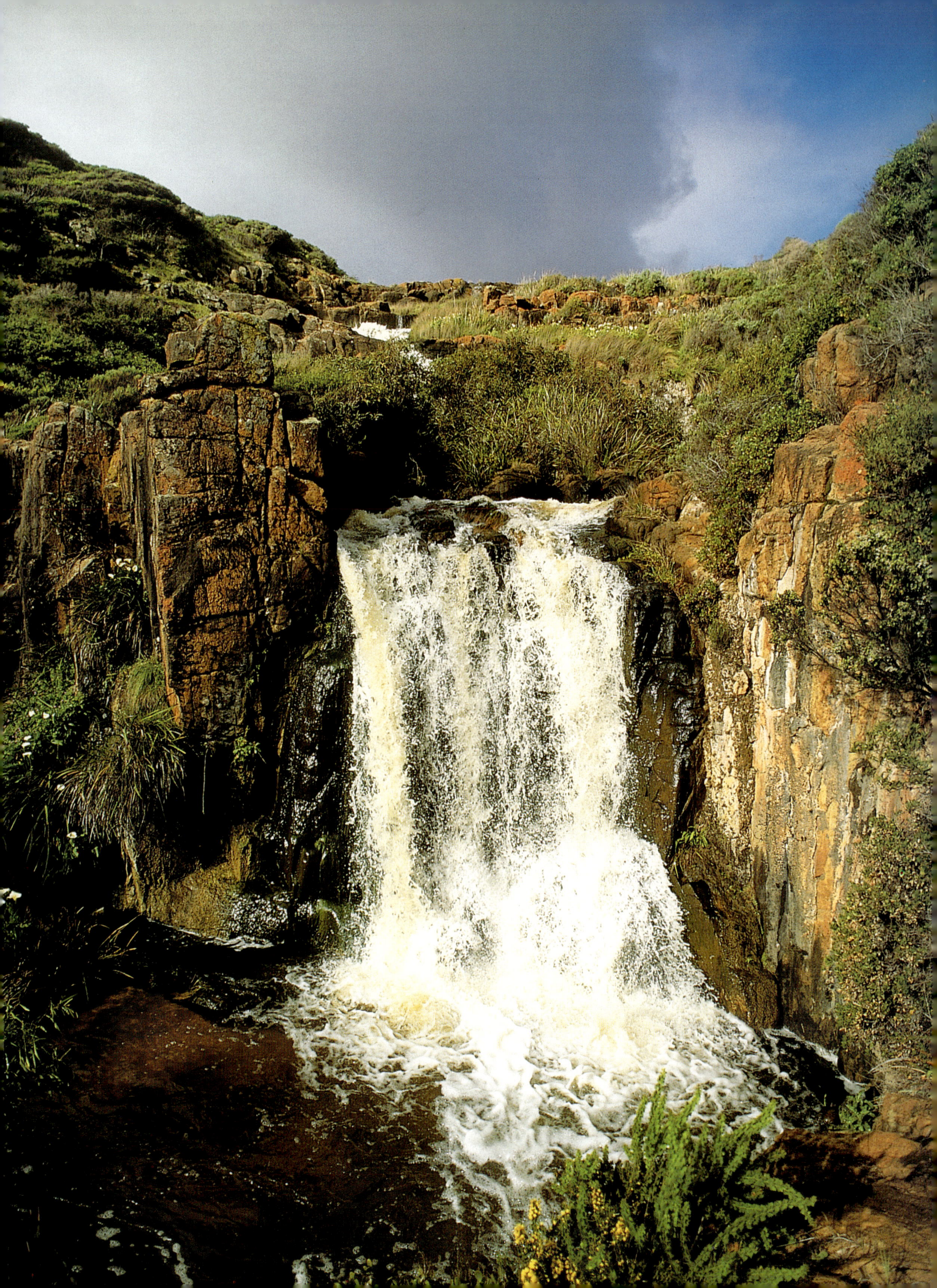

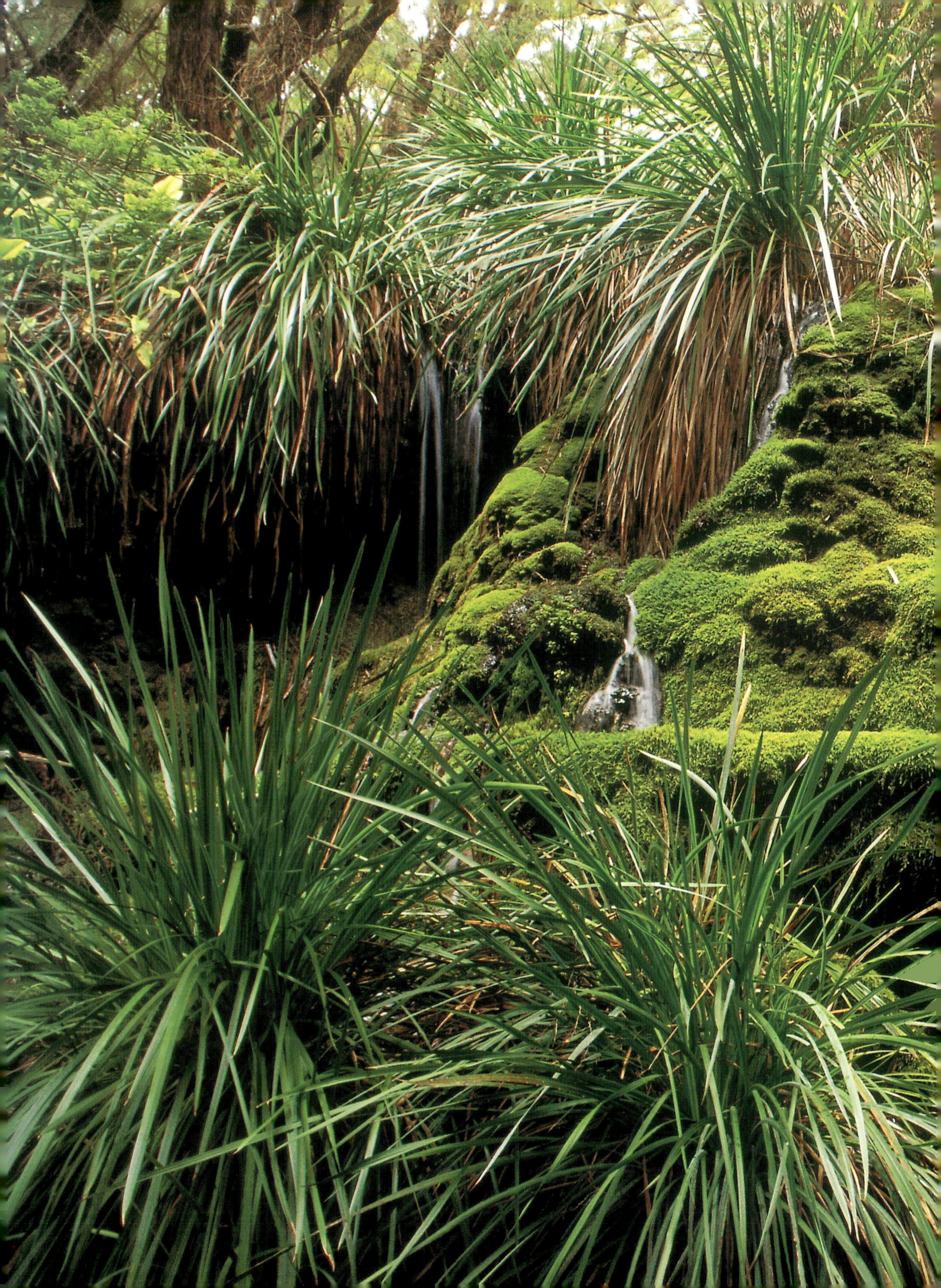

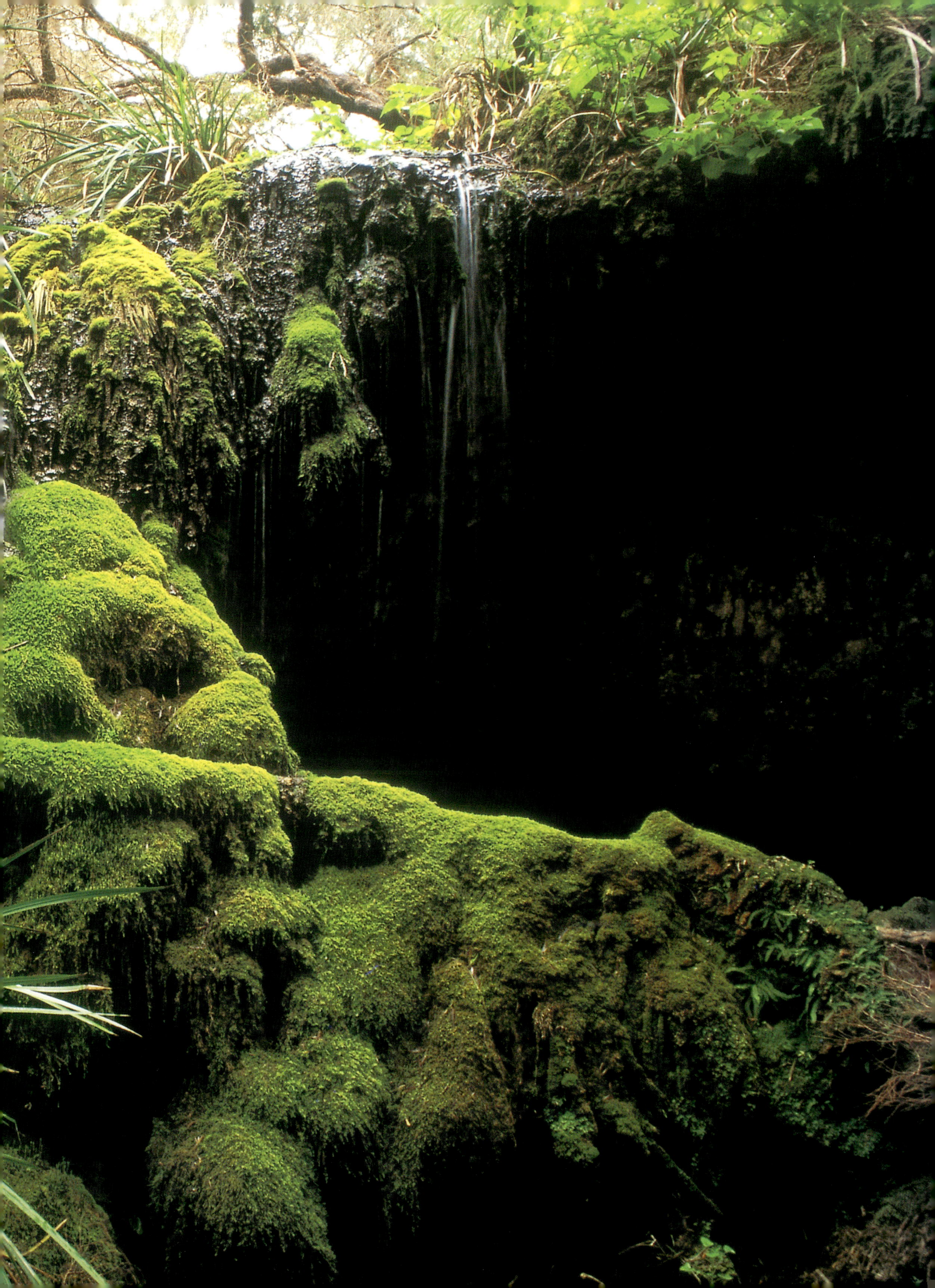

However, despite the apparent good intentions of Molloy and John Bussell, trouble was not far from the surface, inevitably erupting in 1841, when settler George Layman, the head of Wonnerup House on the Vasse Estuary, was speared to death. Seven Aborigines, none of whom was the killer, were hunted and shot. As the indigenous people lost more of their traditional hunting grounds, they naturally turned to the introduced livestock of the new settlers for food. Later in the century and into the twentieth century, the relationship deteriorated further as more settlers arrived, imposing significant cultural changes on the independence of the indigenous people and introducing discriminatory laws and layers of bureaucracy that sought to exert unnecessary control.

With Ellensbrook bursting with children, stock and residents, the Bussell family began building Wallcliffe House, above the Margaret River as it winds its way towards the sea. Its distinctive architecture must have looked positively palatial at the time with its many bedrooms, dining, reception and kitchen areas. The shingled roof and the rich jarrah floorboards are made from local materials. The home and surrounding gardens were faithfully restored in the 1990s by businessman and developer Mark Hohnen, and the house is now owned by another prominent Western Australian businessman, Michael Chaney.

One of the grandest homes in Margaret River was Basildene Manor, built by the Willmott family in 1912. This classic two-storey timber and stone building with polished jarrah boards at the entrance has been gradually restored and extended in recent years, while retaining the integrity of the original design.

A major development in the architectural style of the Capes region was that created by the settlers who came as part of the Group Settlement Scheme in the early 1920s. Using the abundant local timbers they created a simple and practical style of house. The small and modest weatherboard construction is a testament to simplicity. The distinctive features of this style are a passage from front to back with bedrooms off to the side, and a sloping roof, which creates a front verandah. Many of the original group houses have been restored and survive today. An early example is the small cottage at Brookland Valley winery on Caves Road. It was built in the 1880s and became a standard design for group settlers some years later.

Through much of the first fifty or sixty years of the twentieth century there were few new influences on the architecture of the area, but then in the sixties came the first stirrings of the new wave. It was the ocean waves they were chasing, but the surfies and 'alternative lifestylers' also needed somewhere to live — permanent and not so permanent.

Right: Wallcliffe House, built by Ellen and Alfred Bussell in 1865 and now owned by Michael and Rose Chaney.

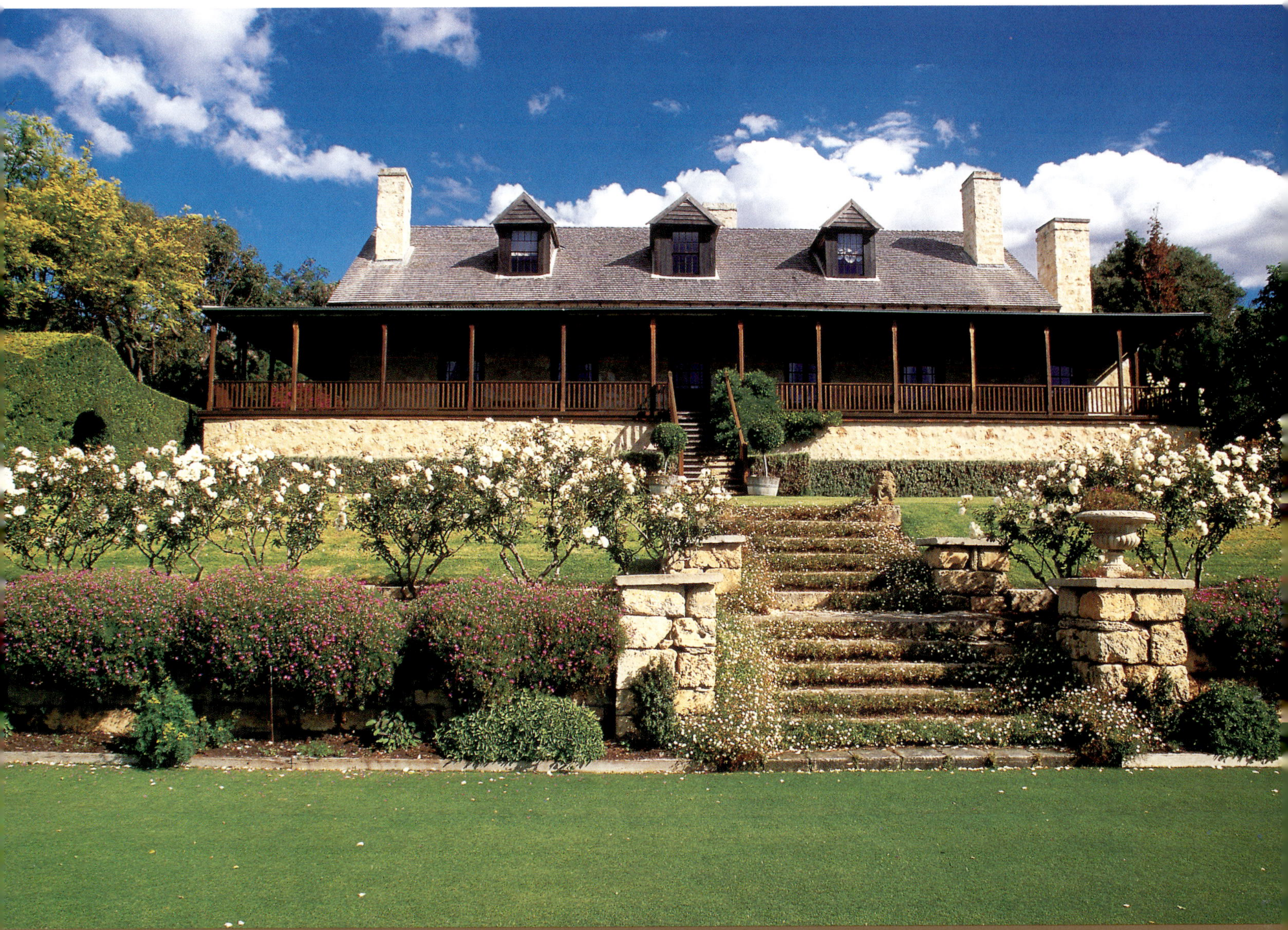

Above: Betty and Neville Earl raised their five children in this house near Cowaramup.
Right: Basildene Manor, built for Percy and Margaret Willmott in 1912 and now a popular guesthouse close to the township of Margaret River.

The structures that emerged were basic and generally created with second-hand materials of all shapes, sizes and previous uses, along with whatever the local landscape and environment could provide — gravel, timber and limestone. Some of these rather basic structures still exist, but many have been replaced by more sophisticated dwellings, stylish creations using granite and limestone and local jarrah and marri, with corrugated iron for roofing and internal walls.

Even more creative forms of architecture have crept into the landscape, some wildly outlandish, some simple and quaint, but most refreshingly inventive. Natural or easily obtained materials such as corrugated iron, concrete, straw, mud, timber and granite are brought together by talented artisans and professional architects to create the rich architectural fabric of Margaret River.

In the early seventies, as the fledgling wine industry was just starting to find its feet, a new style

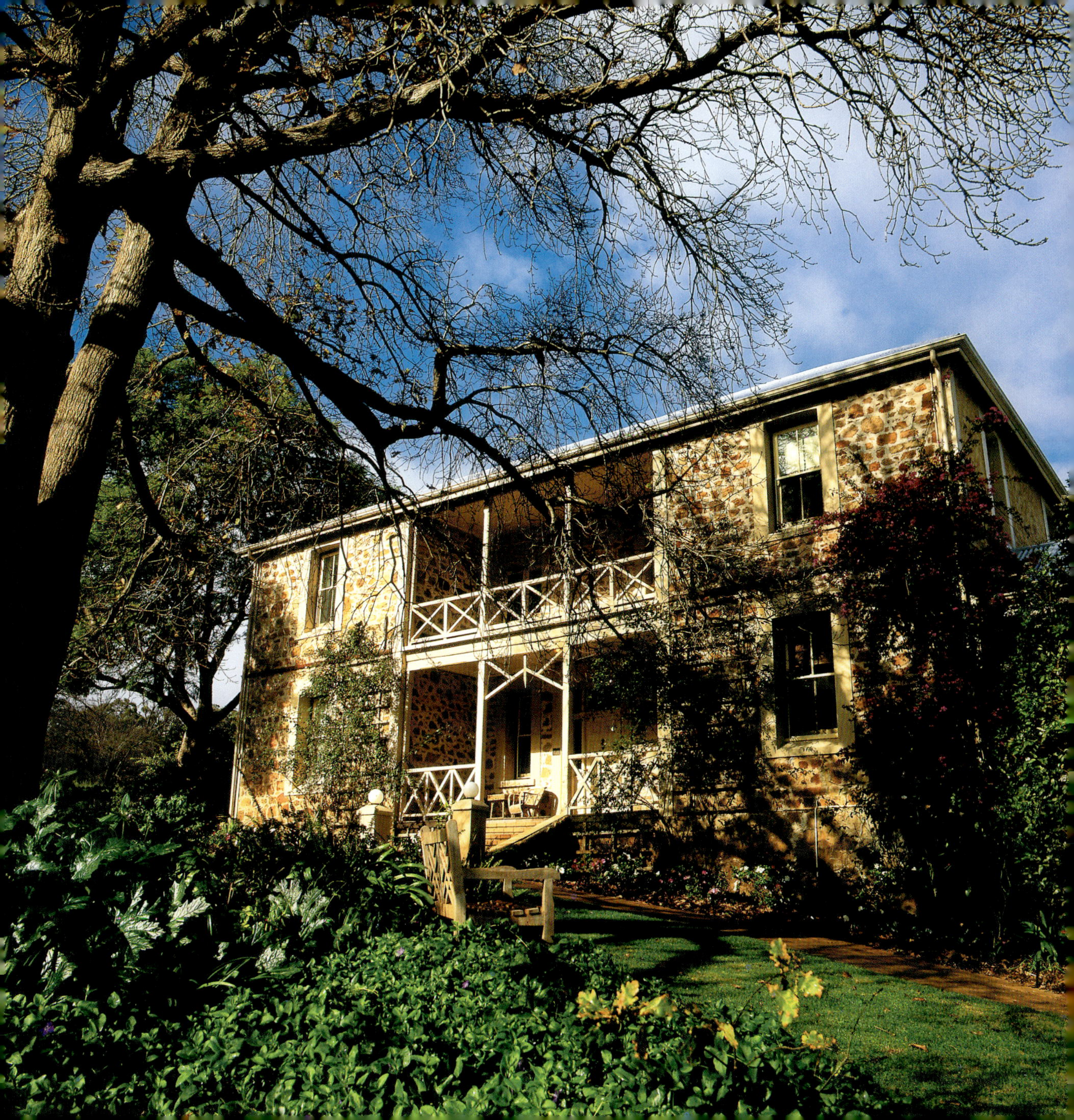

Above and right: Duncan Hancock's house.

of architecture, based on the use of rammed earth blocks and bricks, also began to establish a foothold. This material was perfectly suited to the basic winery need for insulation and temperature constancy. It draws on the abundant reserves of gravel and loam to create the thick building blocks, and on the range of excellent timber to provide a functional and beautiful finish. The result is sturdy, yet rustic, and maintains a harmonious blend with the surrounding environment. The natural brown gravelly loam colour is an extension of the soils on which these structures have been built.

Together, the effect is a distinctive and modern Margaret River architectural style, perfectly illustrated in wineries such as Cape Mentelle, Pierro and Lenton Brae, which are aesthetically pleasing as well as providing a pragmatic solution to the winemakers' need for an efficient working environment.

125

Above: Howard Park vineyard and cellar door at night.
Right: At Gunyulgup Gallery.

126

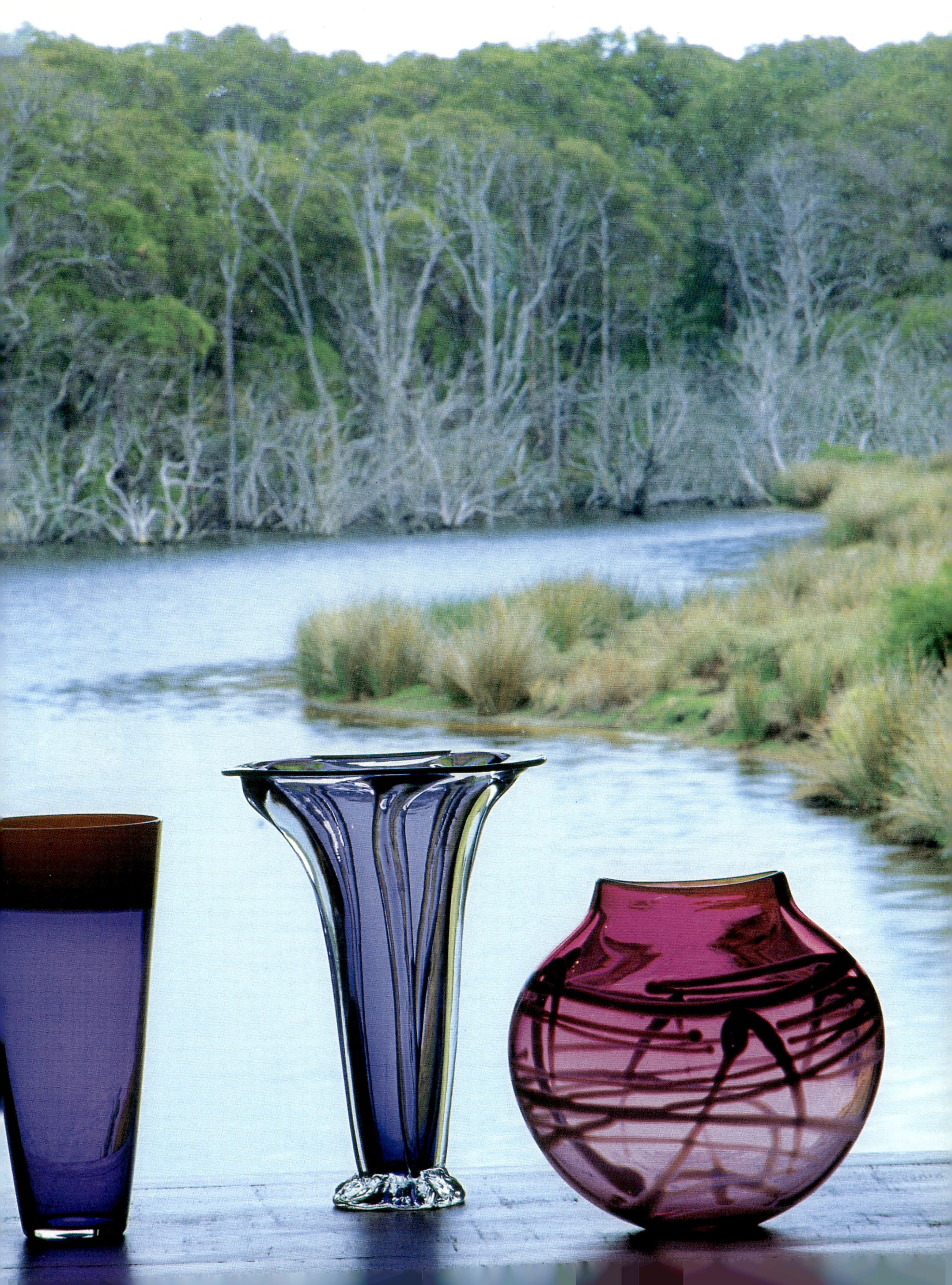

Above: The art gallery at Leeuwin Estate features the original paintings from their Art Series wines.
Right: St Thomas More Catholic Church, Margaret River,
designed by Chris Wilcox and built in the rammed-earth style so popular in the region.

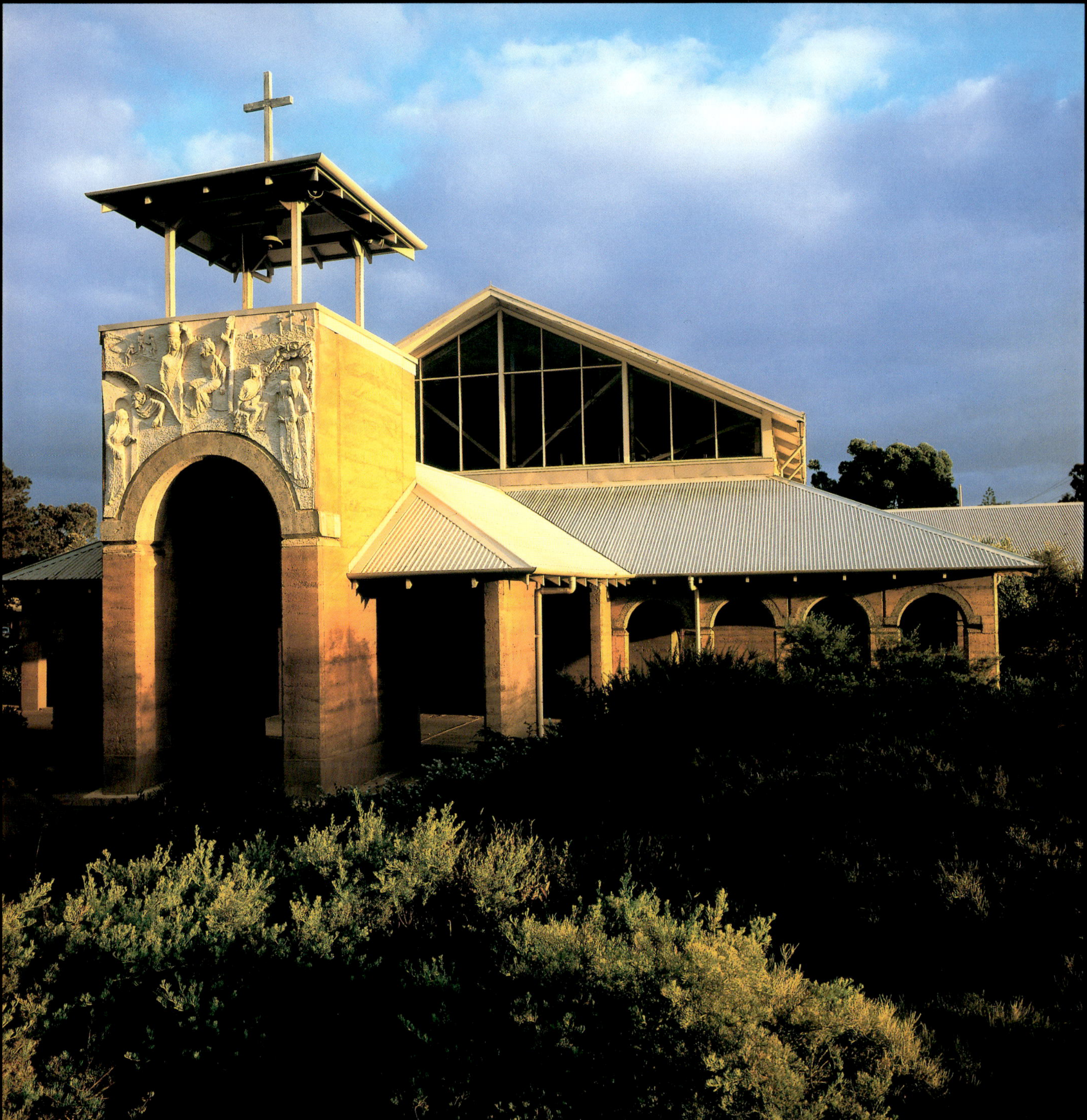

6. The people

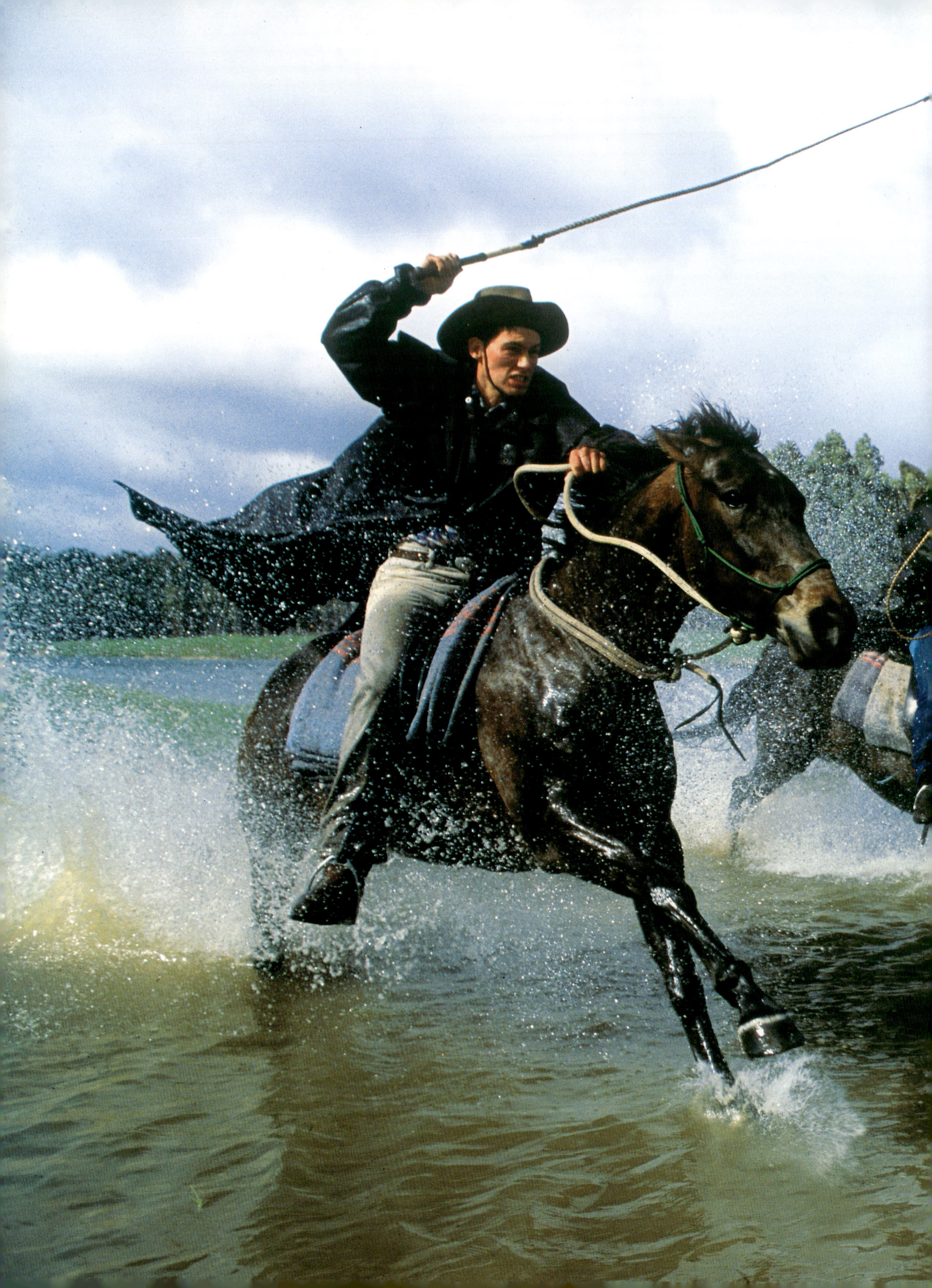

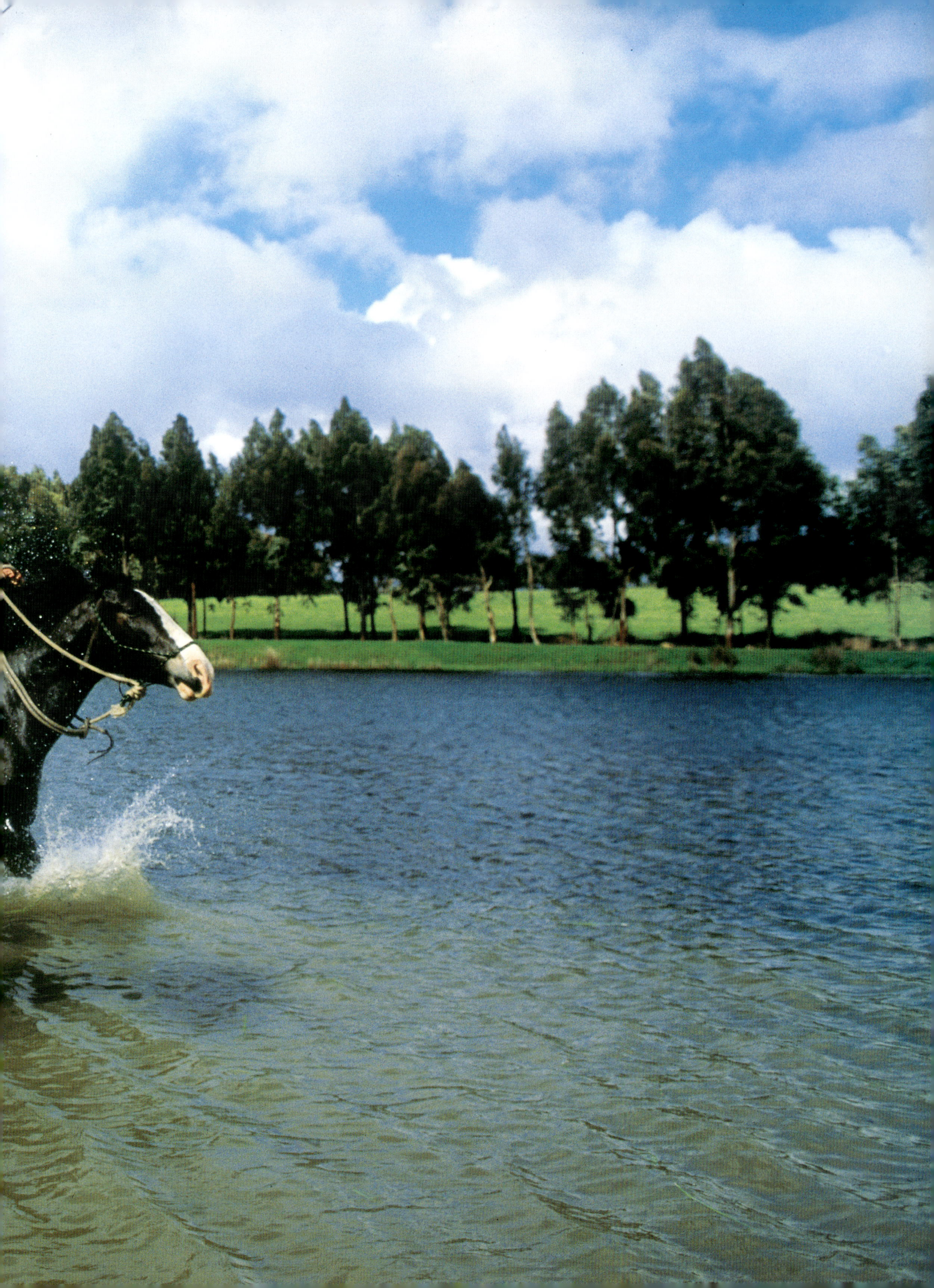

For the past fifty years or so, the call of the surf has lured young men and women to Margaret River. Initially, the awesome reputation of the best breaks drew them to its beaches, on weekends or for their holidays. Since the 1970s, however, the development of a local wine industry has transformed the area, initially by providing increased employment. Those who love the surf and want to come to Margaret River to live have been attracted by the availability of casual work. Seasonal and part-time employment — much of it outdoors, in vineyards and wineries, at cellar doors and in winery restaurants — has enabled many to take up the relaxed lifestyle that the region offers. Since the 1990s, the dramatic increase in tourism — once again largely fuelled by the national and international success of Margaret River wines — has brought with it the need for a viable hospitality industry and the infrastructure to satisfy the demands of overseas and interstate visitors, as well as locals.

Given the carefree lifestyle that is possible here, it is hardly surprising that there are some with little visible means of support who like to dally in the region. Some of these have found cheap accommodation by sharing with others or camping out in the forests or in their cars by the beach.

There are significant environmental issues still facing Margaret River — most of which are concerned with containing the urban sprawl — at places such as Prevelly, Bunker Bay and Smiths Beach. The days when the forestry industry threatened trees, however, are long gone, and so are many of the environmentalists, who have moved on to places where there are still trees to be saved — to Pemberton, Walpole and Denmark.

There are those whose families have farmed in Margaret River for generations who have accepted, even loved, the toil and dawn-till-dusk hours that are an inevitable aspect of the work of the farmer. Certainly, they have delighted in the peace and tranquillity of farmland surrounded by the bush. While they talk of the constant struggle, they remember their life on the land as a happy one.

The substantial price rises that have accompanied the increased demand for viticultural land have made farming uneconomic for all but the largest and most mechanically efficient dairy farmers. Low returns from beef and dairy farming, together with significantly higher land rates that resulted from rises in property values, have meant that those wishing to remain on the land need an alternative or supplementary income. Although reluctant to leave behind a lifestyle and an area that they have loved, selling out has become for many a necessary — and lucrative — option. The pain of leaving, however, is palpable. Second-generation farmers, Moya and John Dempster, have a second income that enables them to remain on their farm. They comment that few who leave ever come back. Except for funerals.

The loss of so many of the region's farmers has had at least one unforeseen effect. Kangaroos, for a long time culled by locals whenever their numbers grew beyond acceptable levels, have increased to plague proportions and have become a serious problem for vignerons.

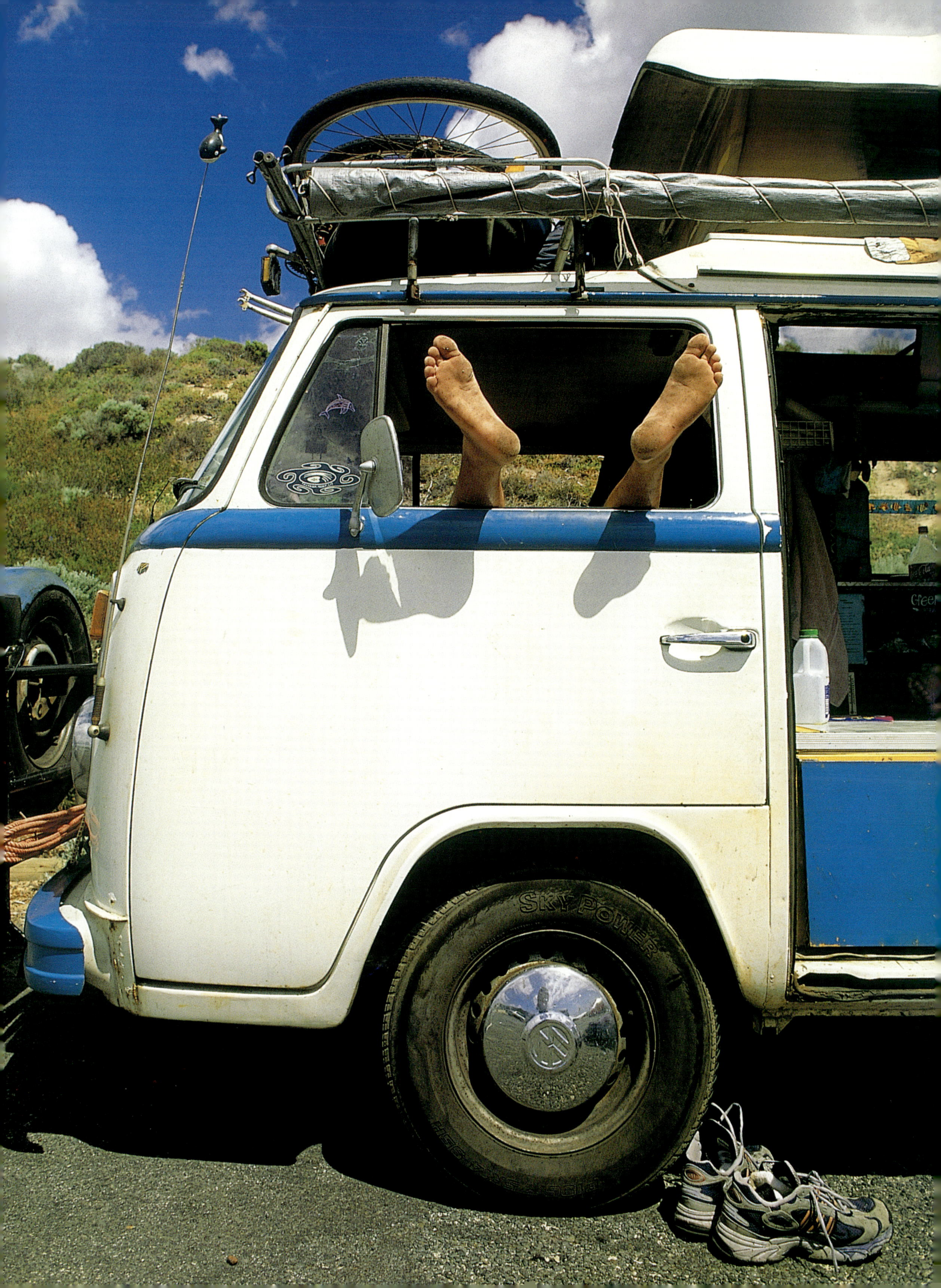
SKY POWER

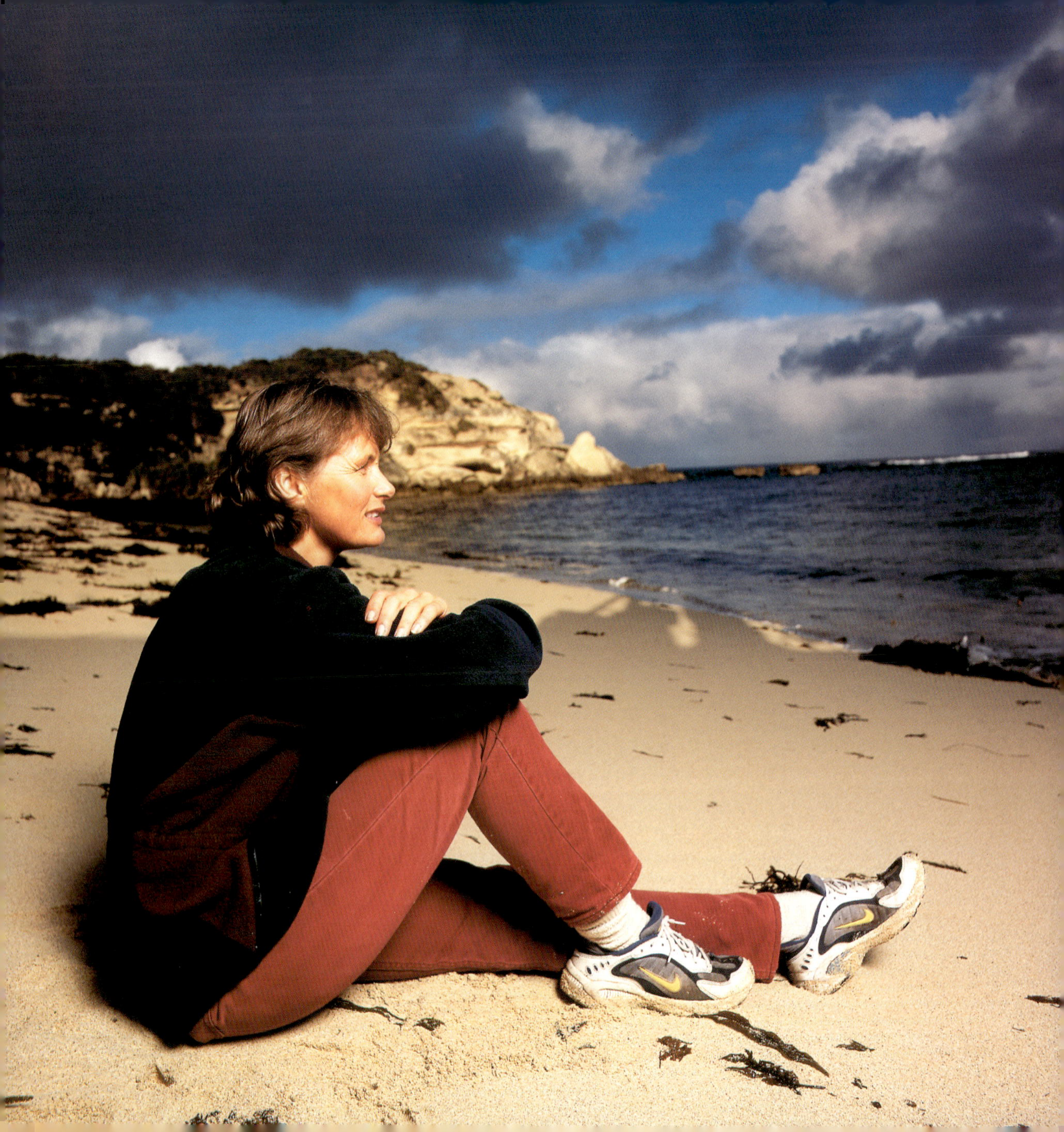

Page 131: Canoeing down the Margaret River on a Bush Tucker tour.
Page 132: Sam Watson and Sascha Watson, who train people in horsemanship,
at full gallop on their family's Margaret River property.
Previous page: Relaxing at Prevelly.
Left: Shane Gould at Gnarabup.
Above: Margaret River chefs get their rocks off fishing at Gracetown.

Above: The Wise Family Band. From left to right: Louisa, Rowena, Lucy, Ruth and Scott.
Right: Breakfast with the family of local vet, Stefan Kurys-Romer.
Clockwise from left: Uta, Stefan, Lilian, Moritz, Lorenz and friends.
Stefan, an Olympic sailor for Germany, and Uta emigrated to Australia to live in Margaret River.

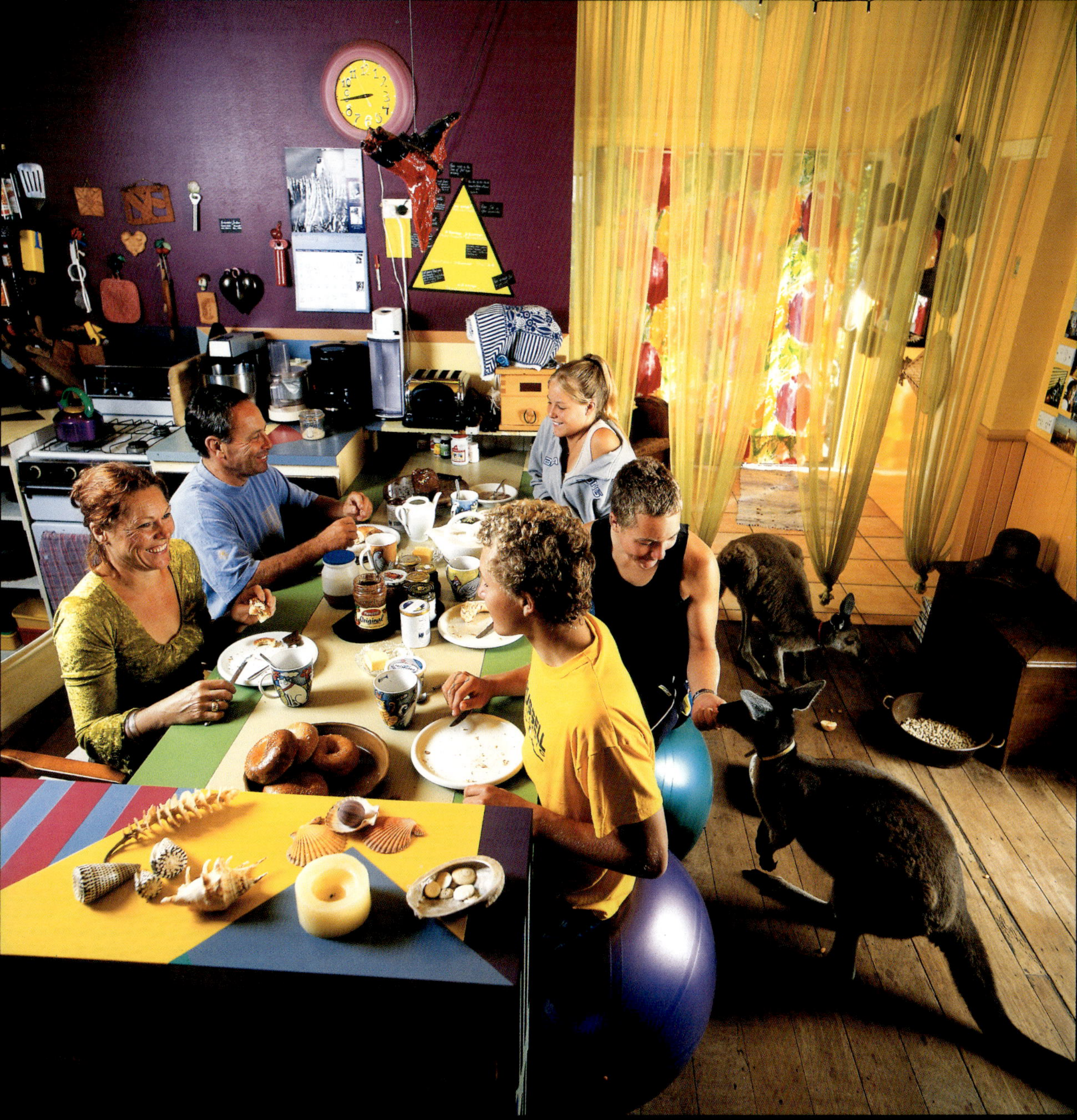

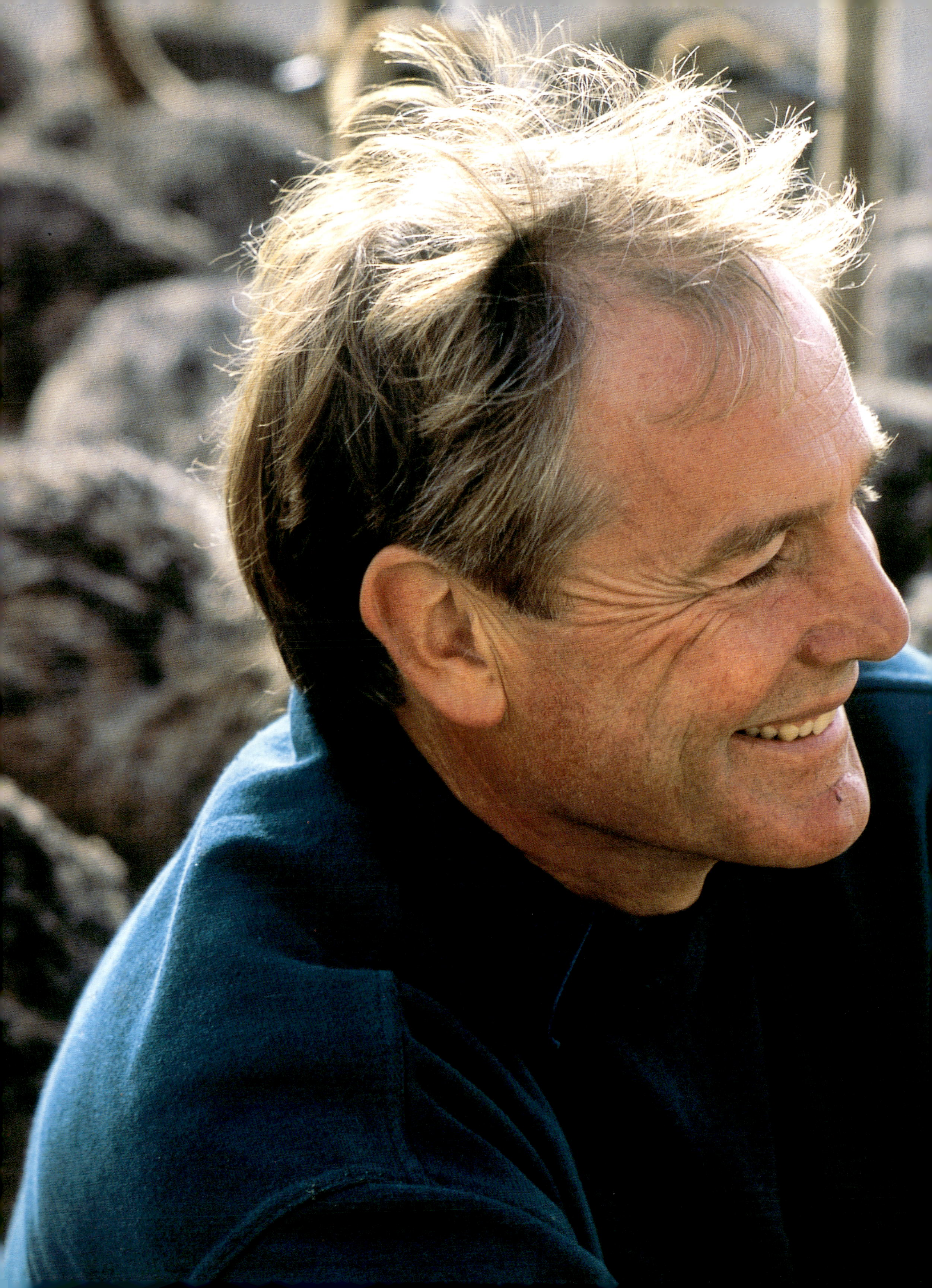

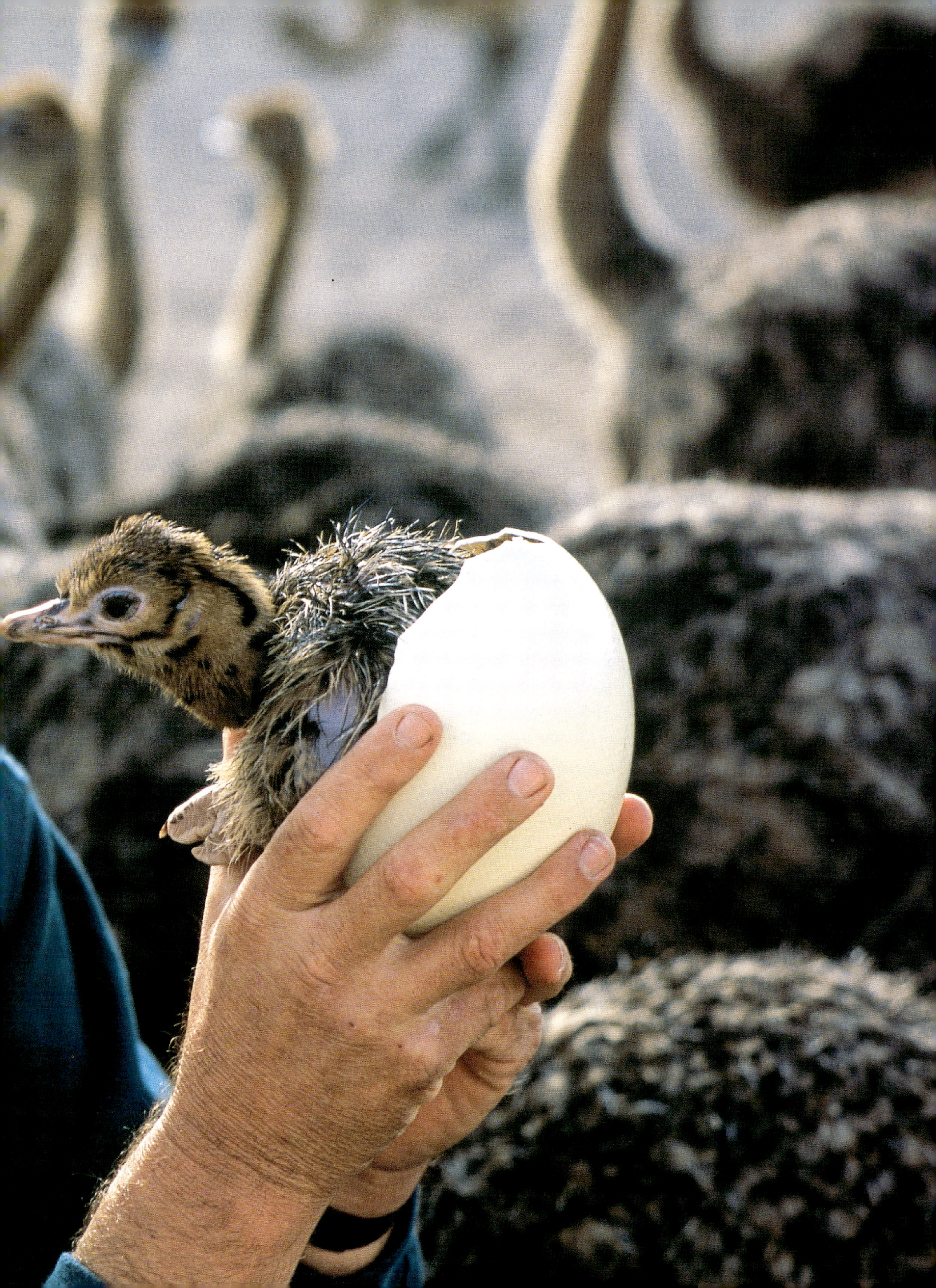

Almost all of the artisans attracted to Margaret River came in search of the surf and stayed as potters, furniture makers, wood-turners, glassblowers, jewellery makers and metal workers. They sought the clean air and water of the region, and the tranquillity that came with its remoteness. They loved the landscape, especially the trees, and delighted in the feeling of being close to the land. Potter Ian Dowling says that this group has sometimes been confused with hippies who came to the area. He claims that few of the artisans have left. 'Dropping out was never an option that they considered. These are hard workers, risk takers, driven people. They need to be working with their hands, have to be making things, and they never lose that.'

Many of those who came to Margaret River in the last thirty years of the twentieth century relished the opportunity to build their own homes. They saw the readily available materials — wood, clay, gravel, rock — and took up the challenge. Diversity and experimentation have been two resulting themes.

The perspective of the alternative lifestylers in Margaret River is vividly captured in Shane Gould's compelling autobiography, *Tumble Turns*. She describes the continuing lure of the surf and her delight in the tranquil surroundings of her farm, while making it clear that the 'simple, subsistence lifestyle was a lot of work.' Gould discusses the financial reality of running the farm, the ten years it took to build their house, the need to take on part-time work within and outside the region to survive, and the rigours and joys of raising children.

Previous page: Rod Gaskell was a farmer in South Africa and France before starting Wulura Ostriches in Yallingup. Here, a new arrival is caught at the moment of birth. Right: Allan Fox, glassblower, hard at work at Fox Glass Studio.

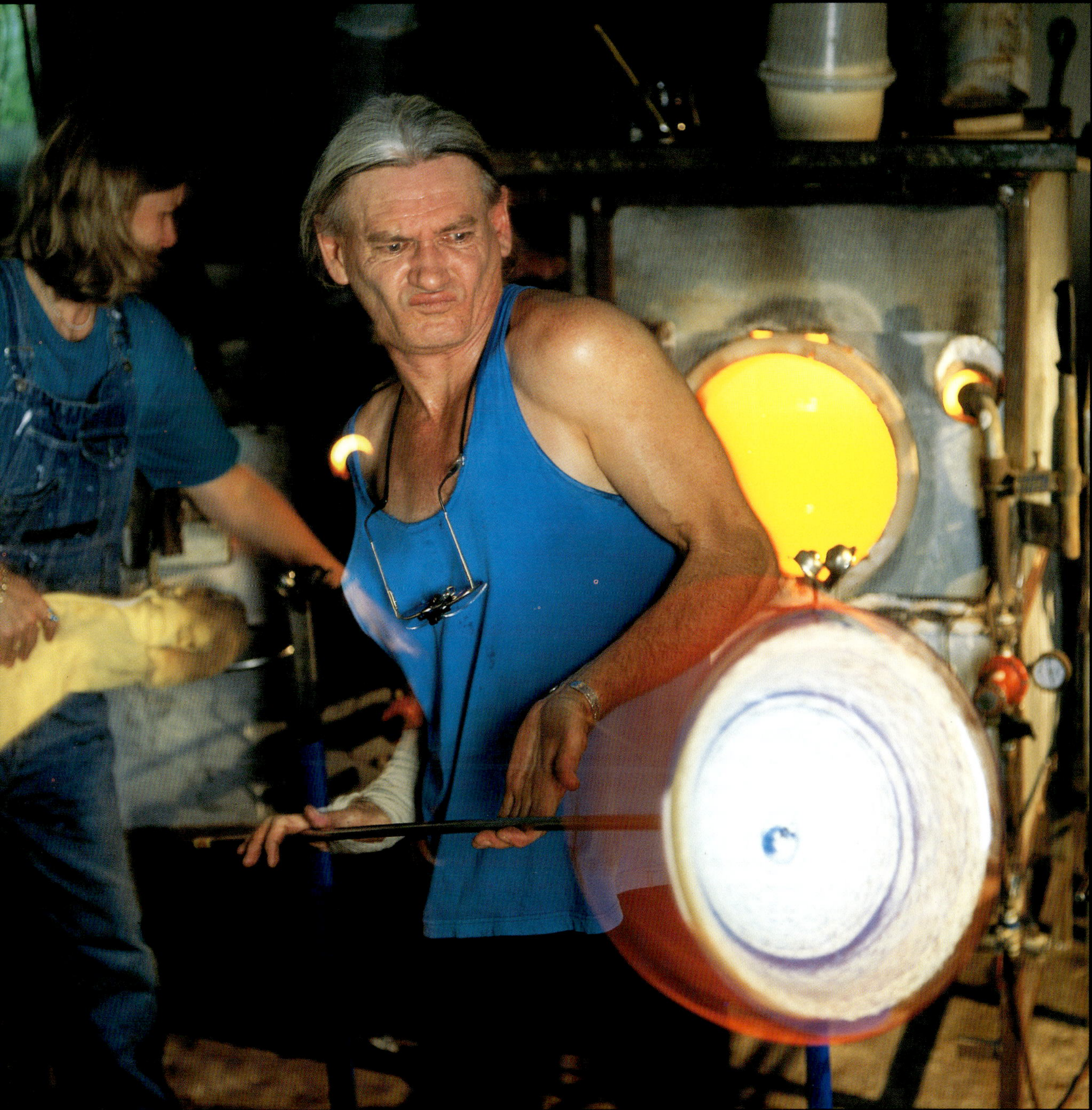

Today, many Nyungars maintain cultural and family ties with their traditional lands. The Wardan Aboriginal Cultural Centre at Injidup (eight kilometres south of Yallingup) serves as a community centre. It features an outstanding Aboriginal art gallery, and offers regular guided bushwalks of the area to the public as well as occasional functions such as the corroboree and traditional feast held to celebrate the Birak (summer) season.

Times change. With the build-up of population following the success of the wine industry and the development of infrastructure to cope with significantly increased numbers of tourists, many of those who came to Margaret River seeking a quiet and peaceful alternative lifestyle are moving further south to more sparsely settled places like Karridale and Augusta.

Surfing, once the preserve of fanatical young men and women, has attracted more widespread interest and support. Almost everyone does it; super-fit middle-aged swimmers — labelled by the young 'the geriatrics' — can be seen surfing off the Point early each morning. While you can still find an errant vineyard worker who misses work or a graphic designer who doesn't make a deadline because the surf is particularly enticing, there is an increasingly stronger work ethic and a greater sense of competition among the young. The appearance of so many coffee shops and cafes on the main street of Margaret River in the late 1990s is regarded as reflecting the coming of the yuppies.

Right: Artist Trevor Woodward at home.

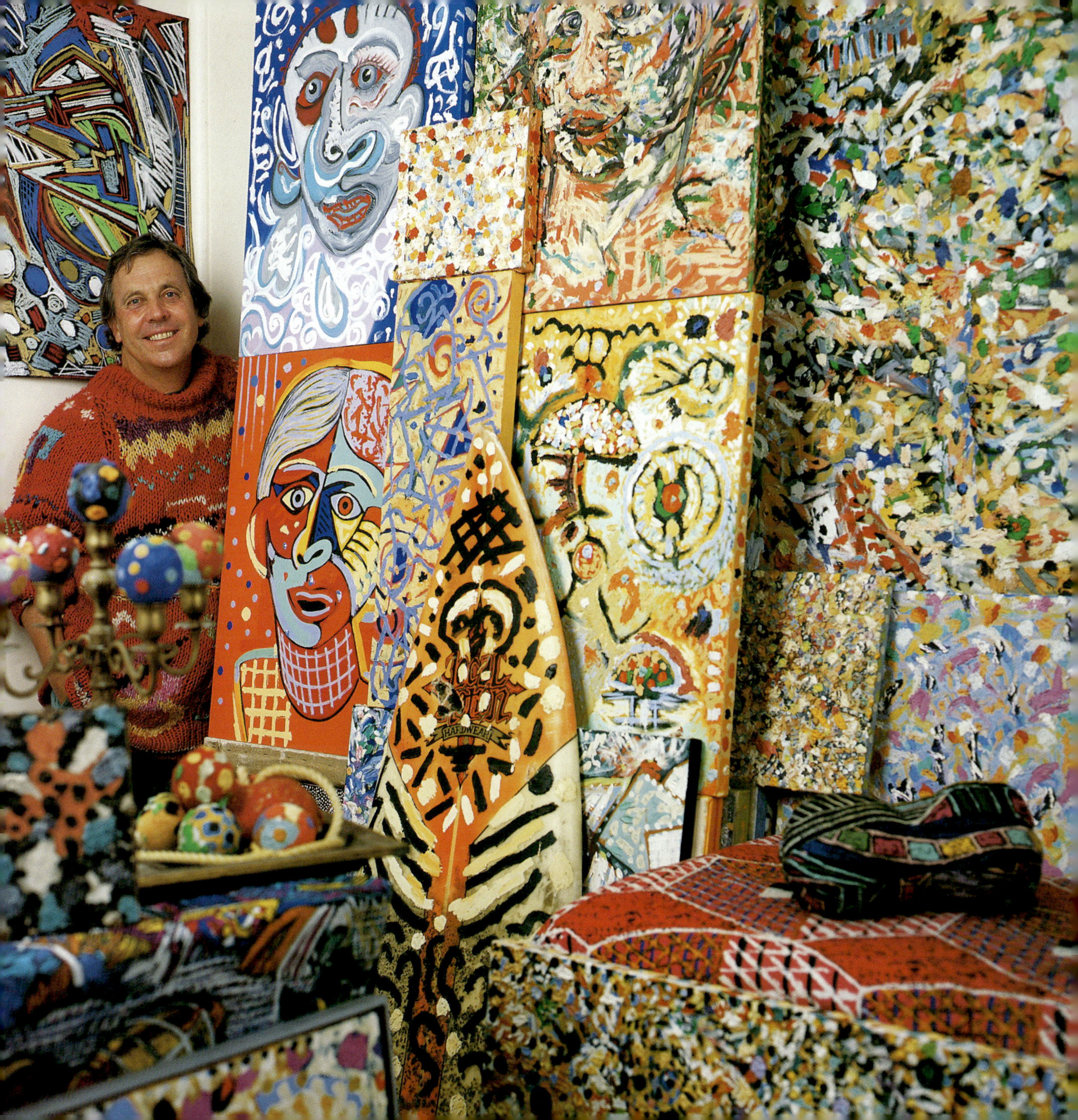

Above: Wood designer Greg Collins in his Margaret River studio.
Right: Vilma Webb and Frances Gillespie at the Wardan Aboriginal Cultural Centre near Yallingup.

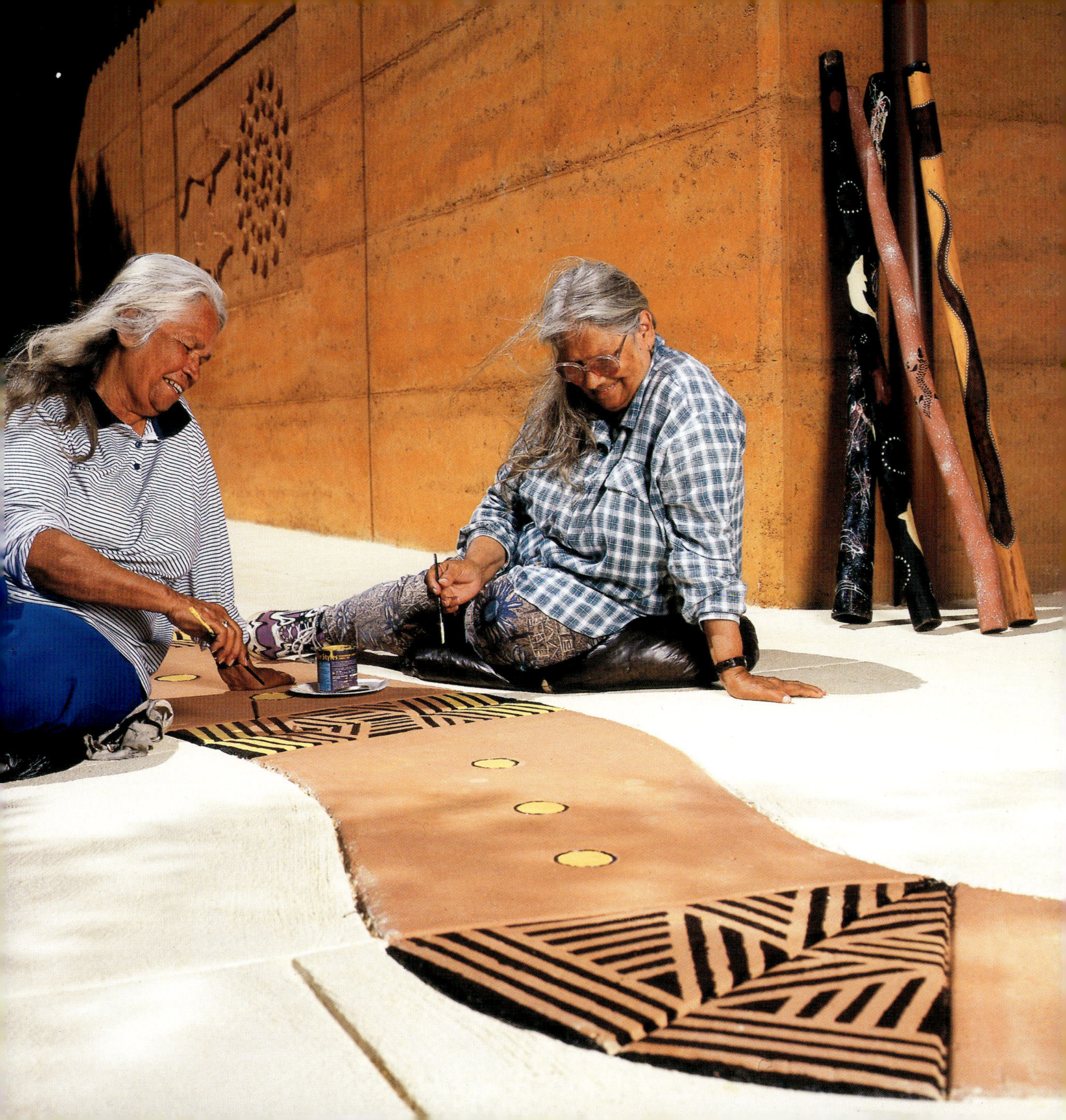

7. The food

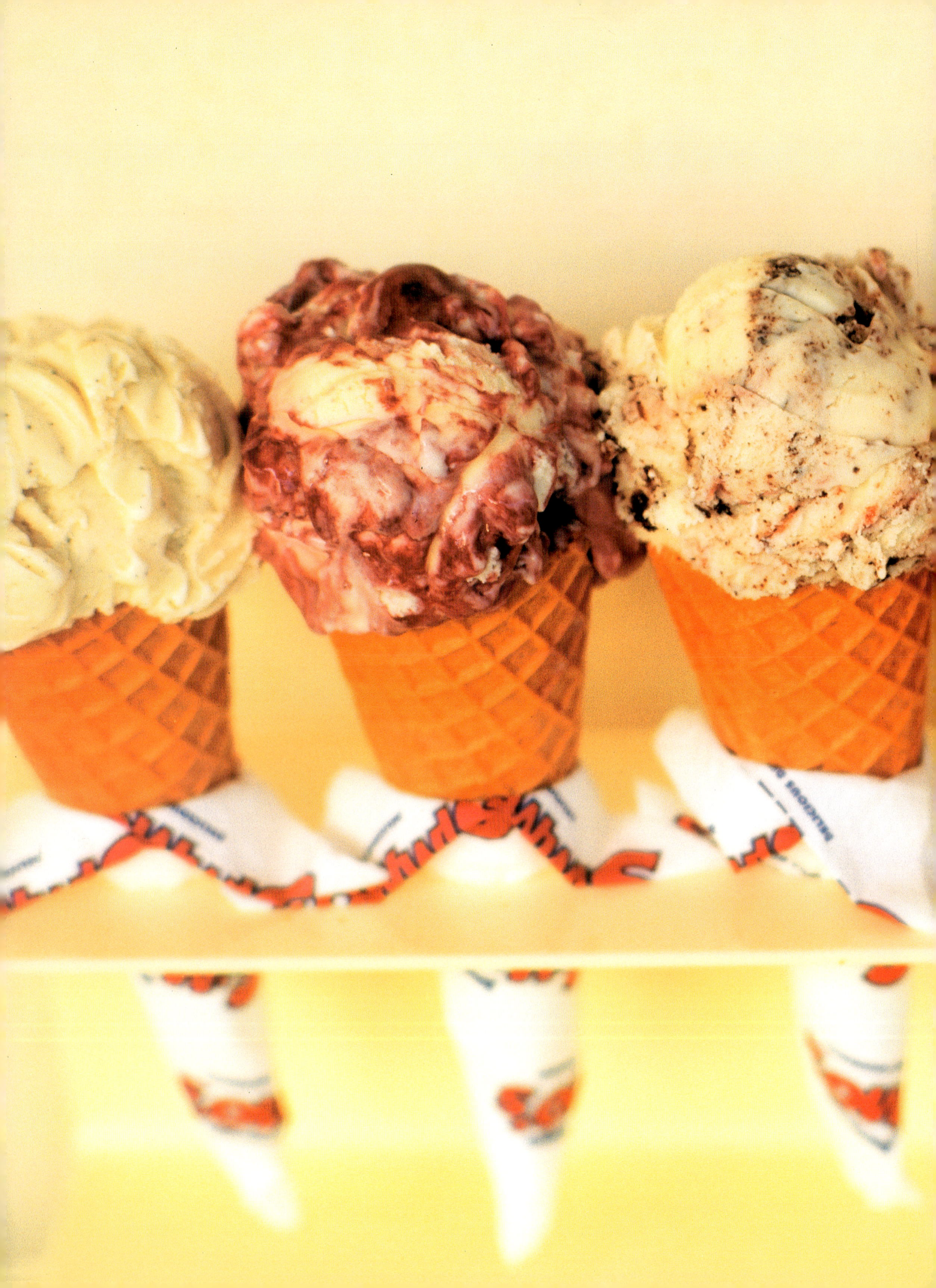

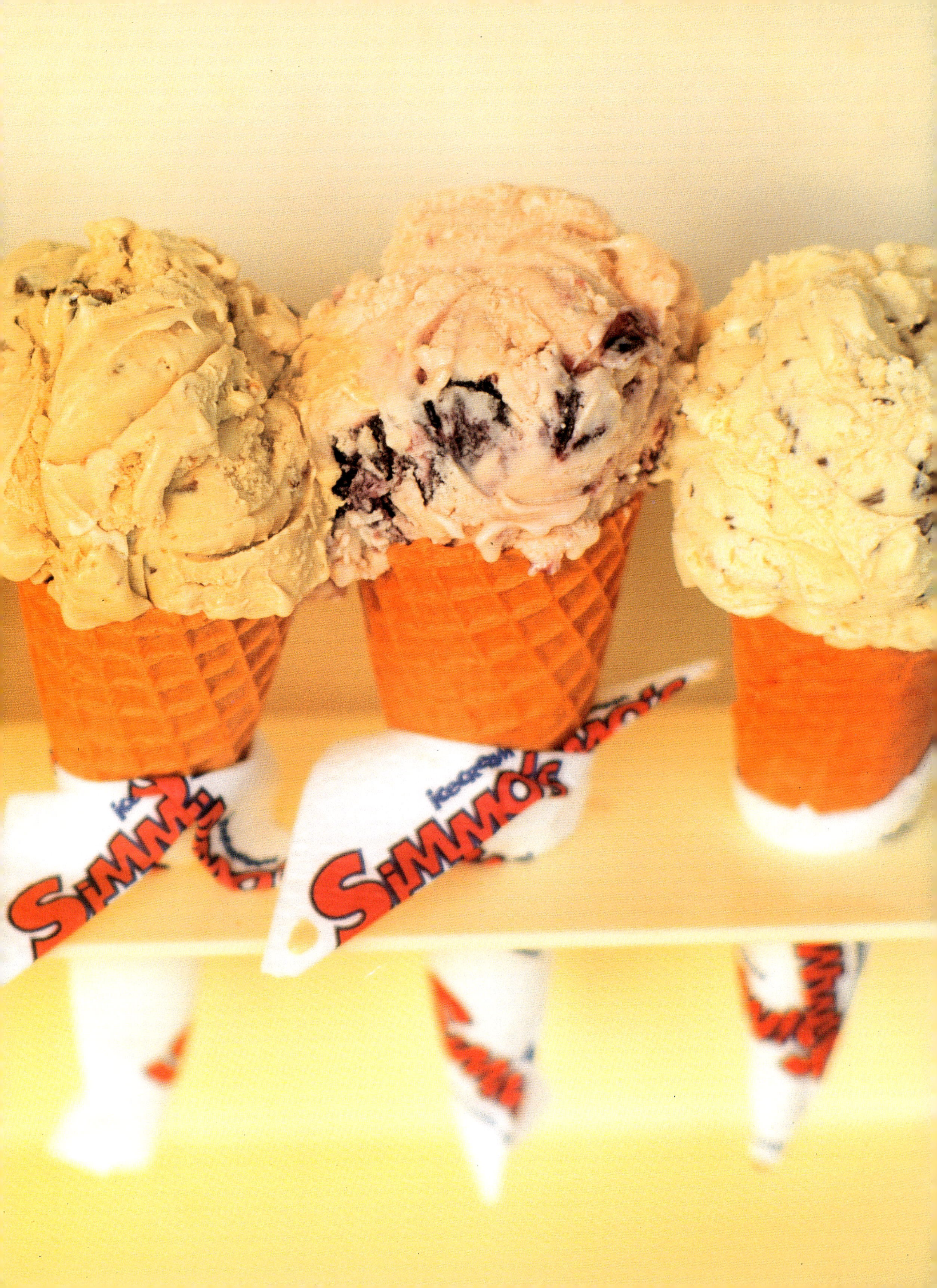
SiMMO'S

From the time of the first European settlement at Augusta in the early 1830s until the beginnings of the dairy industry in the 1920s, subsistence farming — where families produce just enough food to enable them to survive — was the most significant form of food production in Margaret River. In the early days at Augusta the settlers struggled even to subsist, due to their lack of experience and expertise, as well as the difficulties involved in clearing the land and the poor soils they encountered. During this period, fishing, hunting and gathering native plants played an important part in their survival.

For the next forty years, there were a small number of settlements and farms scattered throughout the region whose inhabitants eked out a bare living. This was supplemented, where possible, by selling any surplus production to American whalers. Ellen and Alfred Bussell showed what was possible, firstly at Vasse, then at Ellensbrook and finally at Wallcliffe, by producing and selling butter, milk and cheese, vegetables and meat. From Wallcliffe, they supplied these goods to workers in the timber mills at Quindalup and Augusta.

The establishment of the timber industry in the South-West from the 1870s provided a boost to the economy, transport infrastructure and employment. For the first time, significant numbers were attracted to the area. Because of this, the timber industry was a factor in the successful establishment of the beef and dairy farms in the Augusta region in the 1860s. The rich karri loam soils of Boranup and Karridale were utilised by many of the timber workers who kept vegetable plots and livestock to supplement their income and diet. In the 1880s, timber mill proprietor Walter 'Karri' Davies established the first major horticultural project in the area, a large (approximately fifteen hectare) vegetable garden at Karridale.

Although the South-West had shown its potential for beef and dairy production, these could not be regarded as well established industries, even as late as the 1920s. The state government introduced the Group Settlement Scheme to formally establish a dairy industry and increase the population of the area. Individual tales of the hardship of the Group Settlement years in the Margaret River region give a vivid picture of families struggling to produce in order to survive, running cows, pigs, chickens, ducks and horses; hunting the local wild animals — kangaroos, rabbits, possums and birds (pied currawong and parrots) — and growing their own vegetables and fodder for their animals. With time and experimentation they were able to sell off any surplus to neighbours, while milk and cream went to one of the local dairies.

Although many regard the personal cost of the Group Settlement Scheme as high, it can be counted a success in many ways. Imports of food from the eastern states (especially vegetables, eggs, ham and bacon, and dairy produce) fell substantially during the 1920s. By the end of that decade, there was a viable dairy industry with seven factories being operated by the South-West Dairy Farmers' Co-operative. Within ten years, the number of cows in Western Australia doubled while butter production trebled, and trebled again in the 1930s. The population of the South-West increased significantly and its infrastructure was enormously improved.

Page 149: Quinces and quince jam at the Berry Farm.
Previous page: At Simmo's Icecreamery.
Above: Cattle at Gralyn in Wilyabrup.

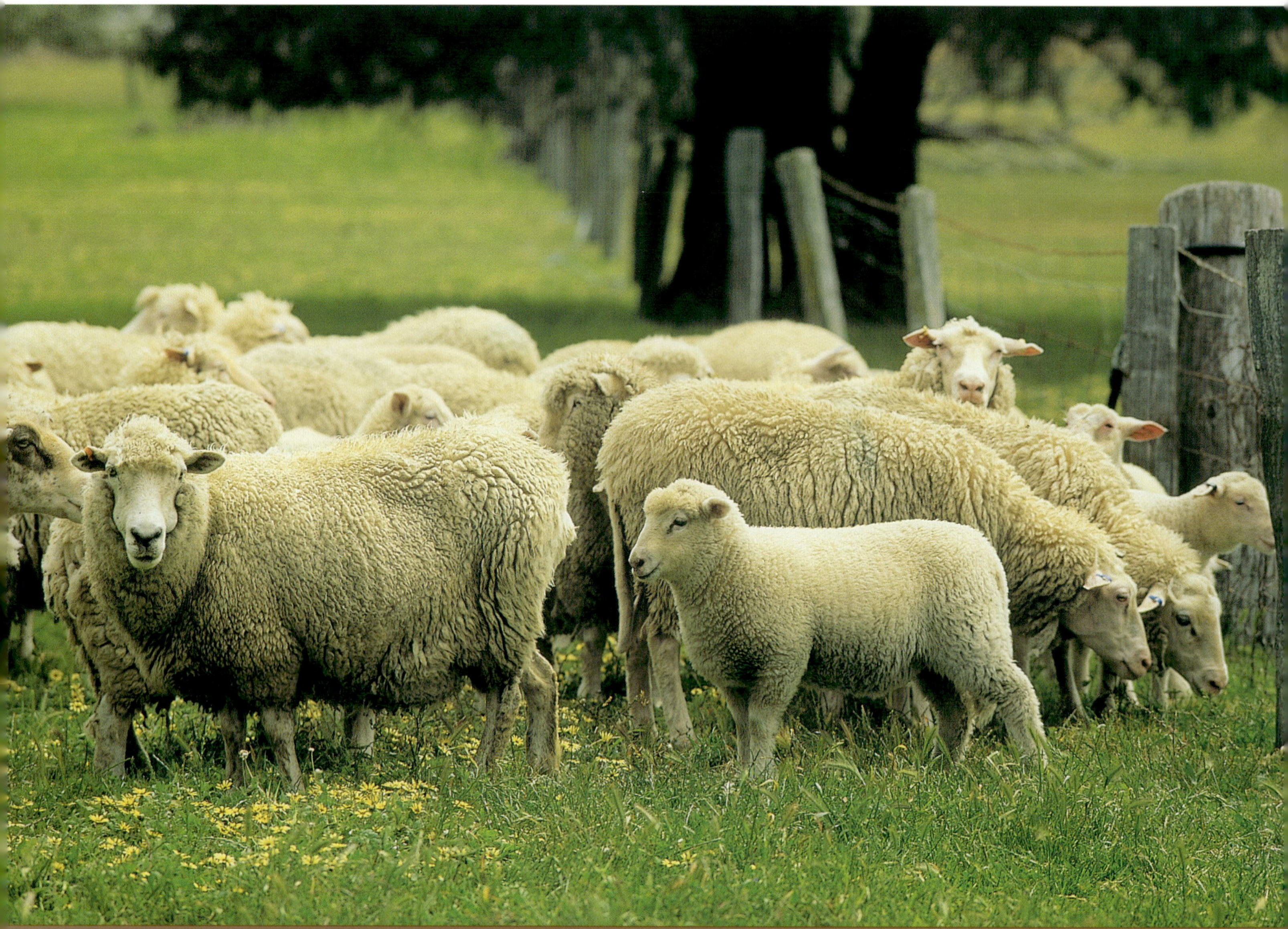

Left: Sheep at Cloverdene Farm, Karridale.
Above: A tray of meseta, a fresh sheep's milk cheese from Cloverdene.

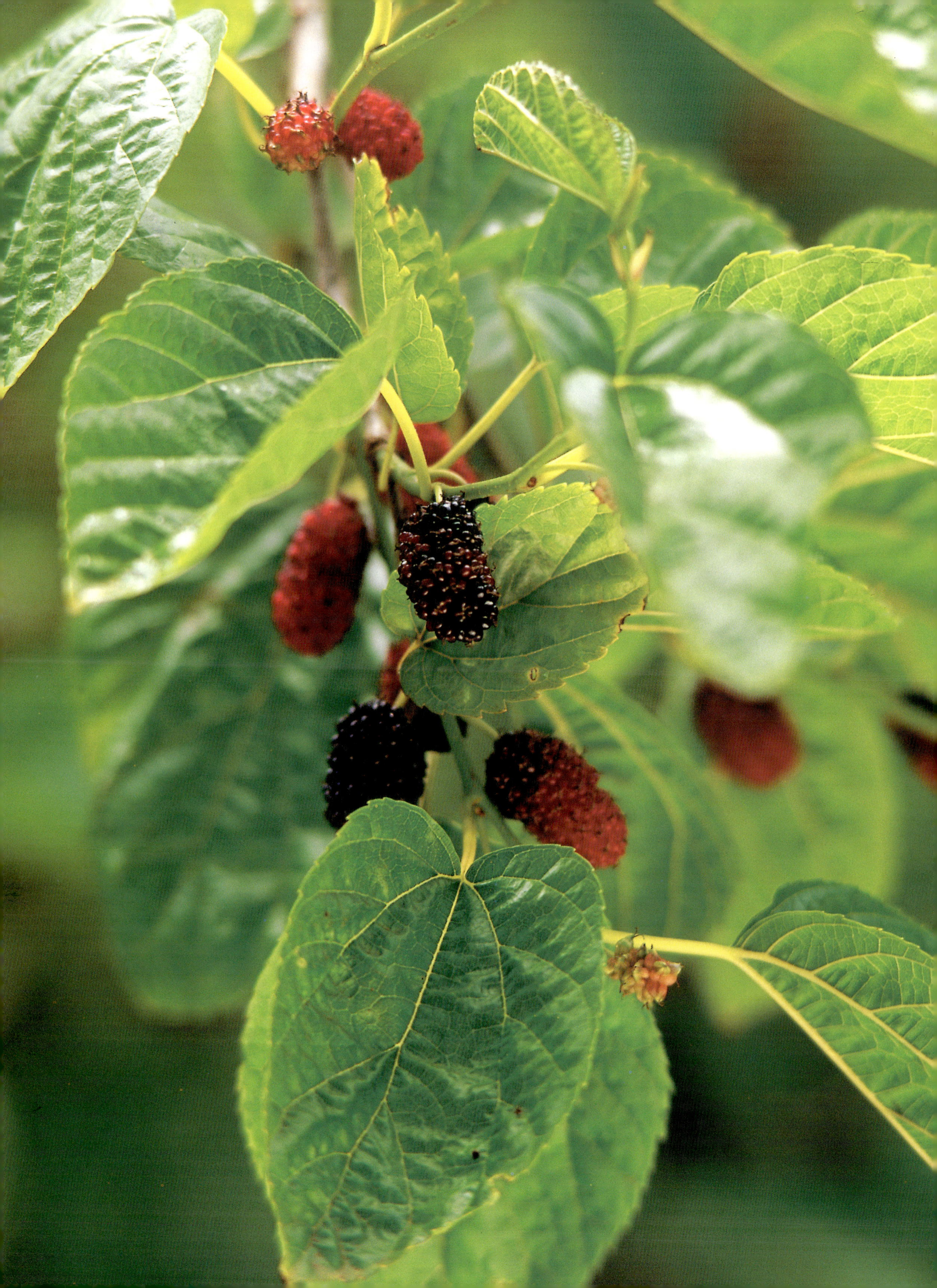

Left: Mulberries at the Berry Farm.
Above: Art or commerce? A new take on the Hay Shed Hill motif.

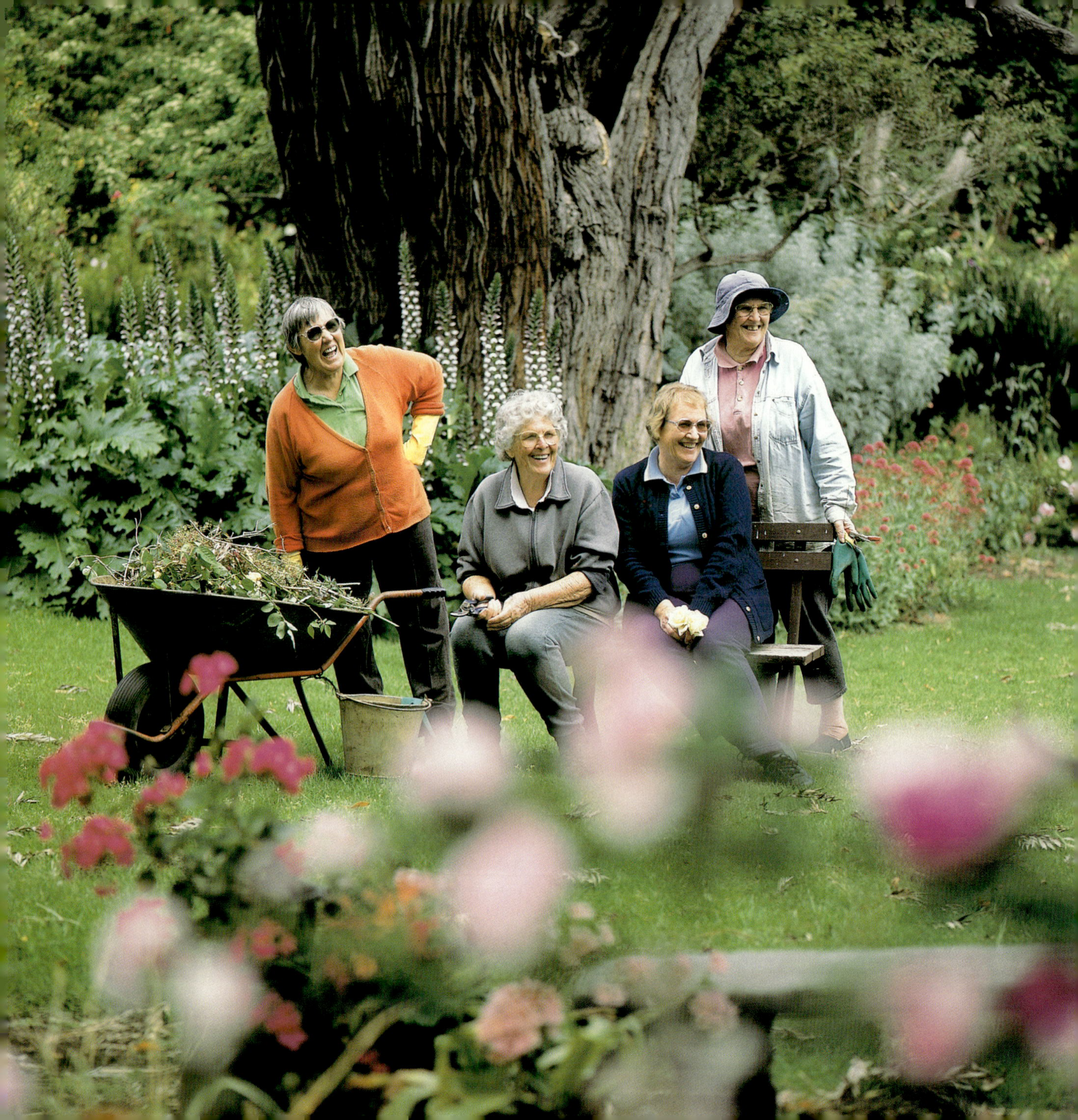

Left: The Peirce sisters. Left to right: Shirley, Barbara, Valerie (Rangnow) and Zoe.
Above: The Community Garden, Margaret River. Left to right: May, Stephen, Dylan and Carroll.

A property on the Margaret River where it crosses Caves Road has been in the Peirce family for more than a hundred years. Barbara, Zoe and Shirley Peirce still live there, and talking to them provides a fascinating picture of the region from the 1920s to the 1960s, during which time the family ran a small dairy farm. They milked up to fifty head of cattle, kept pigs and chickens, and had a vegetable and a flower garden. In addition they grew hay and oats as fodder for the cattle. Meat was only available on the rare occasions when they killed a cow or a pig; even then, some was bartered and some salted for future consumption. Chickens were killed only at Easter and Christmas. They traded butter and bread for fish with two Aboriginal families — the Isaacs and the Harrises — and as girls they shot rabbits with a .22 rifle. Barbara and Zoe Peirce talk about walking three miles to the beach to bring home a bag of winkles that they'd collected from the seashore. The whole family was involved in the work of the farm and their father regularly looked for outside work, for instance with the Road Board, to supplement their income. Most of their neighbours were dairy farmers, although some were vegetable or potato producers. Timber was still the region's main industry at the time.

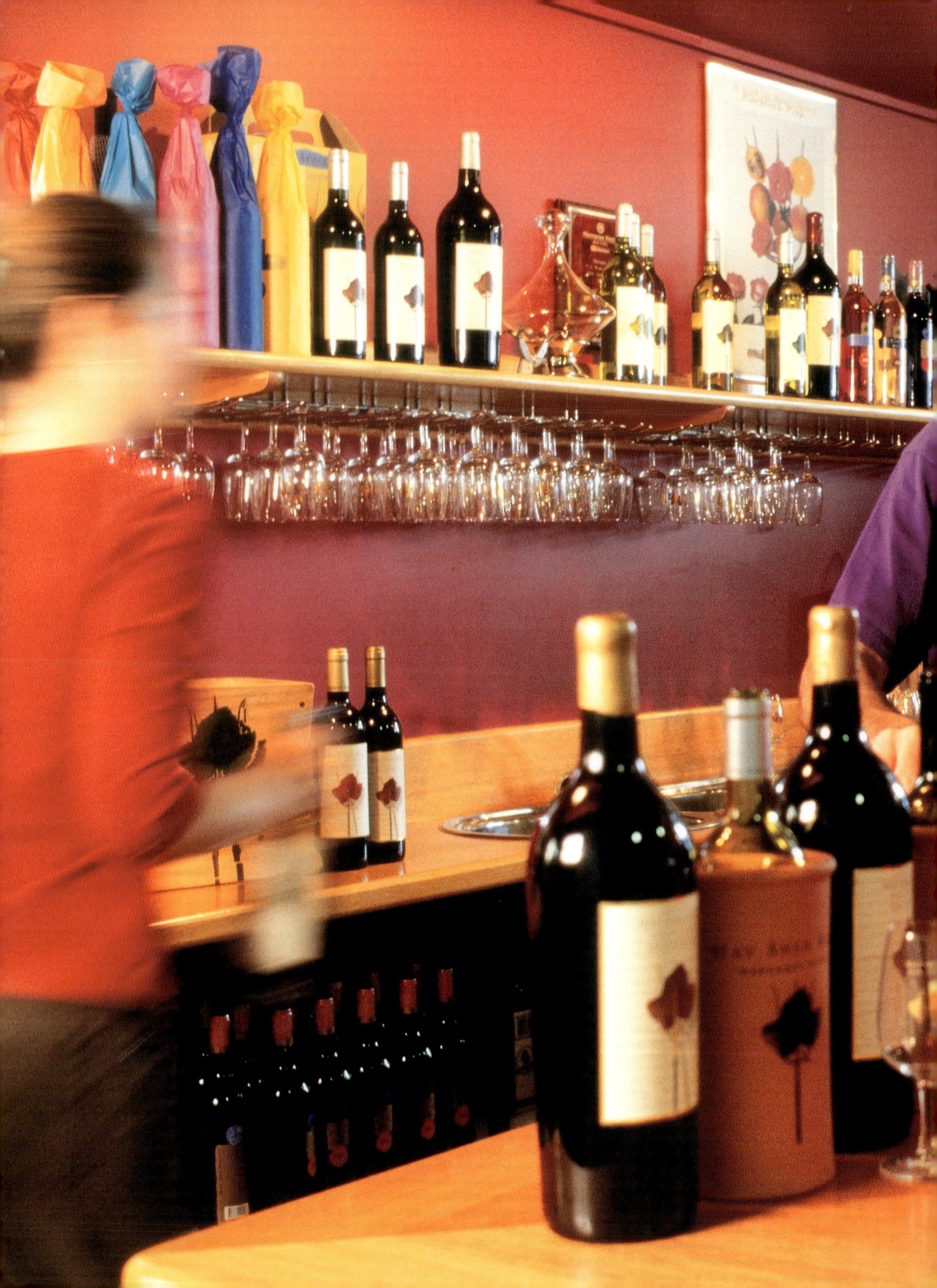

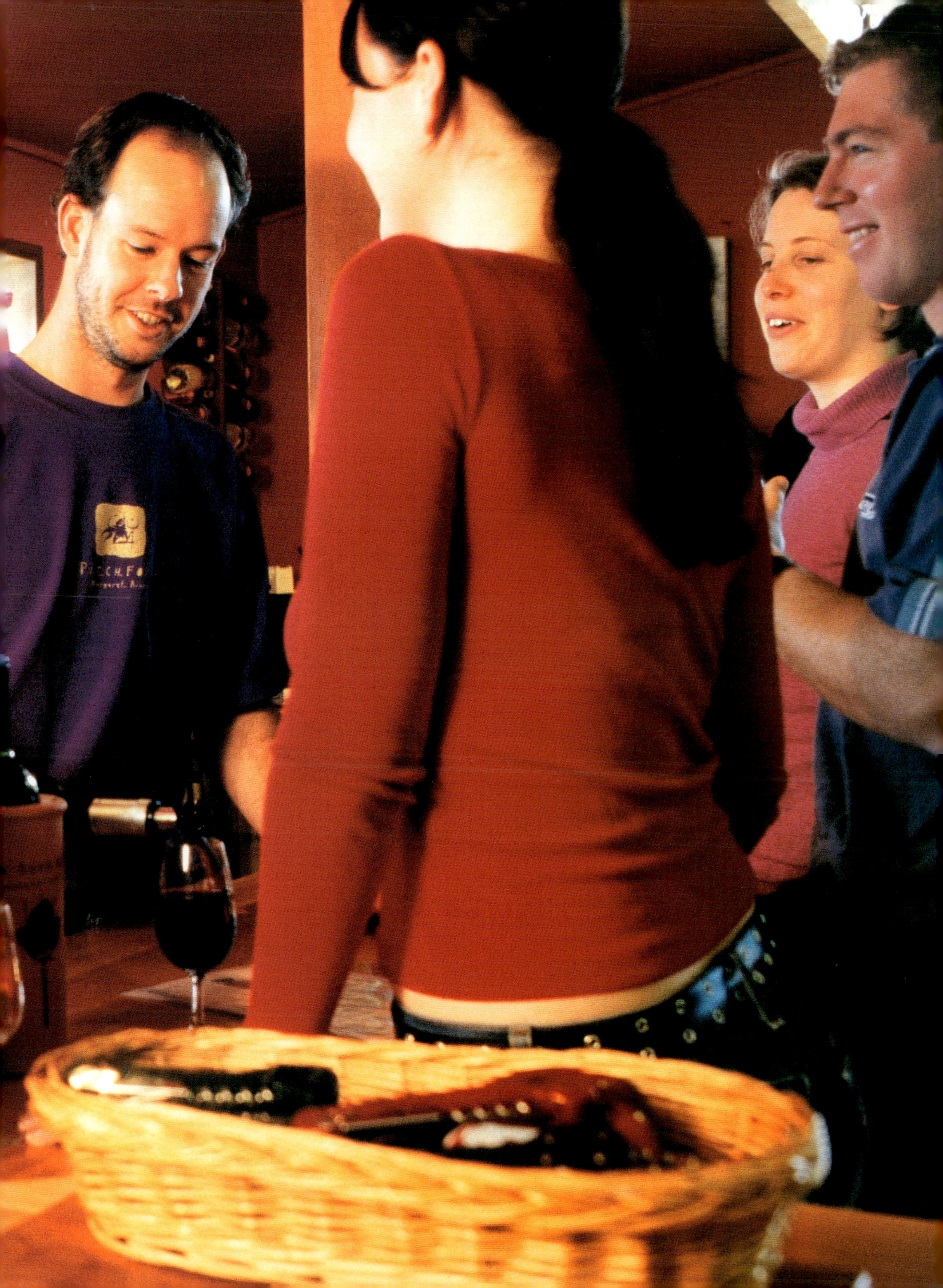

Previous page: The cellar door at Hay Shed Hill.
Above: The restaurant at Leeuwin Estate.
Right: Olives at Stellar Ridge.

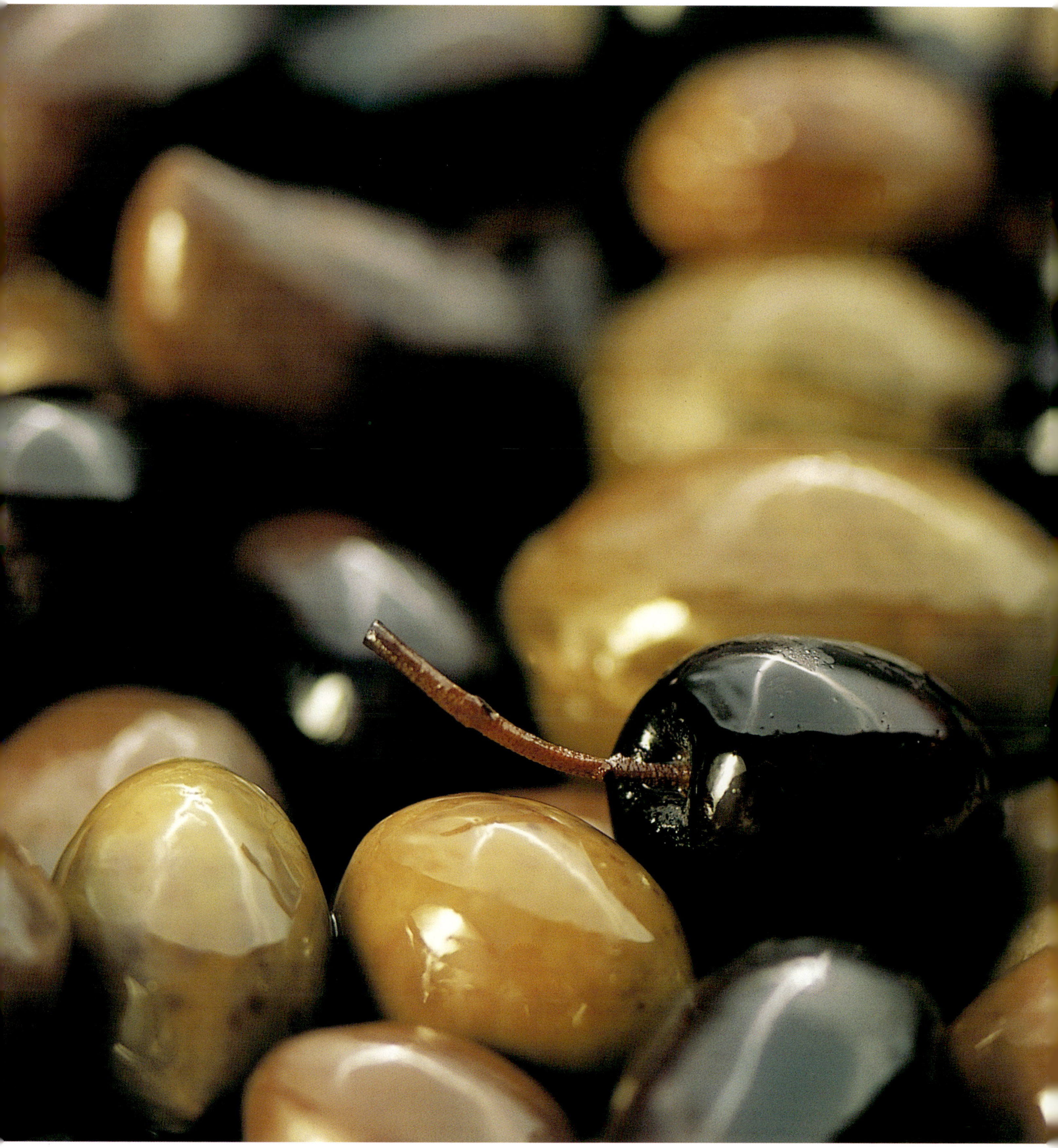

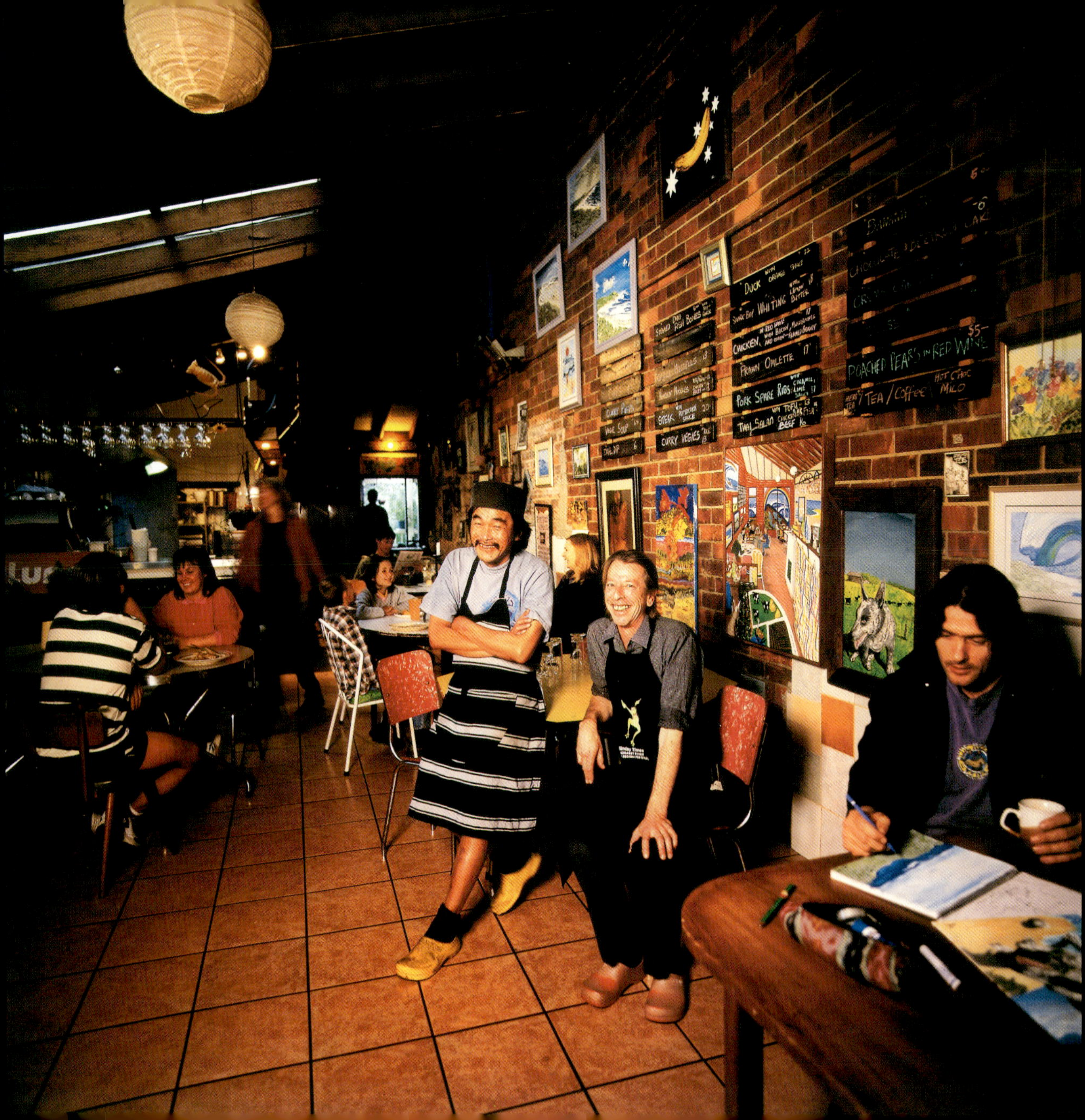

The recent deregulation of the dairy industry has led to many of the smaller farmers selling out and moving on. The subsequent consolidation has left fewer but larger operators, and the industry is stronger than it has ever been. There is a degree of optimism in the beef industry thanks to reasonable prices. However, most agree that it has been difficult to make an adequate return from beef farming in recent times. Certainly the number of cattle produced in the region is significantly less than it was twenty or thirty years ago.

Among those attracted to the region by the climate, its proximity to the ocean and the possibility of an alternative lifestyle, were people who wanted to buy a property and make a living from it. Many professional people came wanting to 'get their hands dirty'. Those who have succeeded did so because they realised that a willingness to work long hours, a sound business head and an ability to adapt to the needs of the marketplace, are each as important as the desire to grow produce. Hence, the Lindsays of the Berry Farm decided that growing fruits was not in itself a recipe for success. They now value add by making jams, relishes and sauces, have diversified into fruit wines and vinegars, and attract customers by offering morning and afternoon teas and lunches.

For many years, holiday makers have been attracted by the natural beauty of Margaret River. It has been the catalyst of the emerging wine industry, juxtaposed with the natural beauty, however, that has resulted in Margaret River becoming a significant international tourist destination. As the need for tourist infrastructure — especially quality accommodation, restaurants and cafes — has grown, so the food industry has flourished.

The expectation that a memorable experience will influence decisions about buying wine has encouraged Margaret River to embrace the concept of the winery restaurant more thoroughly than any other Australian wine region. More than a dozen wineries attract visitors to their cellar doors by offering a wide range of quality dining experiences, often in a natural bushland setting.

Local chefs recognised an opportunity to gain an advantage over their competitors by sourcing the freshest and best local produce, so they eagerly sought close relationships with outstanding growers. With the exception of the Scott River Growers at Karridale, which produces vegetables on a large scale, most of these growers have been small operators. In some cases they were hobby farmers looking for a relaxed lifestyle who needed to make a return on the land. They have tended to specialise, for example, in growing baby vegetables, chestnuts, limes, chillis or asparagus, or new products in response to the demand from chefs. Marron, ostrich and venison have been raised successfully and are widely used. The Cloverdene farm at Karridale produces outstanding yoghurt and sheep's cheeses as well as lamb which is sold under their name in some of the region's top restaurants. Others will follow in their footsteps.

Previous page: The Arc of Iris, situated in the main street of Margaret River, is a local institution.
The owners, chef Boon Loh and Glen Latchford, are pictured with local artist John Harrison.
Above: Marron at the Marron Farm.
Right: Marron at Flutes Restaurant.

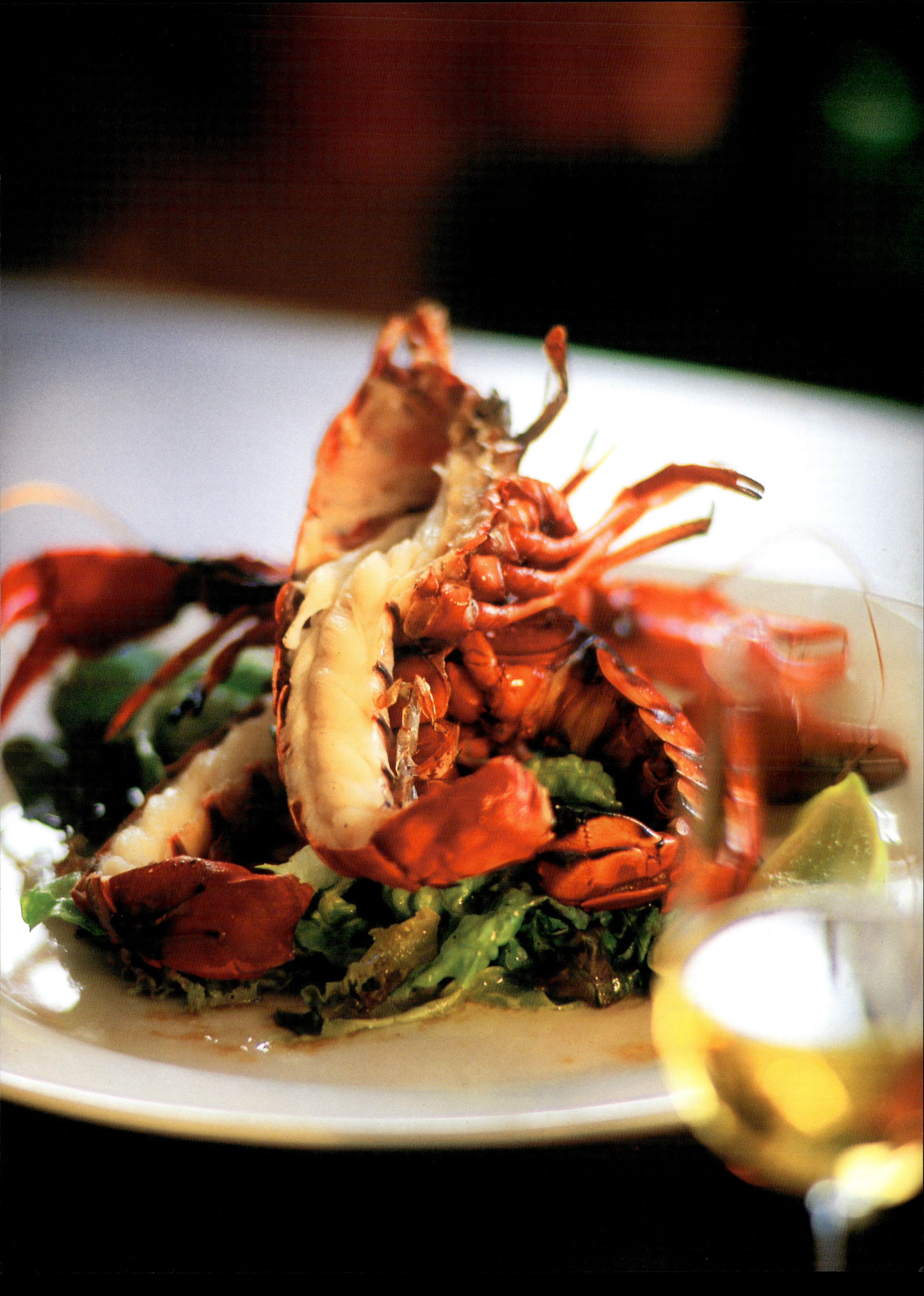

8. The wine

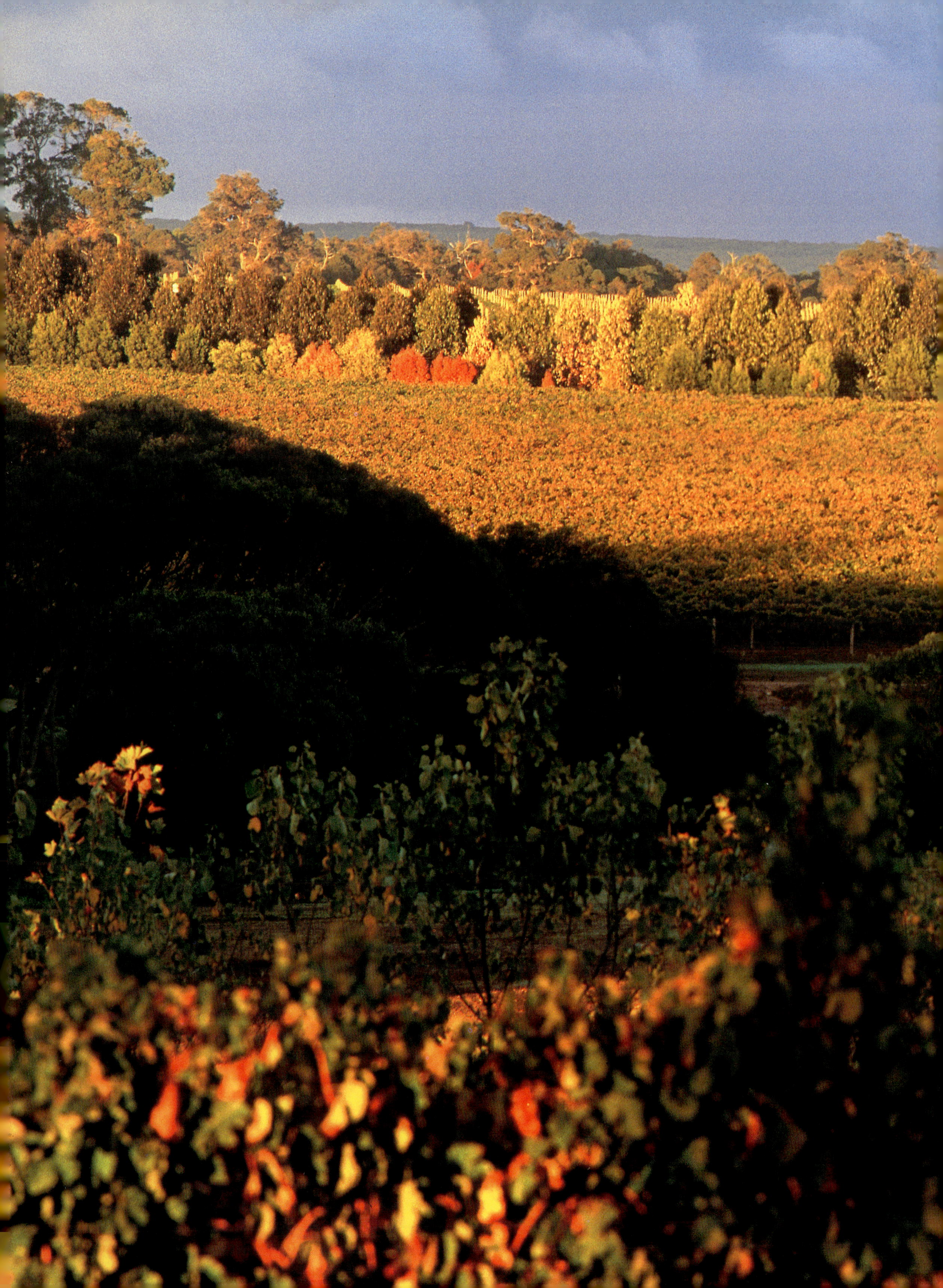

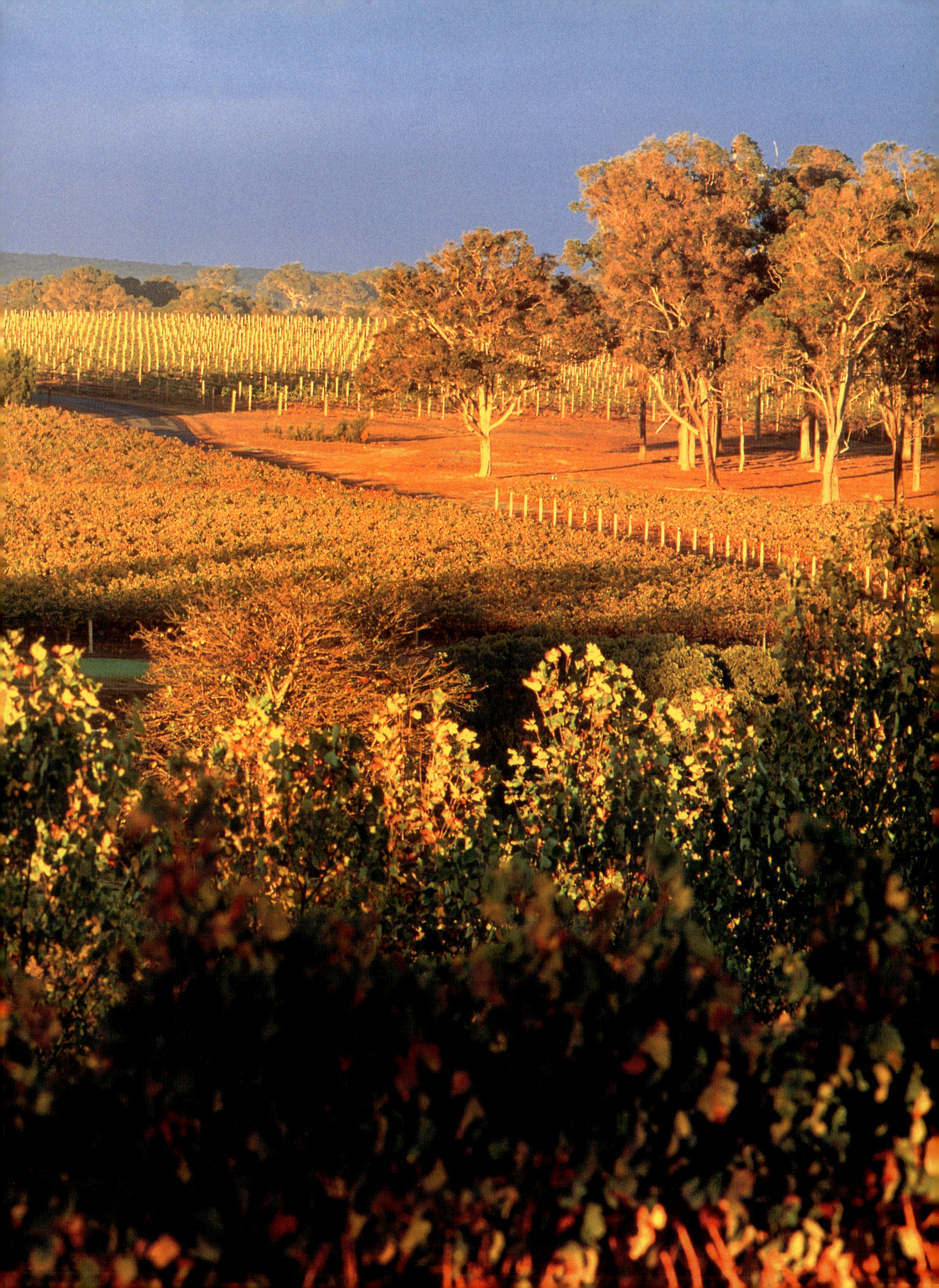

Beginnings

In the mid 1960s Margaret River was quiet, impoverished and quaintly rural. Agriculture was mainly beef and dairy cattle. Many of the roads were made of gravel and in poor condition, and the town looked pretty much as it had for much of the century. Some of the long-time residents of the area can still remember seeing horses hitched to posts in the main street. If you travelled along Caves Road you might run into local youths out shooting kangaroos or rabbits. Even by the second half of the twentieth century, few of the trappings and conveniences of modern life had reached Margaret River. Shops sold only essentials, places to eat were virtually non-existent, and towns closed early.

The sixty or so people who attended a public meeting at the Esplanade Hotel in Busselton in April 1966 may not have imagined that this would be the defining moment in the development of a modern wine industry in the South-West. The historic meeting convened by Kevin Cullen, who owned land on Caves Road, Wilyabrup, brought together local landholders and other interested people to hear about the viability of growing wine grapes in the district. For most of the locals in the sixties, the concept of establishing a wine industry in Margaret River was pure fantasy.

Perhaps the potential significance, or at least a sense of history, was not lost on Cullen even then, in his choice of another local landowner, John d'Espeissis, to chair the meeting. His father, Adrian d'Espeissis, was a government viticulturist and horticulturist in the 1890s and had been responsible for setting up the Valencia vineyards in the Swan Valley.

The main speaker at the meeting was Dr John Gladstones, an agronomist from the University of Western Australia with an international reputation for groundbreaking lupin research. It was his thoughts on viticulture, however, that had sparked the interest of the locals. Gladstones elaborated on his research and described in some detail why the Margaret River area would be suitable for grape growing. Given the depressed state of the rural economy, his suggestion that viticulture could be profitable appealed to many.

Gladstones was not the first to see the possibilities of the southern area of Western Australia; some years before the great Hunter Valley winemaker Maurice O'Shea had pointed to Albany as suitable for viticulture based on his study of climatic and soil information.

Dr Gladstones' interest in the wine industry stemmed from his early visits to Houghton winemaker Jack Mann in the Swan Valley, where Mann allowed him to use a section of the Houghton vineyard for his lupin research.

Page 167: The vineyard at Wildwood.
Previous page: The Howard Park vineyard.
Right: Chardonnay buds during flowering.

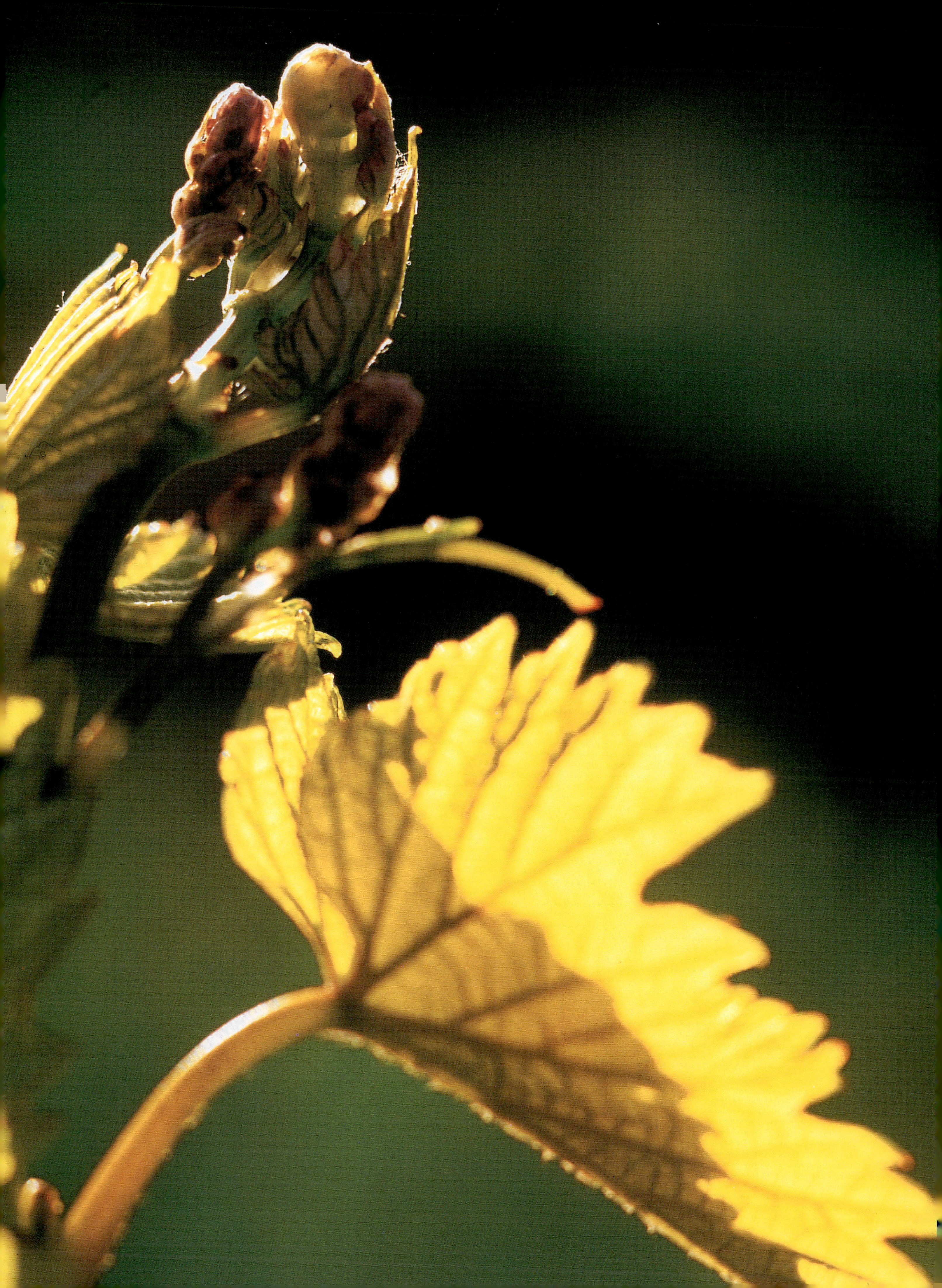

Gladstones was influenced by the distinguished American viticulturist Professor Harold Olmo from the University of California at Davis, who spent eight months at the University of Western Australia in 1955 addressing viticultural problems facing the wine industry in the Swan Valley. During this time he visited the Great Southern and wrote a report suggesting that the country between Mount Barker and Rocky Gully had similarities to the viticultural regions of western Europe and should, therefore, be suitable for producing premium wines. Olmo also pointed to the potential of Margaret River for grape growing because its coastal location meant that it received heavier and more reliable rainfall than the Great Southern. He did, however, note that the incidence of cloud and the likelihood of disease could be significant drawbacks.

Dr Gladstones published two research papers on the topic in the *Journal of the Australian Institute of Agricultural Science* — the first in December 1965, and the second in April 1966. At the meeting, Gladstones painted a more optimistic picture than Olmo.

His parents had a house at Augusta and so Gladstones knew the district well. His intuition had prompted him to think that the area had potential for viticulture. When this was confirmed by thorough research of the soils and climate, he concluded with some certainty that a wine industry was possible. The area around Margaret River and Cowaramup, for example, had climatic conditions quite similar to Bordeaux, with rainfall of more than a thousand millimetres, most of which fell in winter, and modest temperature fluctuations.

Right: The Cullen vineyard.
From top: spring, autumn, winter.

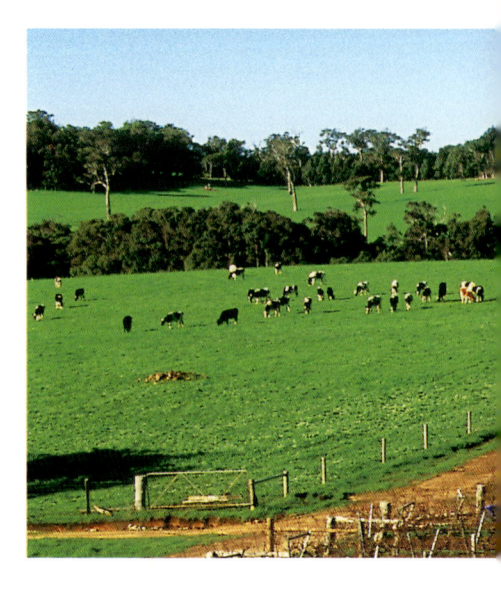

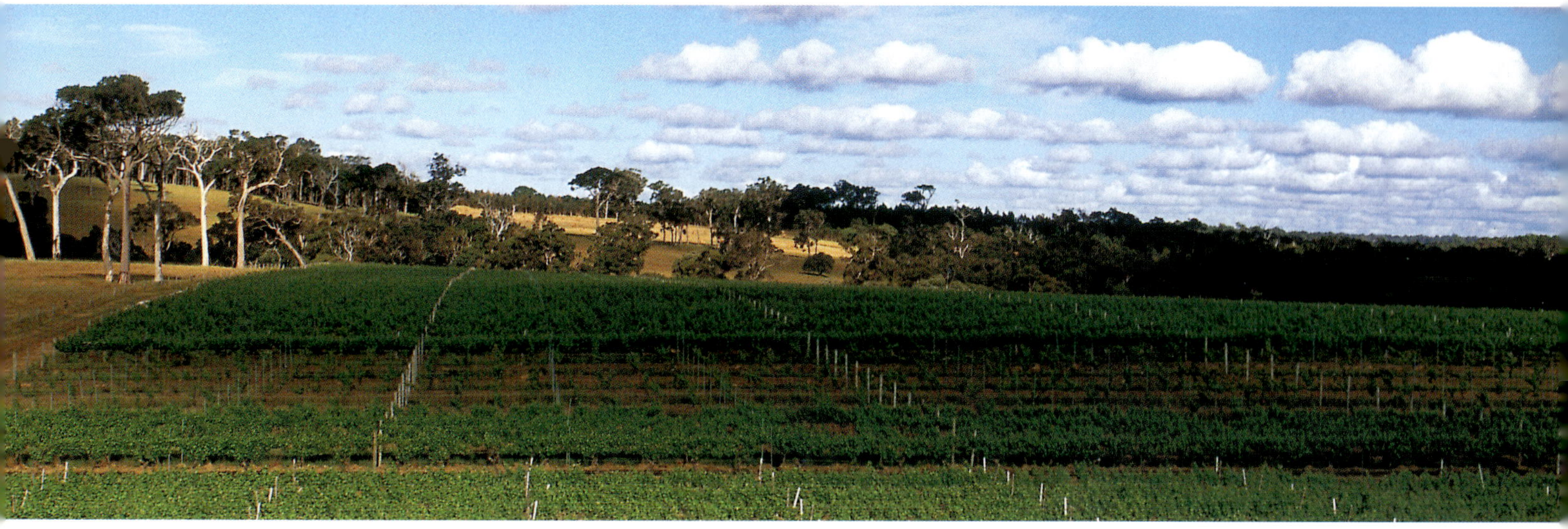

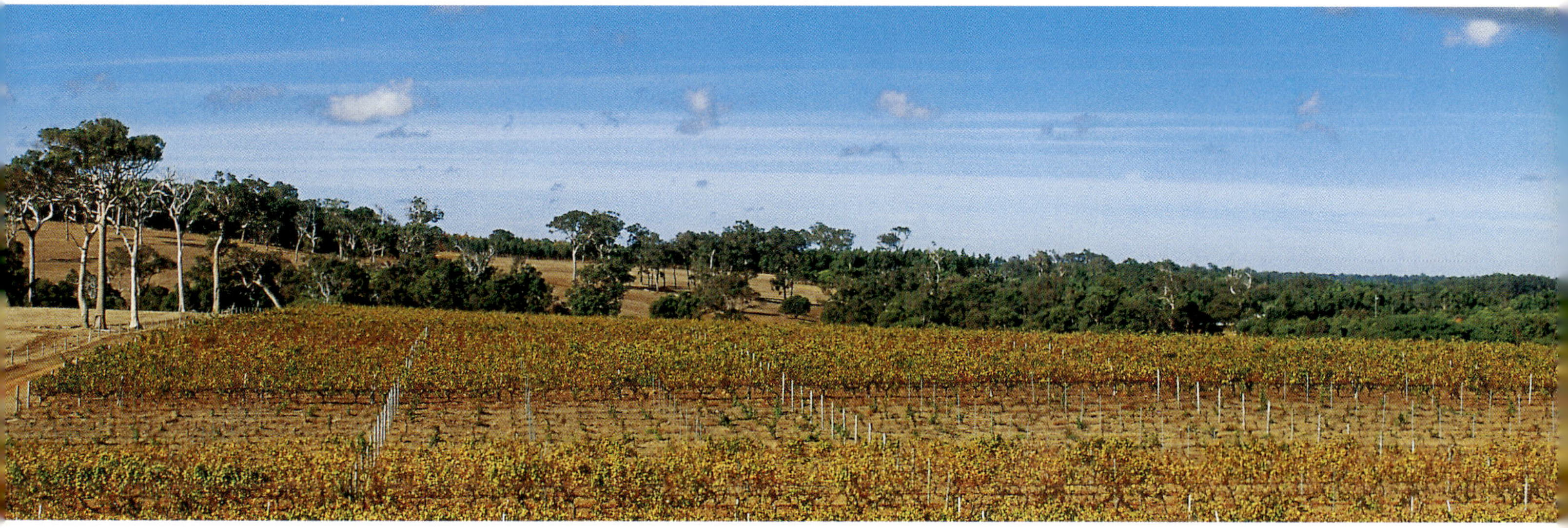

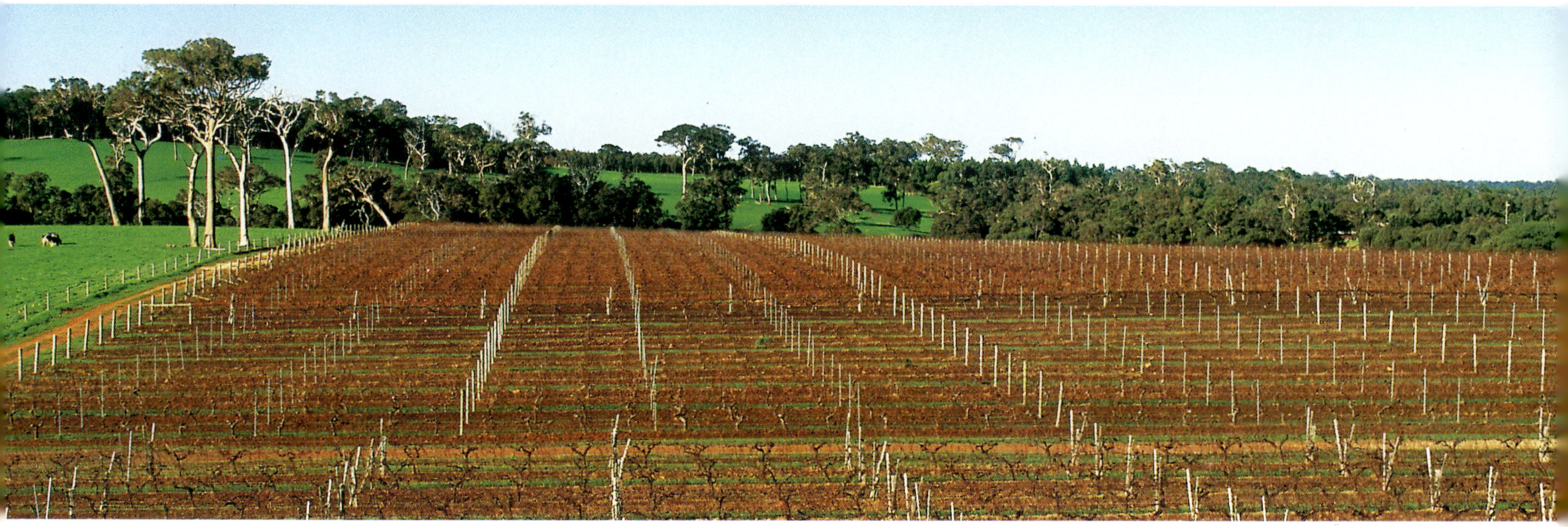

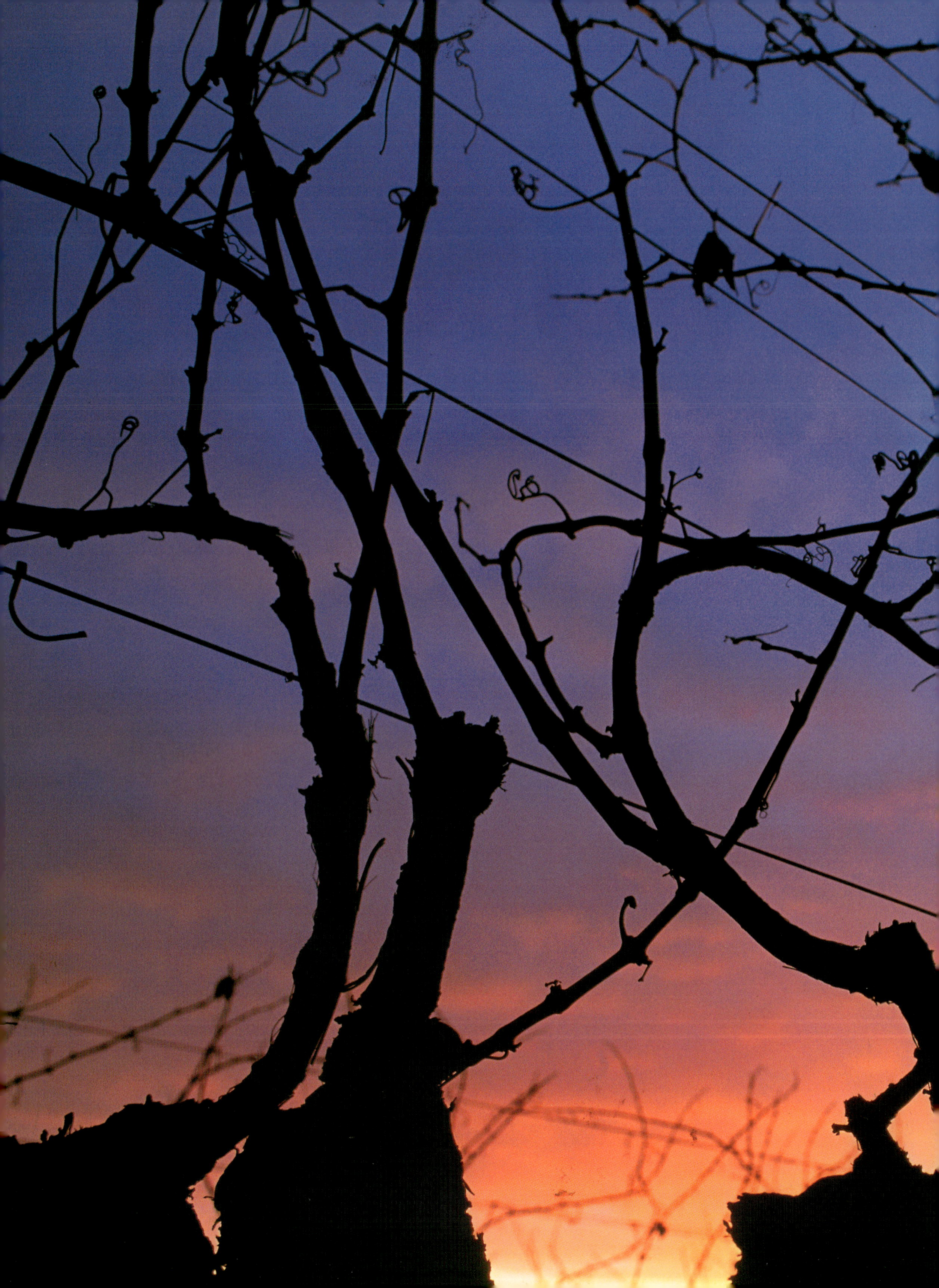

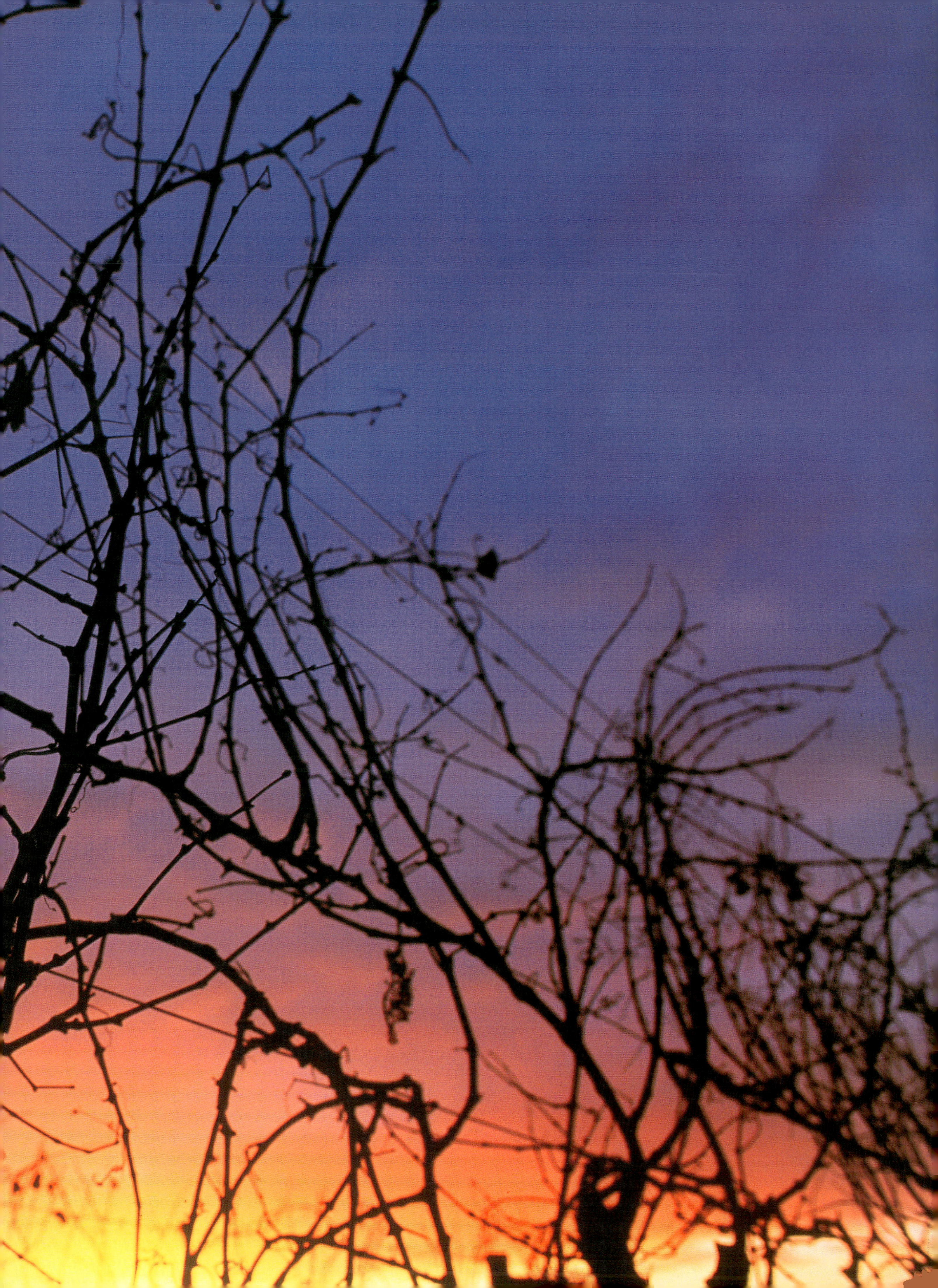

State Viticulturist Bill Jamieson was also at the Busselton meeting. Because of his position and expertise, he was one of the few people available to give advice to those who planted vines in the early days of the Margaret River wine industry. He did this in his own time, defying the politics of his Department which had been seeking to establish viticulture in Mount Barker, rather than Margaret River, in the wake of Olmo's paper. The pioneers of the region pay tribute to the invaluable advice that Jamieson gave them in planting, growing and harvesting vines during the crucial early days.

The Jack Mann Medal is awarded annually by the WA Wine Press Club to people who have made an outstanding contribution to the Western Australian wine industry. It is fitting that its first two recipients were Gladstones and Jamieson.

Gladstones' papers had an impact in the local community and on other wine lovers who were attracted to the area by his comments. Tom Cullity (Vasse Felix, established 1967) came down and bought land to plant a vineyard and was followed by Bill and Sandra Pannell (Moss Wood, 1969), David and Heather Watson (Woodlands, 1973) and Ian and Ani Lewis (Cape Clairault, 1976). Two Swan Valley producers — Evans & Tate (1971) and Sandalford (1972) also bought vineyard land at Wilyabrup. Kevin and Di Cullen — whom Gladstones had encouraged to grow grapes as an alternative to their first choice of lupins — established Cullen in 1971.

Previous page: Cabernet sauvignon vines in winter, before pruning.
Right: Brookland Valley vineyard and Wilyabrup Brook.

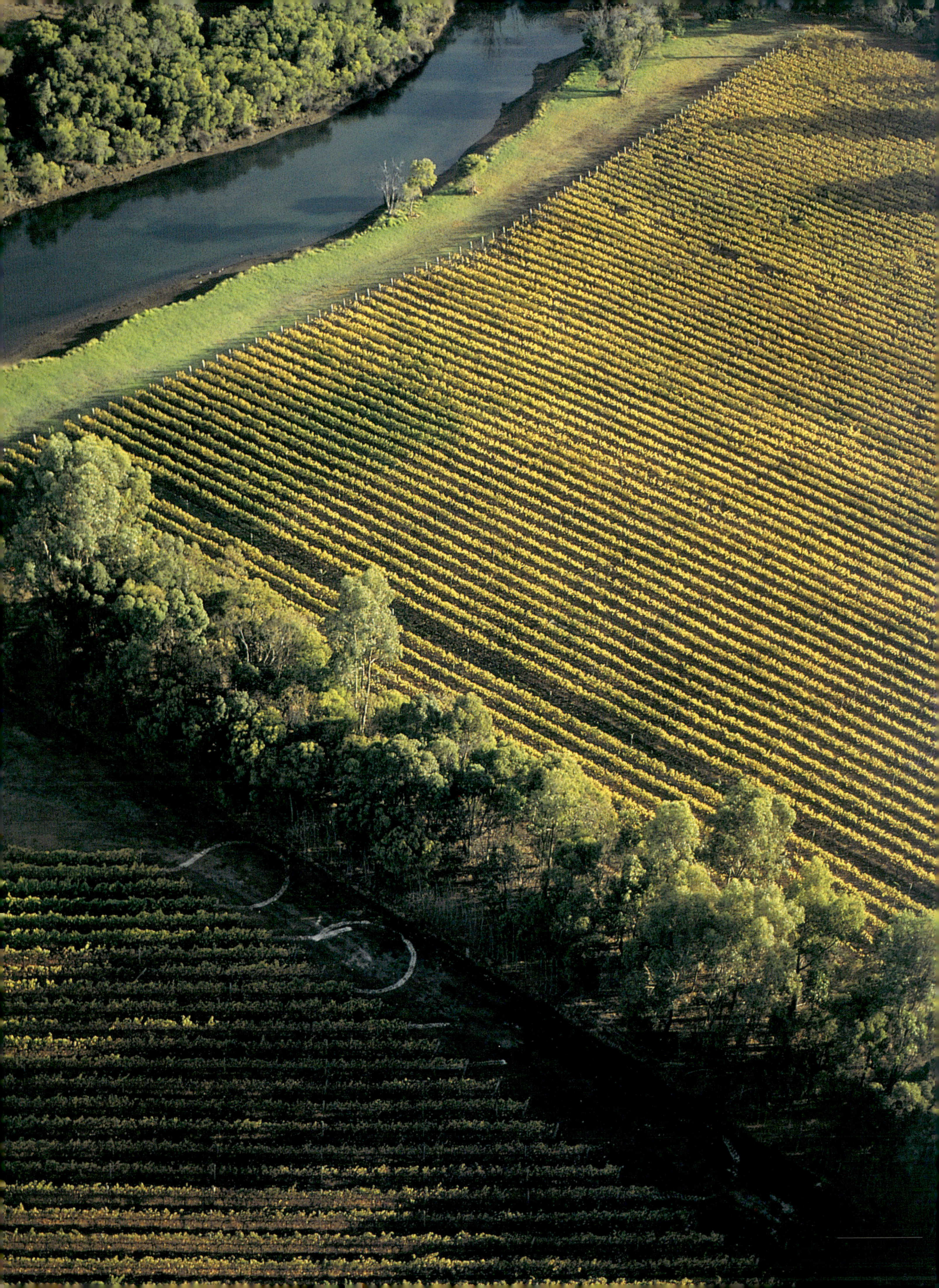

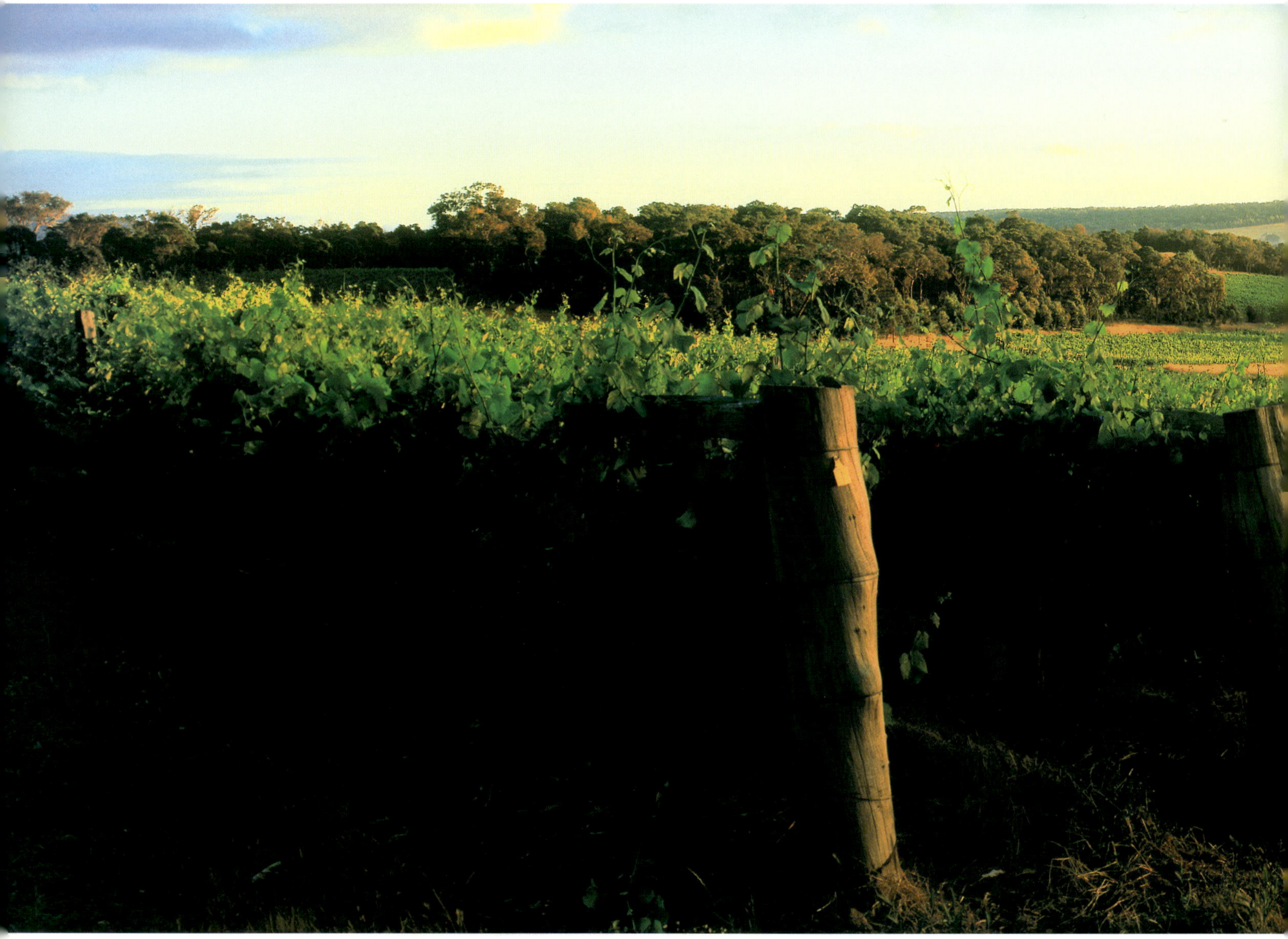

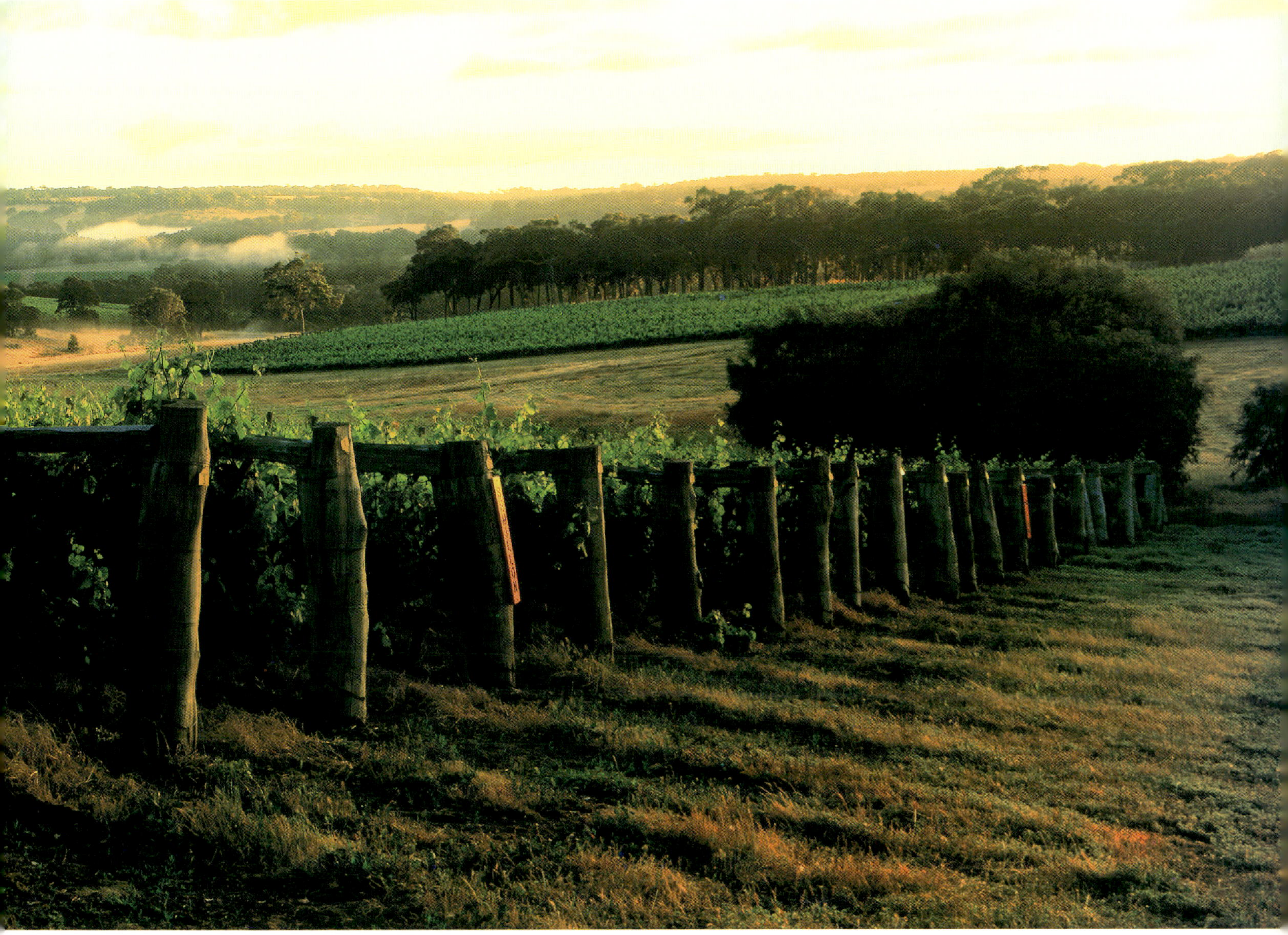

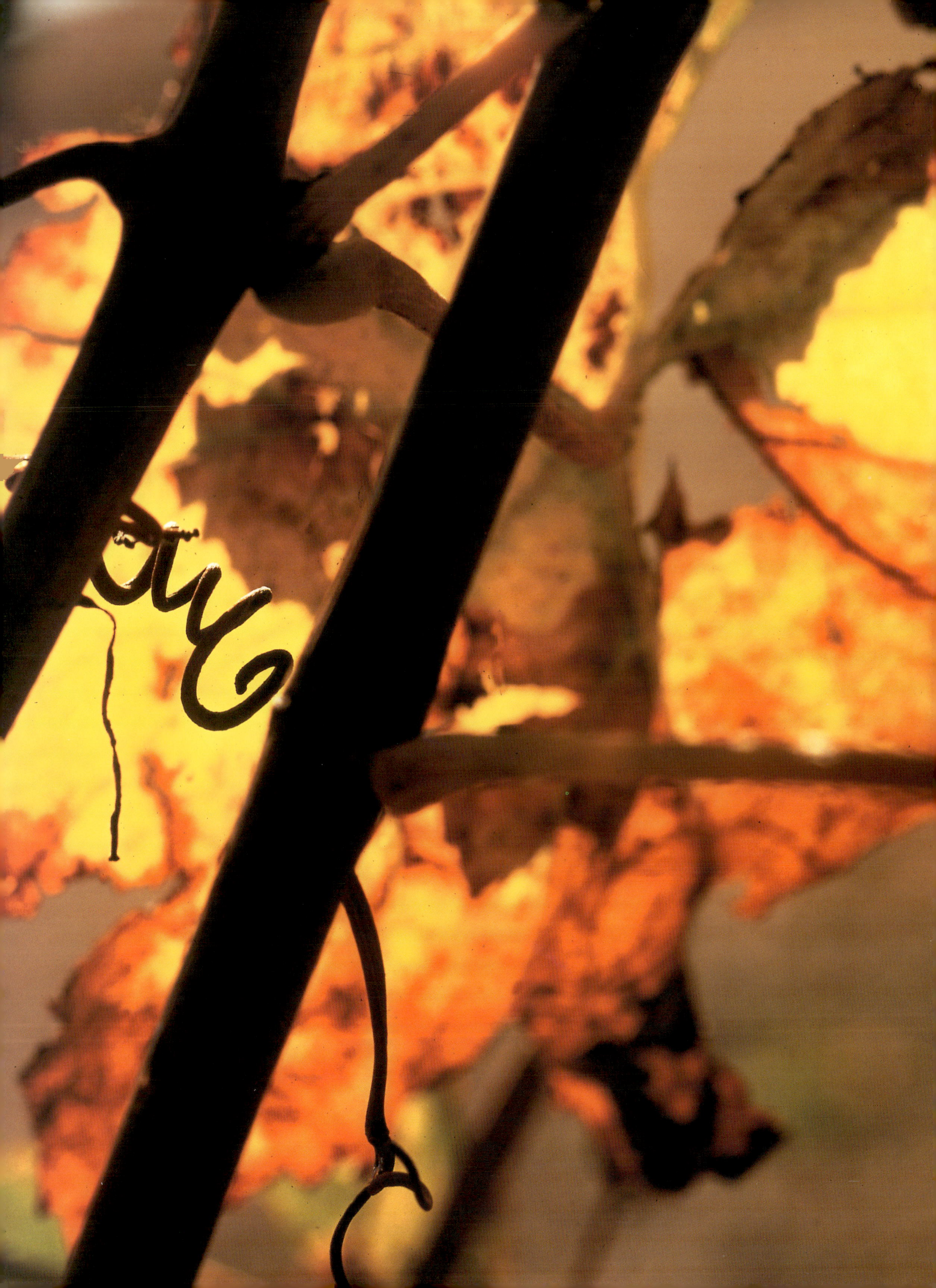

Others who owned land in the area also planted vineyards: David Hohnen (Cape Mentelle, 1970), Maureen and Henry Wright (1973), Jim and Barbara Middleton (Sussex Vale — now Hay Shed Hill — 1973), Merilyn and Graham Hutton (Gralyn, 1975), Tony and Brian Devitt (Ashbrook, 1976) and Marian and Kevin Squance (Willespie, 1976). Denis and Trisha Horgan (Leeuwin Estate, 1974) became established by entering a joint venture with California winemaker Robert Mondavi. These were the pioneers who led the way. Against considerable local scepticism and some political pressure, they gradually began to establish an industry.

Most of those involved in the early days had to maintain their regular jobs, so for people like Tom Cullity and Bill Pannell, it meant driving down at weekends and working from dawn until dark before returning to Perth for a working week.

Perth cardiologist Tom Cullity established the first commercial vineyard in Margaret River at Vasse Felix on Harman's Road South in 1967. He had previously planted a small vineyard and made wine at his brother's property near Collie. Bill Pannell, another doctor, established the second commercial vineyard at Moss Wood in 1969. The story of Pannell's tireless tramping over fences, through paddocks, drilling holes across the countryside in search of the soils espoused by Gladstones is part of Margaret River wine lore.

The 1974 Moss Wood Cabernet Sauvignon won a gold medal at the 1976 Perth Wine Show, making it the first wine from the area to win a gold medal at a nationally accredited wine show.

In the early 1980s, the Australian wine world was beginning to take notice of Margaret River. Successes at capital city shows of the 1980 Moss Wood Cabernet Sauvignon, the 1981 Woodlands Cabernet Sauvignon, the 1982 Cape Clairault Cabernet Sauvignon, and the 1982 Redgate Cabernet Sauvignon all contributed to the region's growing reputation as a producer of quality wine.

That reputation was enhanced in 1983 when Cape Mentelle won the Jimmy Watson trophy at the Melbourne Wine Show. So important is this trophy to wine marketing that, when Cape Mentelle repeated the win the following year, it put the Margaret River region on the wine map. It remains one of two wineries to win back-to-back Jimmy Watsons and one of only three wineries to wrestle the trophy from South Australia in more than forty years. While there is spirited debate over the awarding of a trophy to a one-year-old dry red — a barrel sample of an incomplete wine — the Jimmy Watson remains the pre-eminent trophy on the Australian wine circuit. The dual wins catapulted both Cape Mentelle and Margaret River to a new level. Neither has ever looked back.

Previous page: The vineyard at Wildwood.
Left: Autumn leaves.
Overleaf: The marc from chardonnay grapes.

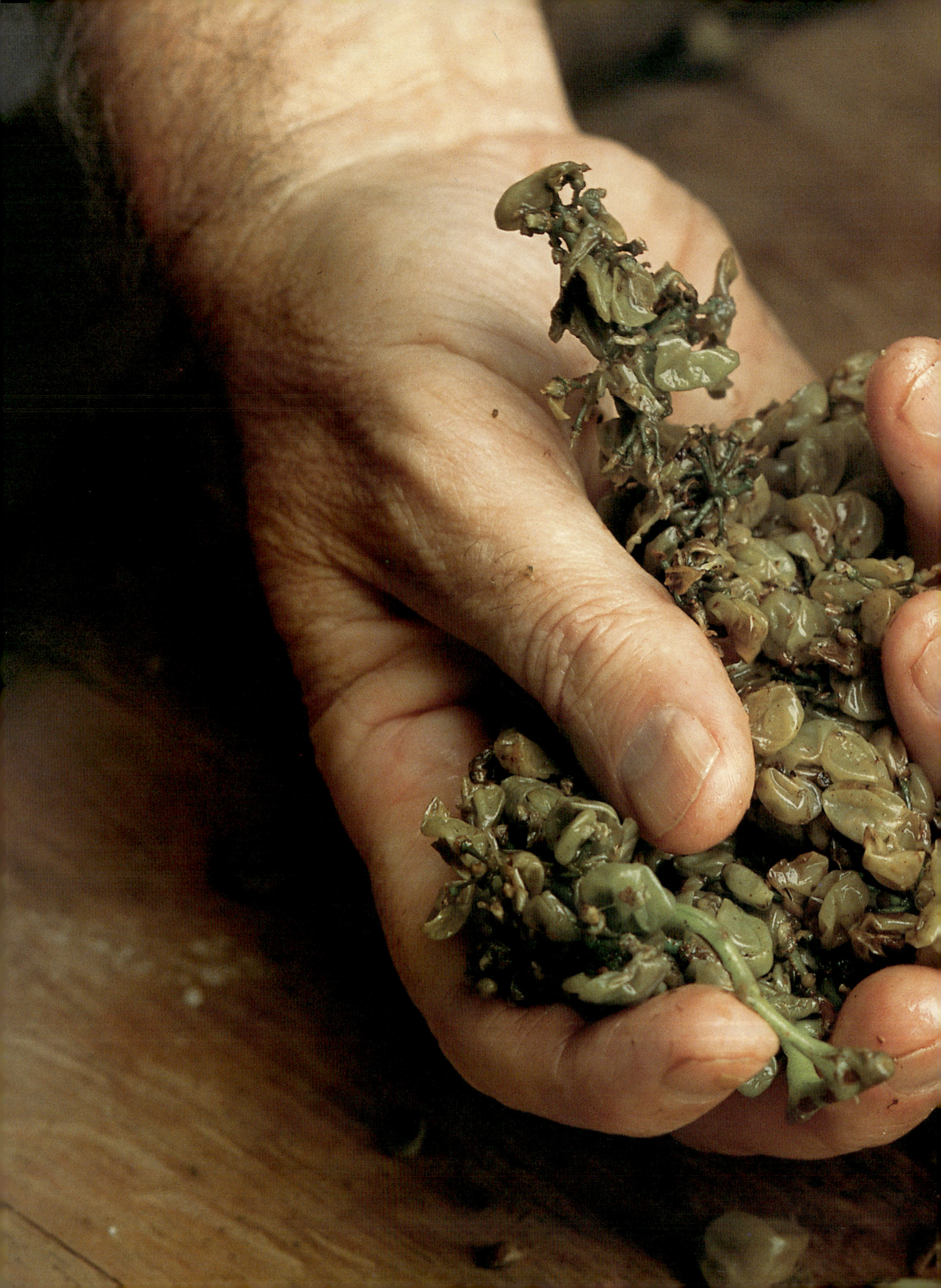

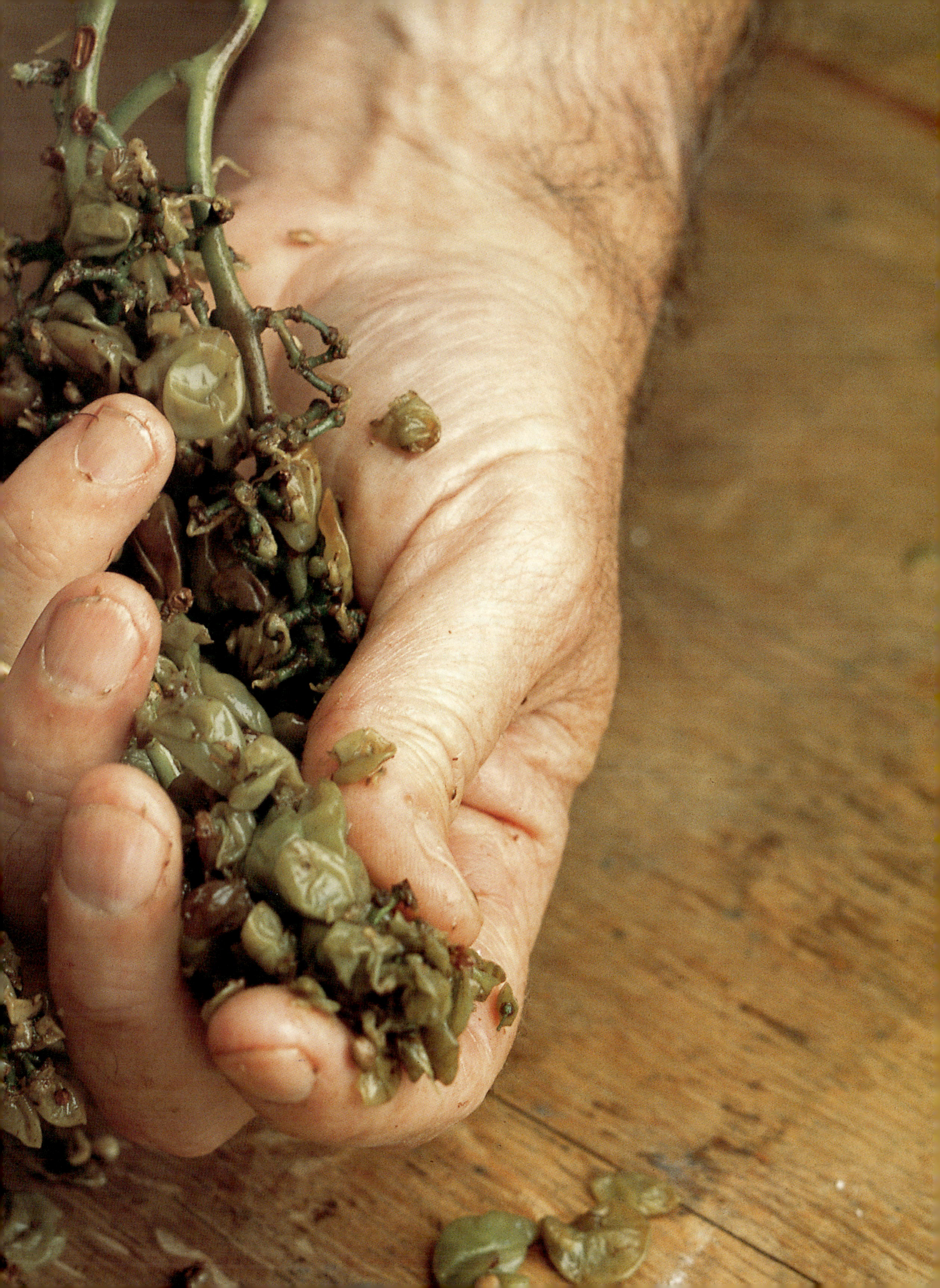

Above: It can be hard, dirty work.
Peta Leiper after shovelling the debris out of yet another tank post fermentation.
Right: Marc — the debris left after the winemaking process,
consisting of grape skins, stalks, pips and pulp.

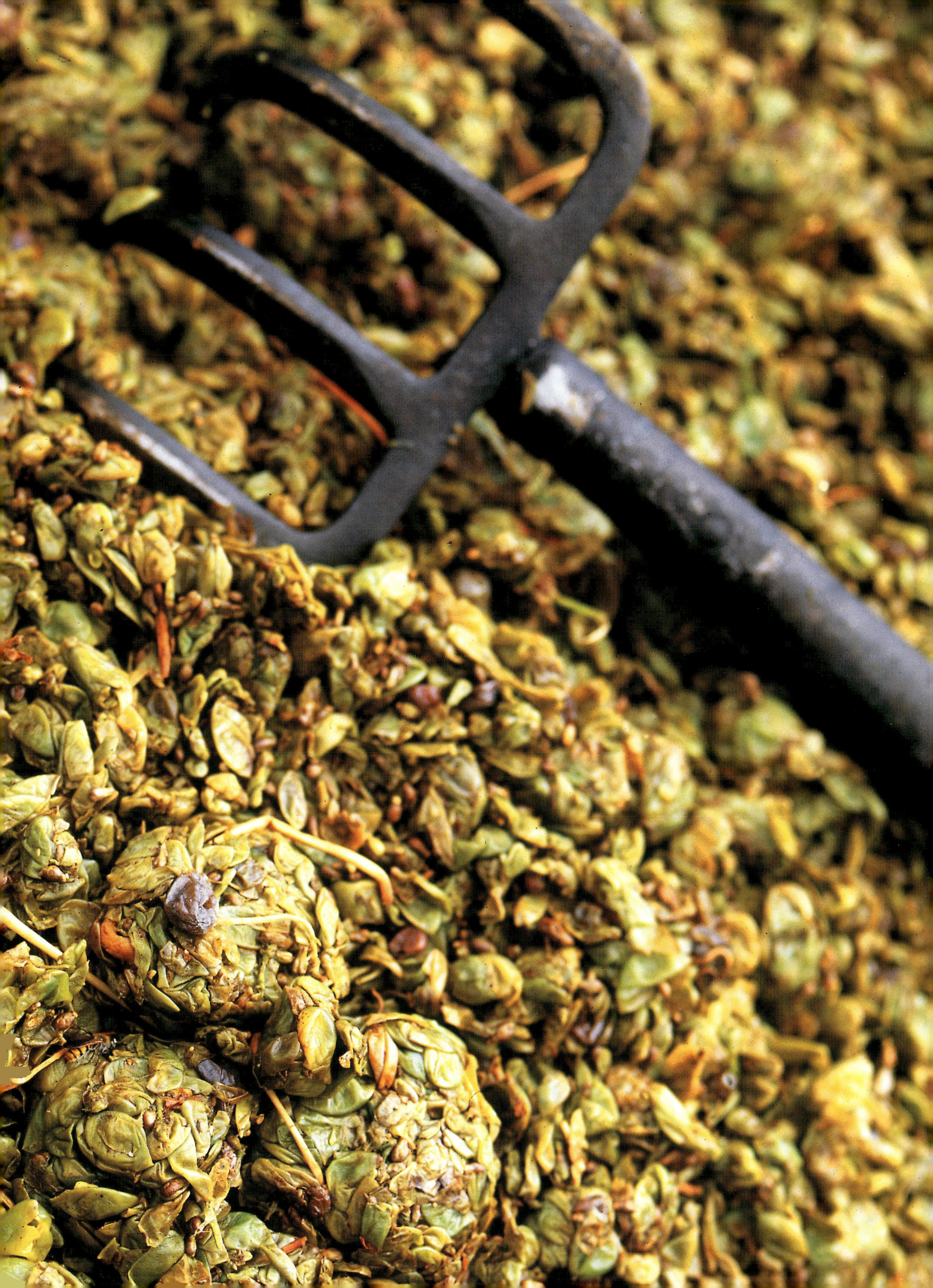

Above: Cape Mentelle winemaker Eloise Jarvis.
Right: Xanadu winemakers. Left to right: Connor Lagan, Jürg Muggli and Glenn Goodall.

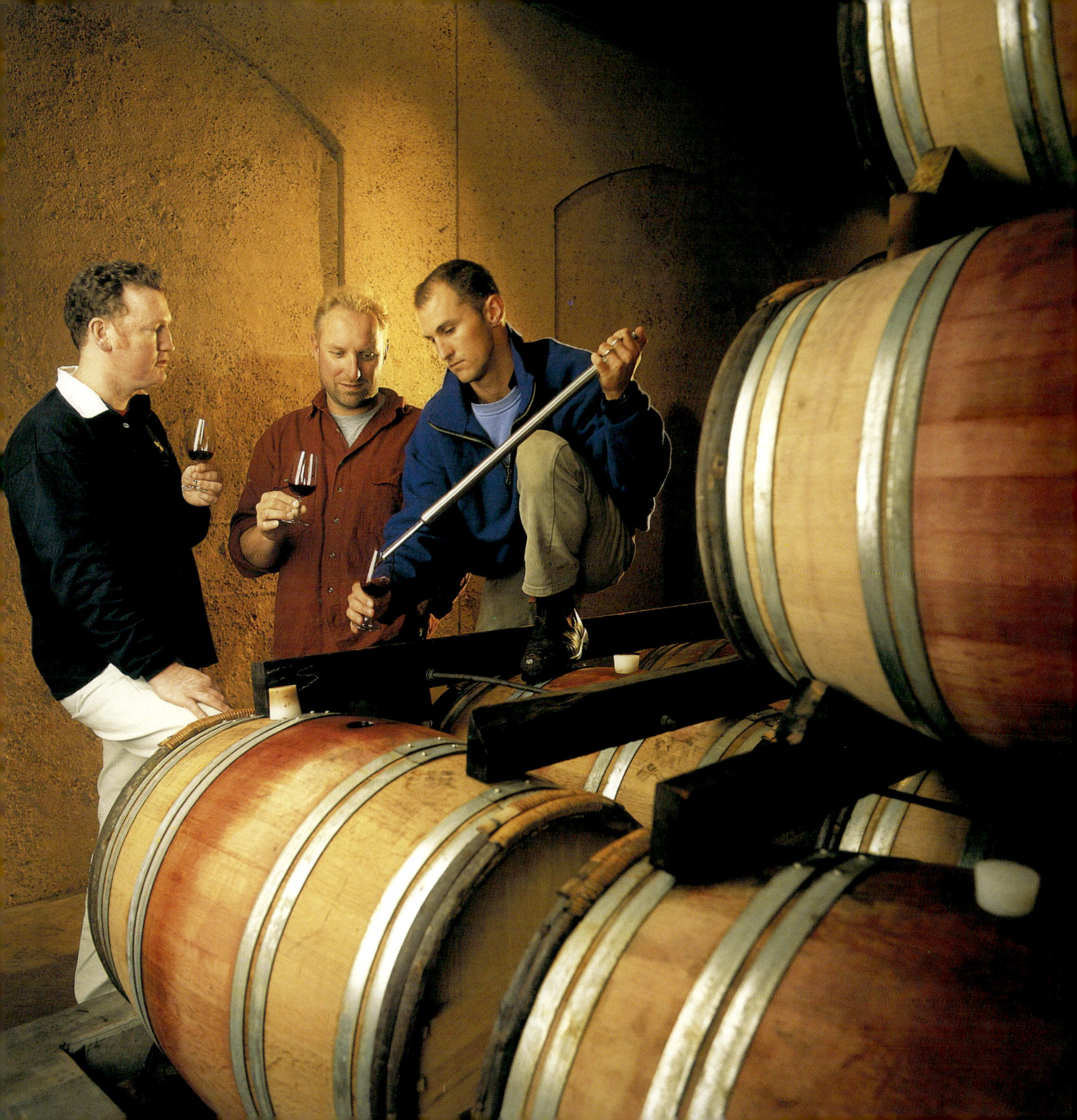

Grape growing

It usually starts about mid to late January. Grape growers start looking anxiously to see if the marri gums have begun to blossom. If the bright sweet blossom appears, you can see them with smiles wider than Cowaramup Bay. If it doesn't, then their faces are as bleak as the rocky outcrops of Redgate Beach. A healthy blossom in the trees means that the birds, mainly the ubiquitous silver-eye, will have something to feast on. If not, birds in their thousands will swoop into the vineyards to dine on ripe grapes, full of sugars and not long from picking.

There doesn't appear to be any logic to it. Some years the marri blossom is there and others it's not. It's one sign that there's a bit more to growing grapes in this area than merely sticking a few rootlings into the ground and waiting for them to produce quality fruit. Perhaps it's the gods, Dionysus or Bacchus, suggesting that if there weren't a few little hurdles, it would be altogether too perfect in Margaret River.

There have been many different strategies to beat the birds over the years. Some have been ingenious, most unsuccessful. The distinctive peregrine falcon on the label of the district's first vineyard, Vasse Felix, tells the story of an early attempt. The falcon was trained to attack any birds which ventured near the vineyard. However, when the cage was opened to release the winged defender, it flew off and hasn't been seen to this day.

Since then, growers have used scarecrows, rubber snakes, air guns and all manner of other clever devices. The regular sound of airguns hasn't been universally appreciated: and some disputes have escalated to local government level. Anyway the birds seem unconcerned, scattering briefly after the pop of the airgun before quickly settling back on the vine until the next bang.

These days, a lot of growers plant sacrificial varieties such as sauvignon blanc around the edges of their vineyards, hoping the birds will be satisfied with them. At Leeuwin, they've planted sunflowers on the edge of one section of vineyard. More often, growers are now using netting. It's expensive, but a lot less costly than losing an entire vintage. Most are no longer prepared to take risks and net even in the years when the marris blossom profusely.

Birds are not the only threat. Kangaroos have taken a strong liking to grapes and it is not unusual to see them tucking into the healthy fruit on the vines. A lot of growers have erected mesh fences to keep the kangaroos at bay.

Then there's the human element. Even when the gods have been kind and the birds leave you alone, there's the perennial problem of getting your fruit picked. When the swell is building faster than the sugars in the grapes, not even attractive pay rates will bring the pickers back.

It is good vineyard practice to pick in the cool of the evening and night to maintain the quality of

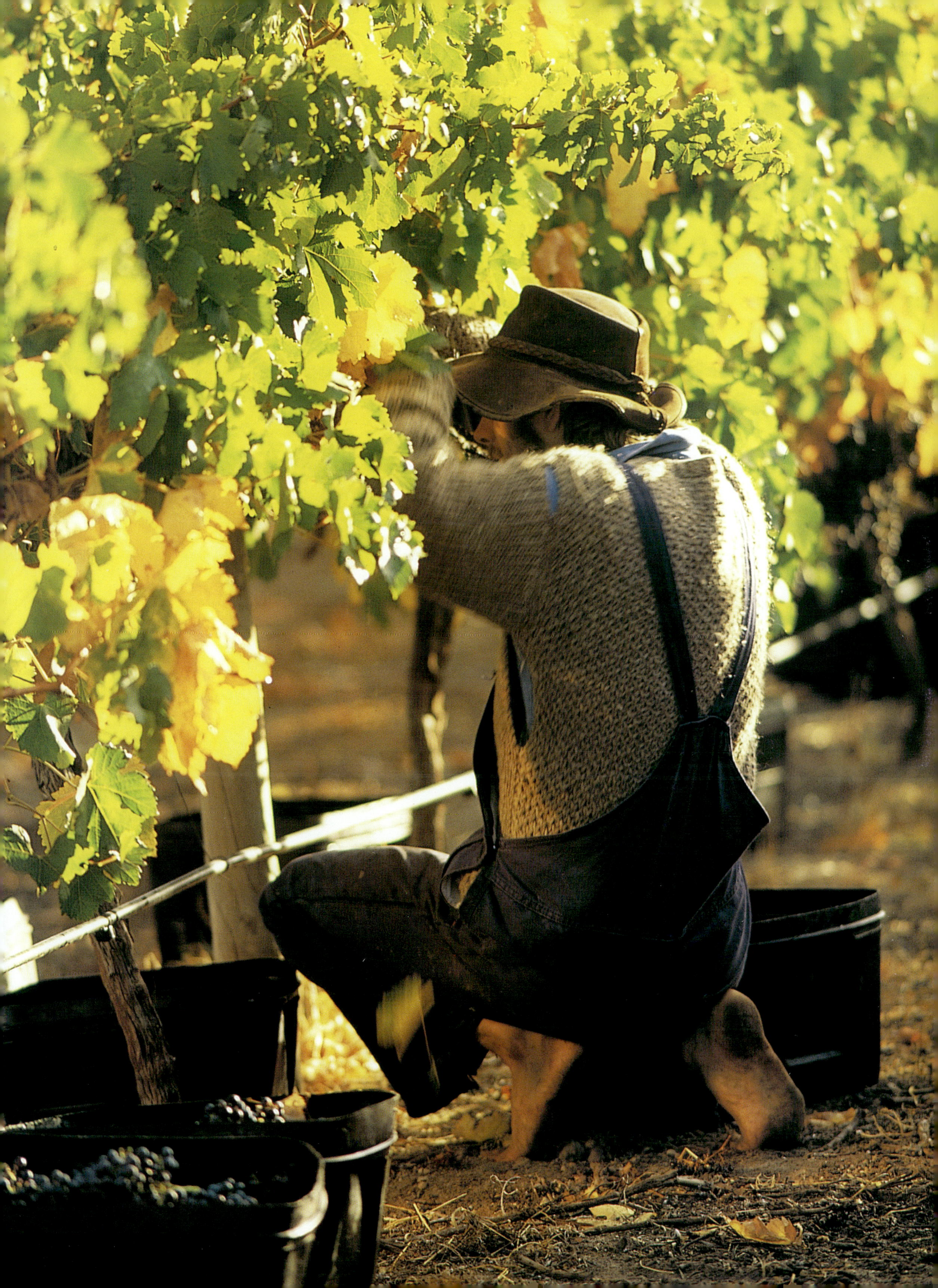

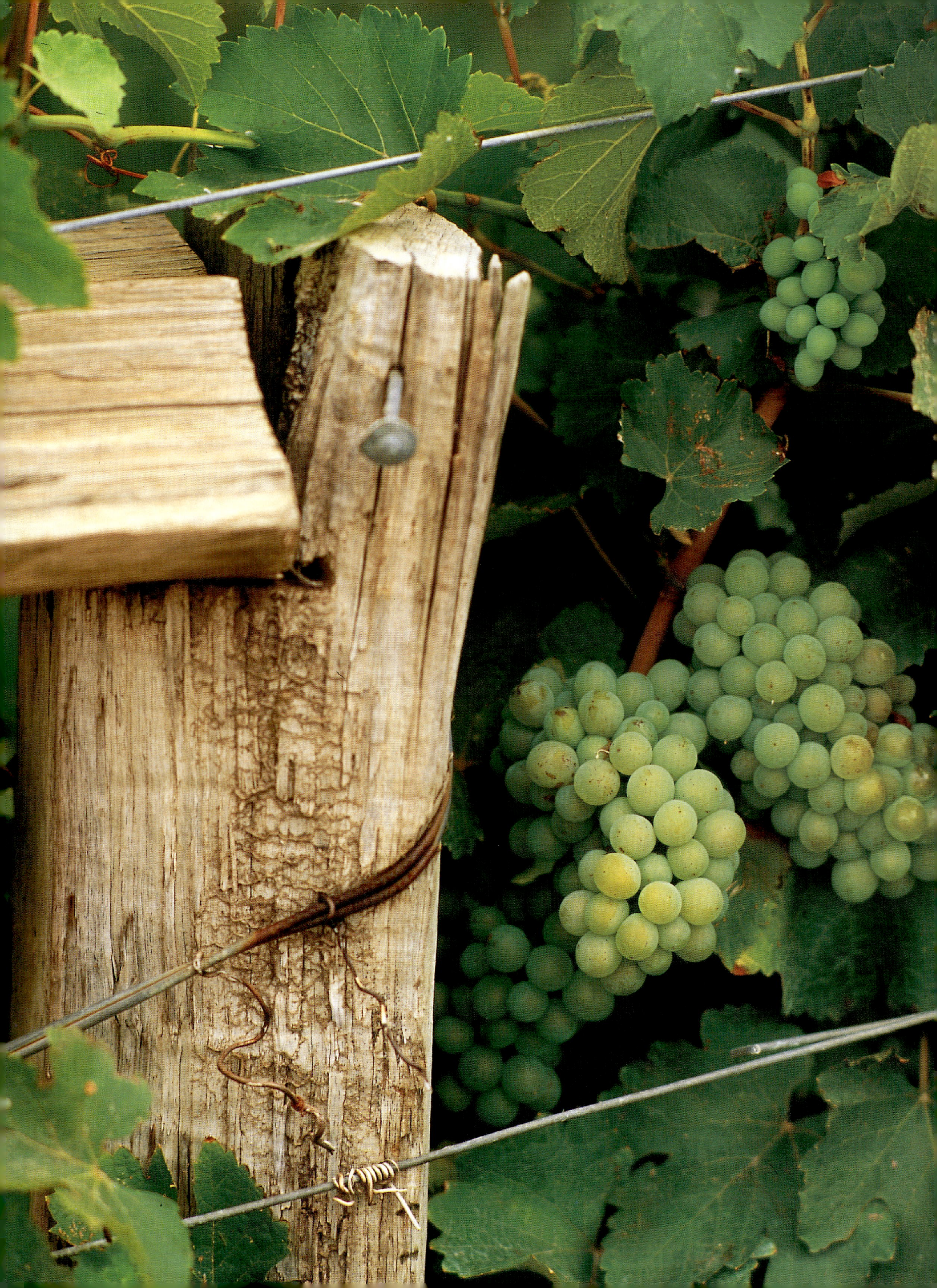

Previous page: India picking cabernet franc at Bligh vineyard.
Left: Chenin blanc grapes.
Above: Chardonnay at budburst.

193

the fruit. But in Margaret River this practice serves more functions than preserving fruit quality: it is to preserve your pickers. Many a long-time grower in the district will tell the story of picking in the morning and then finding his entire picking staff has deserted.

As a result, many simply aren't prepared to take the risk. In the pursuit of certainty, reliability and speed of picking, more have turned to mechanical harvesting. Mechanical harvesting is a little hard on the grapes, but the attraction is that mechanical harvesters don't surf. Some of the premium vineyards will always maintain a hand-picking philosophy, but more and more have chosen mechanical power over manpower.

Above: A serious bow-wow during picking on the Bligh vineyard.
Right: Rob Barker, one of the state's fastest pickers, in action at Moss Wood. Rob spends his winters shearing and summers picking.

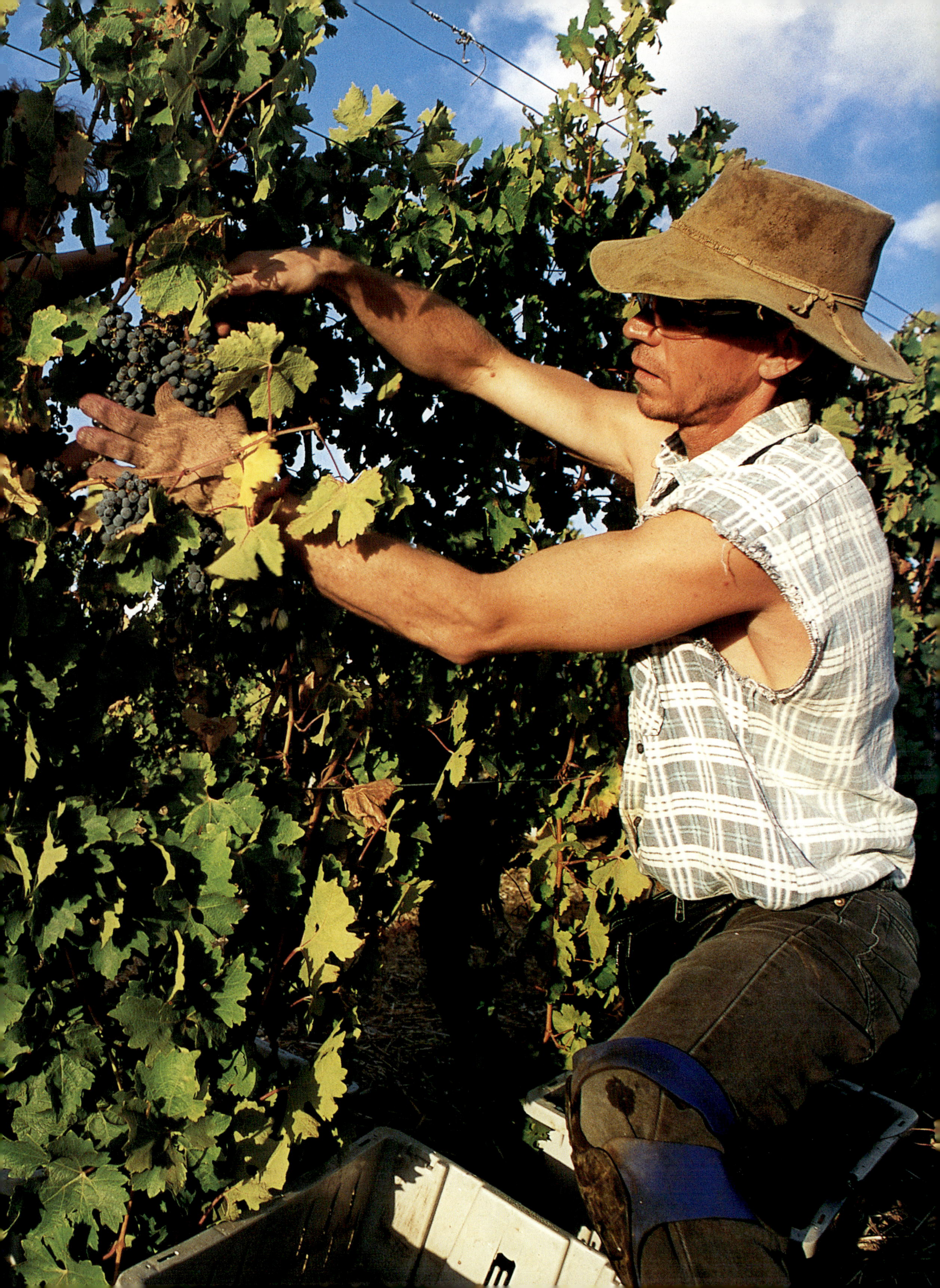

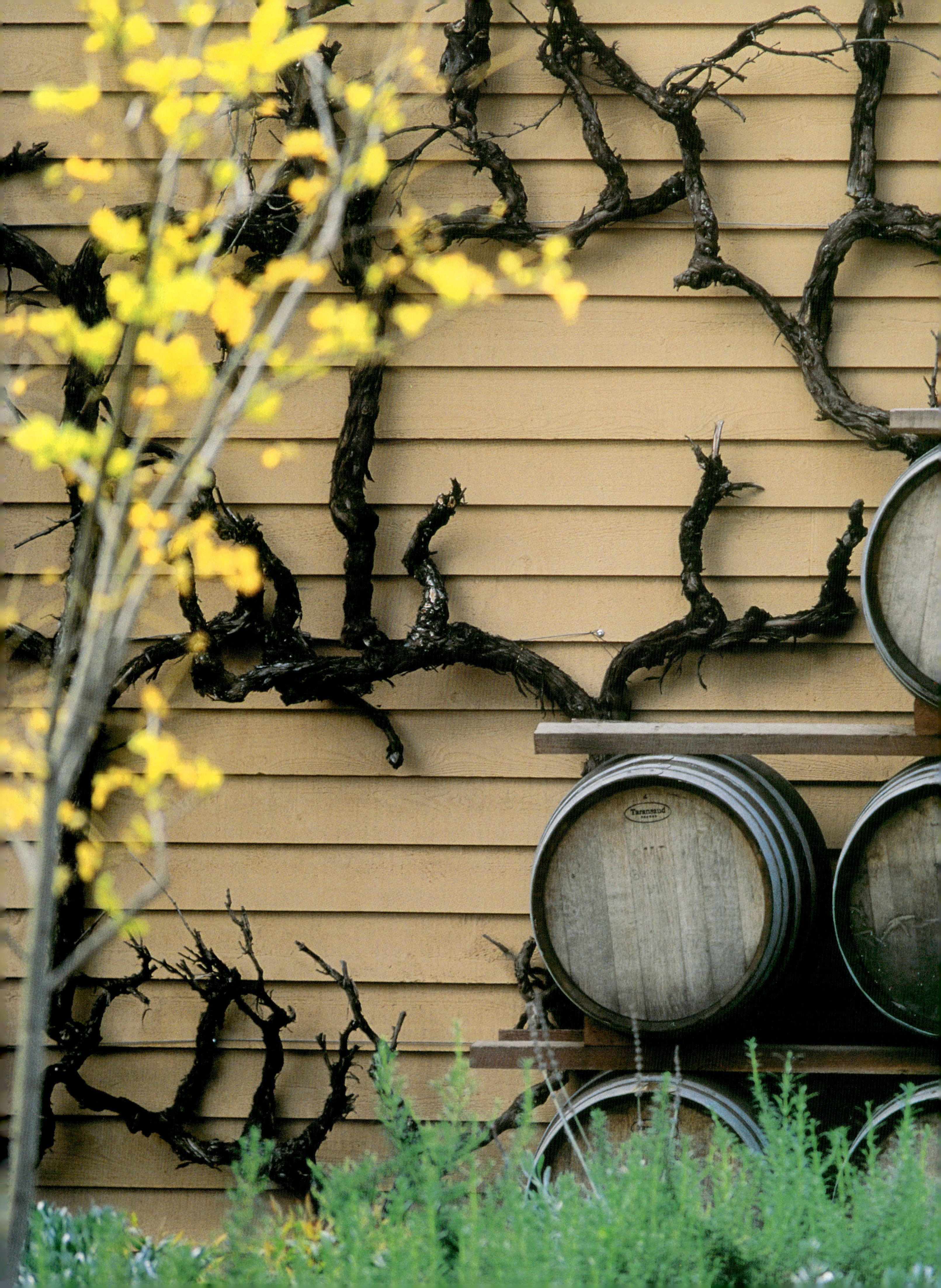
Taransaud

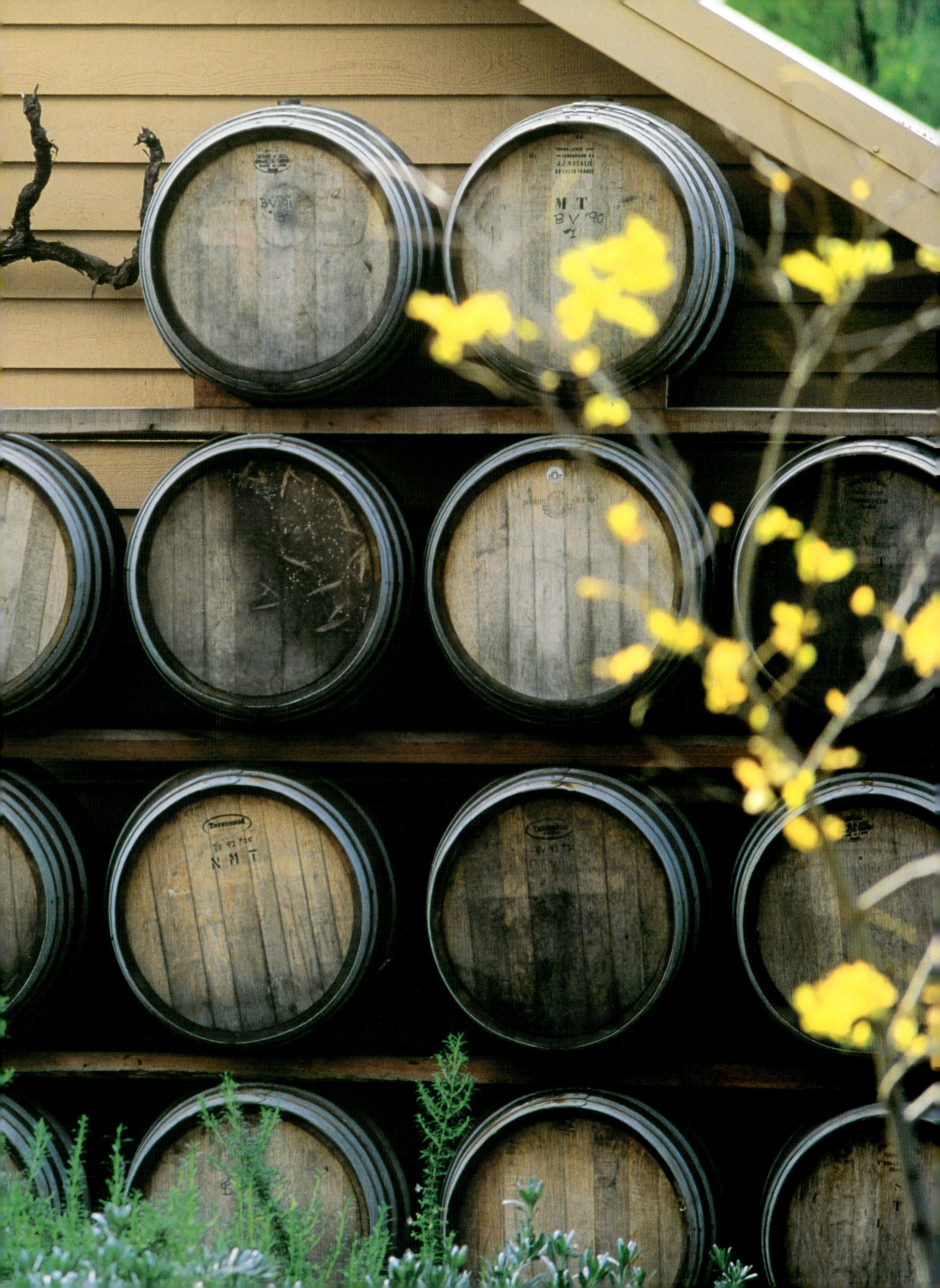
BV '91
M T
BV '90
#1
N M T

Winemaking

To suggest that there are differences between the pioneering winemaking of the 1970s and current practices might be stating the obvious. Few of the pioneers had extensive financial resources and most had another full-time job to help fund their small family wineries; the majority were medical practitioners. While they were driven by the desire to grow grapes and make quality wine, most were untrained and inexperienced in this endeavour. Few of their neighbours were making wine, so they worked in relative isolation. They did receive invaluable advice and support from officers from the Department of Agriculture, but there was no infrastructure; equipment and winemaking supplies had to be ordered from afar. Considering all this, the quality of the early wines they made was remarkable. And it was on the quality of these wines that the region's reputation was founded.

The early winemakers considered it a serious venture but, reflecting back, believe there was also a greater sense of innocence, fun and camaraderie than is possible in today's corporate world. For all that, the pioneers did not come seeking only an idyllic lifestyle: they came believing they could make outstanding, even great wines. For them, winemaking was to become an art as much as a science, and they developed individual wine styles to achieve that objective.

The scale of winemaking in Margaret River has changed dramatically. It is now big business and has the infrastructure to match. There is a great deal of investment in the region and in individual wineries. While small family wineries still exist, and in many cases flourish, the industry has come to be dominated by the corporate world. Improvements in technology have meant access to vastly superior equipment — more efficient crushers, gentler presses, less labour-dependent mechanical harvesters — and improved access to finance has made it easier for wineries to acquire this technology. Larger, more modern and safer wineries have been constructed with facilities such as purpose-built chilling rooms to bring the temperature of grapes down before processing, and dedicated barrel storage sheds to control temperature between fermentation and the time that the wine is ready for sale. Those employed in the industry now need a combination of practical experience and a four-year winemaking or viticulture degree to compete on the labour market.

In the space of thirty years, the wine industry has come to dominate the Margaret River landscape. Little local wine was sold outside Western Australia before 1980. Now, wine from the region is available in most parts of the world.

Previous page: Barrels line the outside wall of the Brookland Valley cellar door.
Right: More debris from the winemaking process: the stalks left after the bunches of grapes are destemmed prior to fermentation.
Overleaf: Ripe cabernet sauvignon grapes at picking.

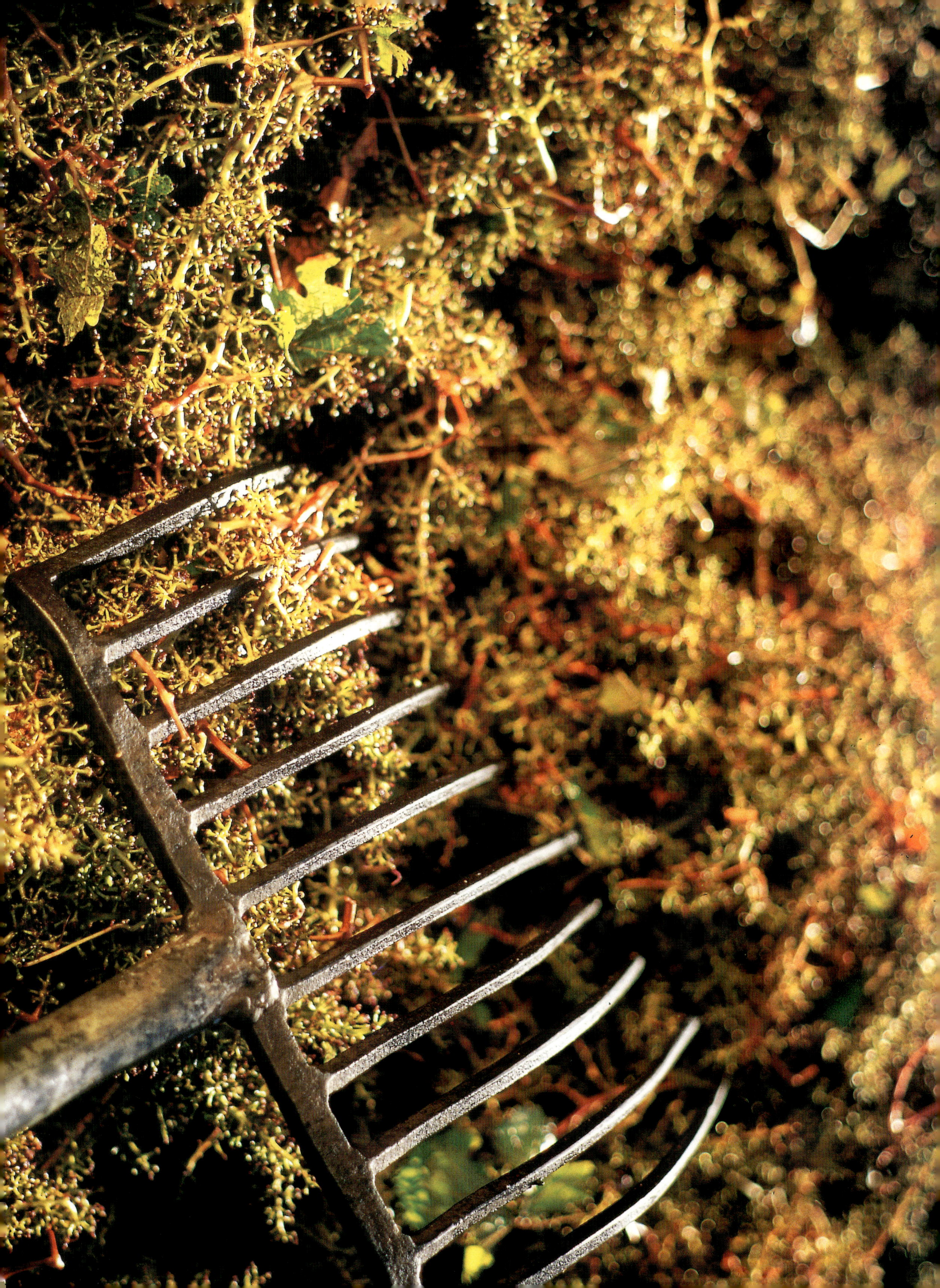

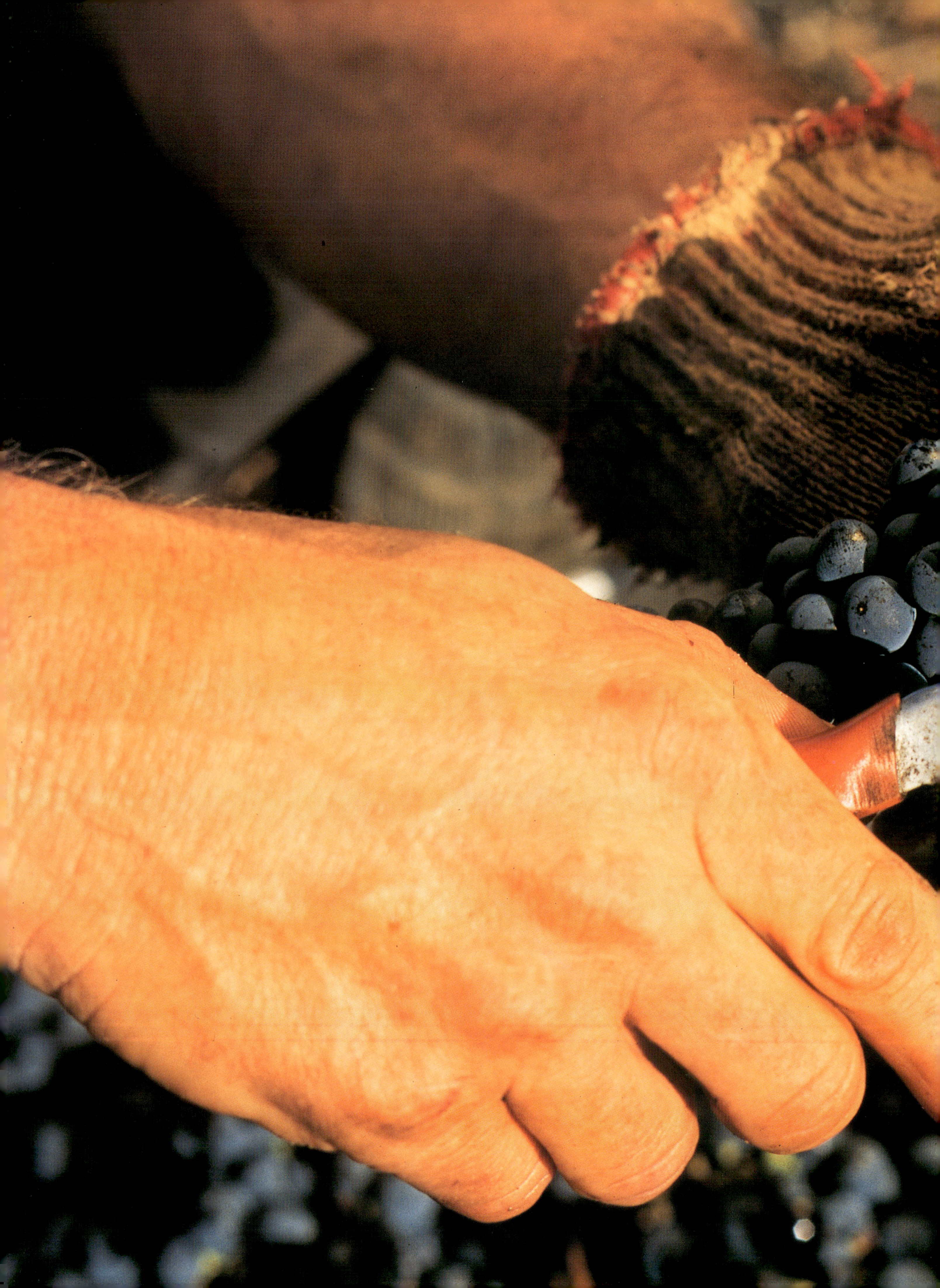

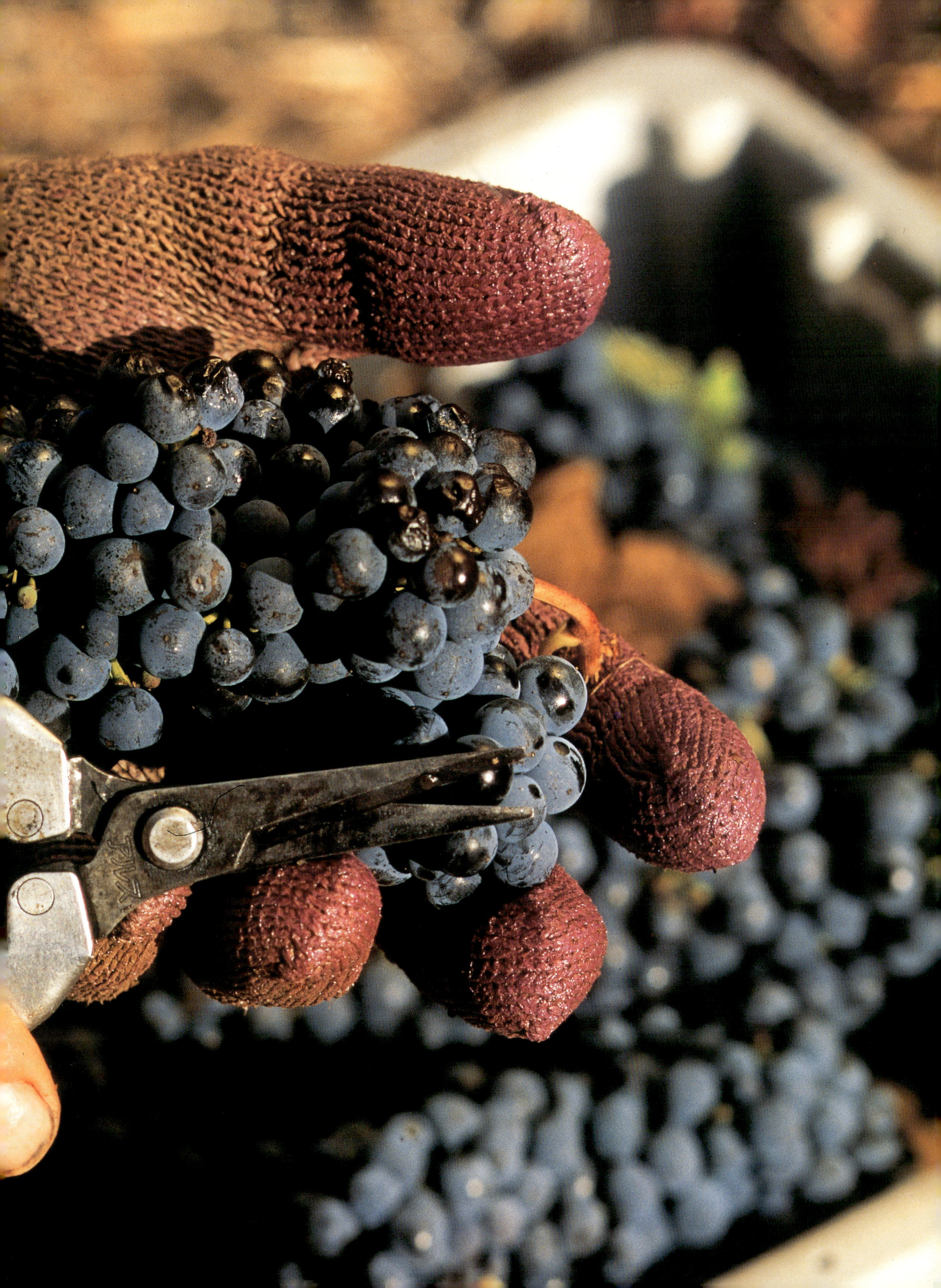

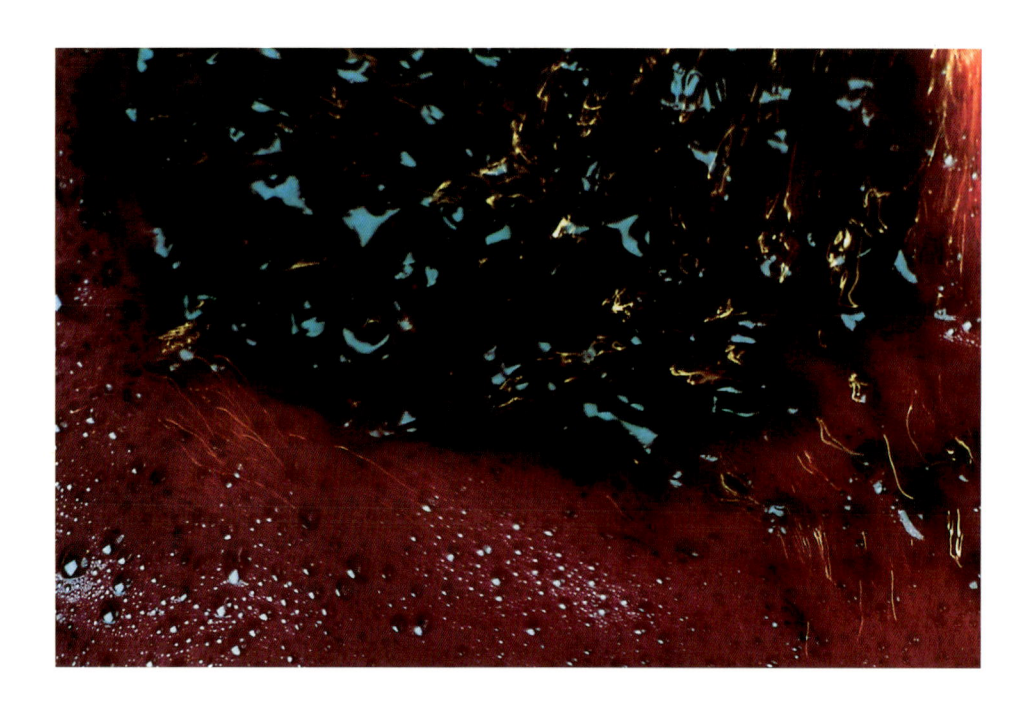

Winemaking practices

It is hard to talk in generalities, but there are some basic changes that have taken place in the art and science of winemaking in recent times. Winemakers are generally more responsive to vintage and tend now to adapt their practices to the particular wine with which they are dealing.

They are also tending to make wines that are less extractive. Where once they would pump over — circulate the fermenting red wine with the grape skins — four or five times a day, they will now pump over only once to produce a finer, more subtle red. Before fermentation, grapes are macerated (softened and broken up in liquid) so that the skins come into contact with the juice at low temperatures. Known as cold soaking, this enables the extraction of colour and flavour without the extraction of tannins. Extended maceration after fermentation enhances the tannin structure of the wine and gets rid of aggressive, gritty, furry tannins and produces finer, better integrated tannins.

Oak maturation probably plays a more significant part in production these days, with a more widespread availability of quality oak. There is a greater use of barrel fermentation and less skin contact before pressing.

Overall, there is a greater confidence in the outlook of the region's winemakers, who no longer aspire to reproduce the wines of Bordeaux or Burgundy. Rather, the men and women making wine in the region are comfortable highlighting the fruit characters and the regionality of Margaret River, assured in the belief that this is what their customers want.

Above and right: Cabernet sauvignon fermenting.
Overleaf: The first stage of making wine. Semillon splashing into the crusher soon after it has been picked.

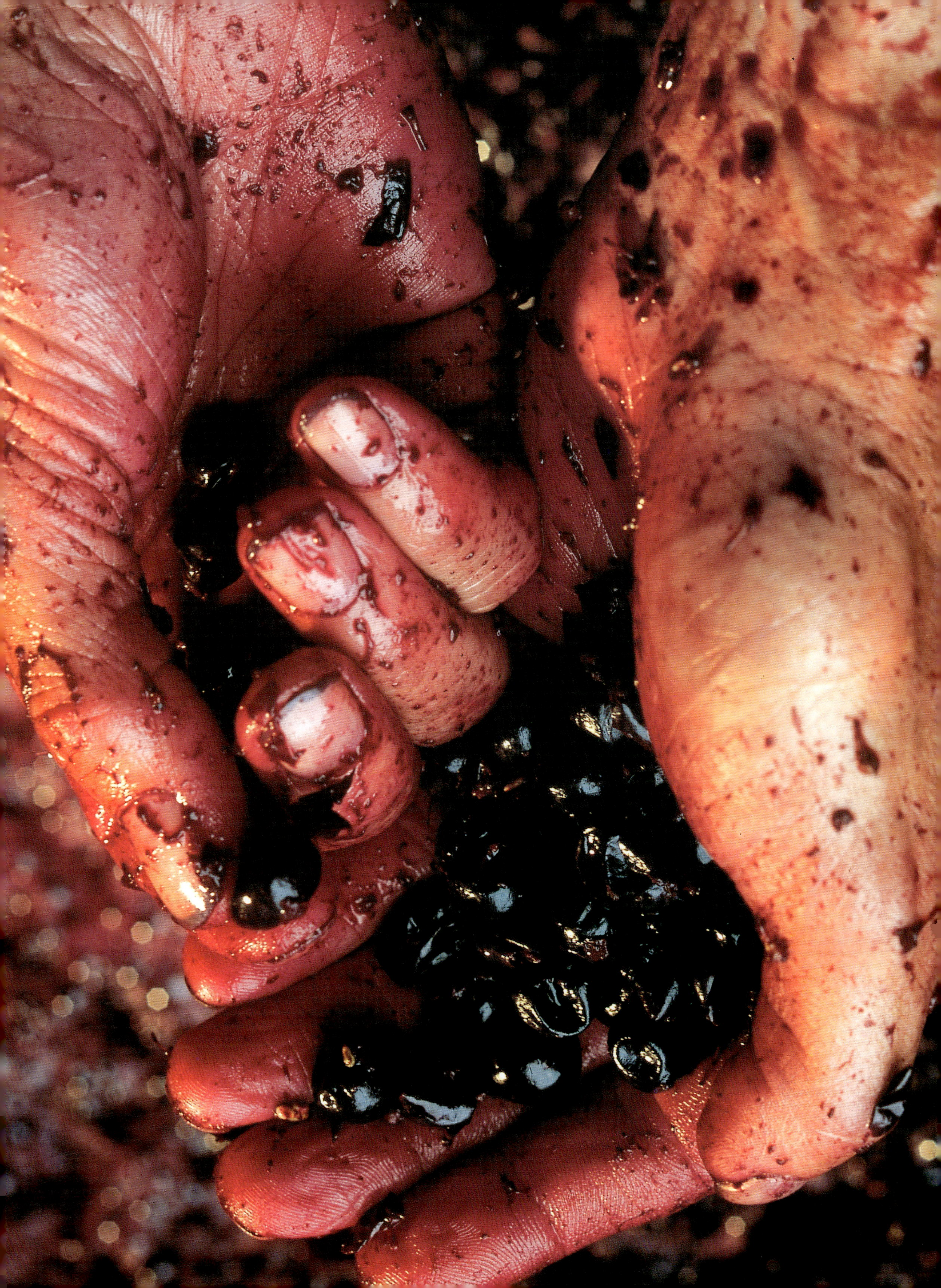

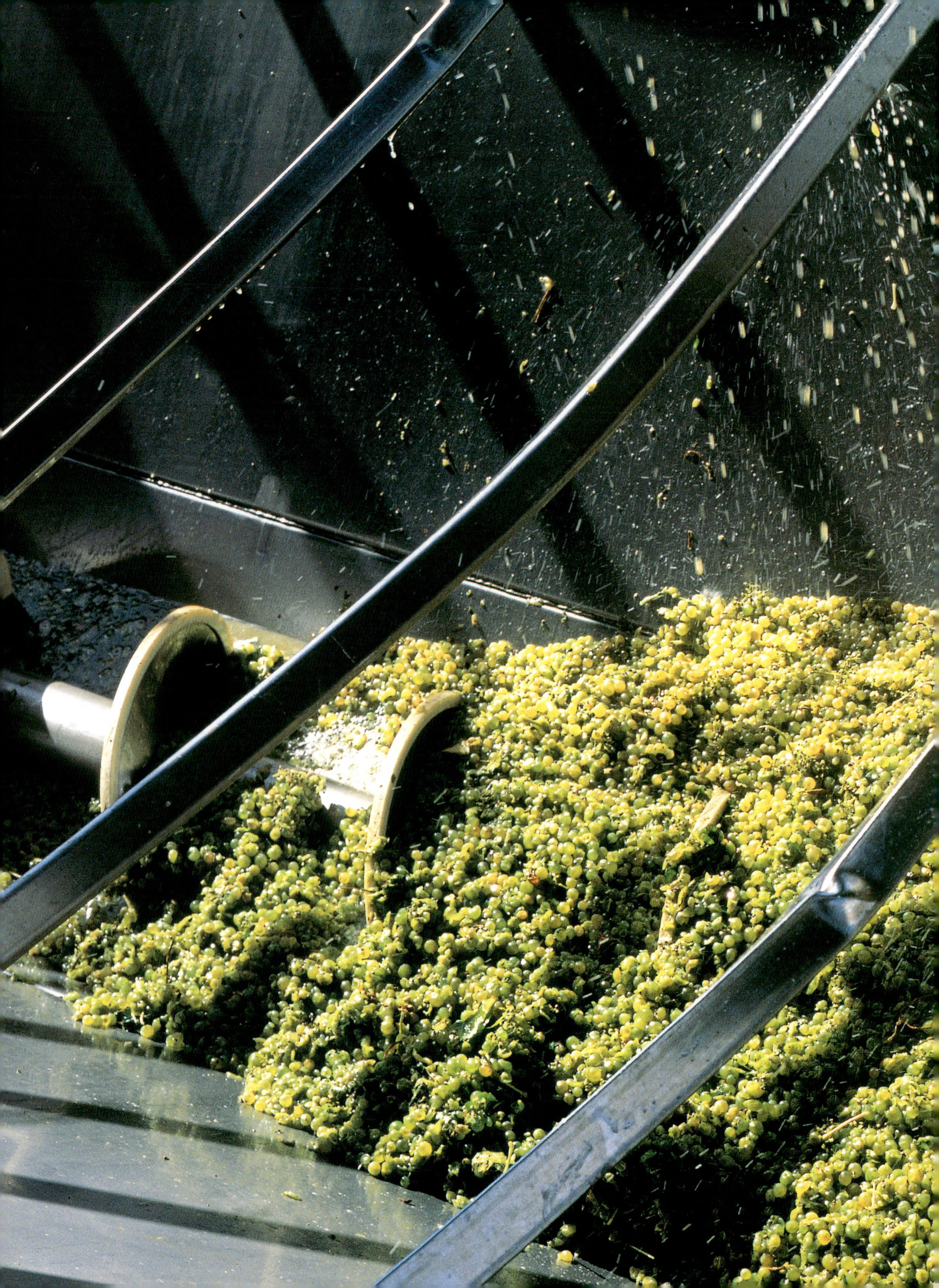

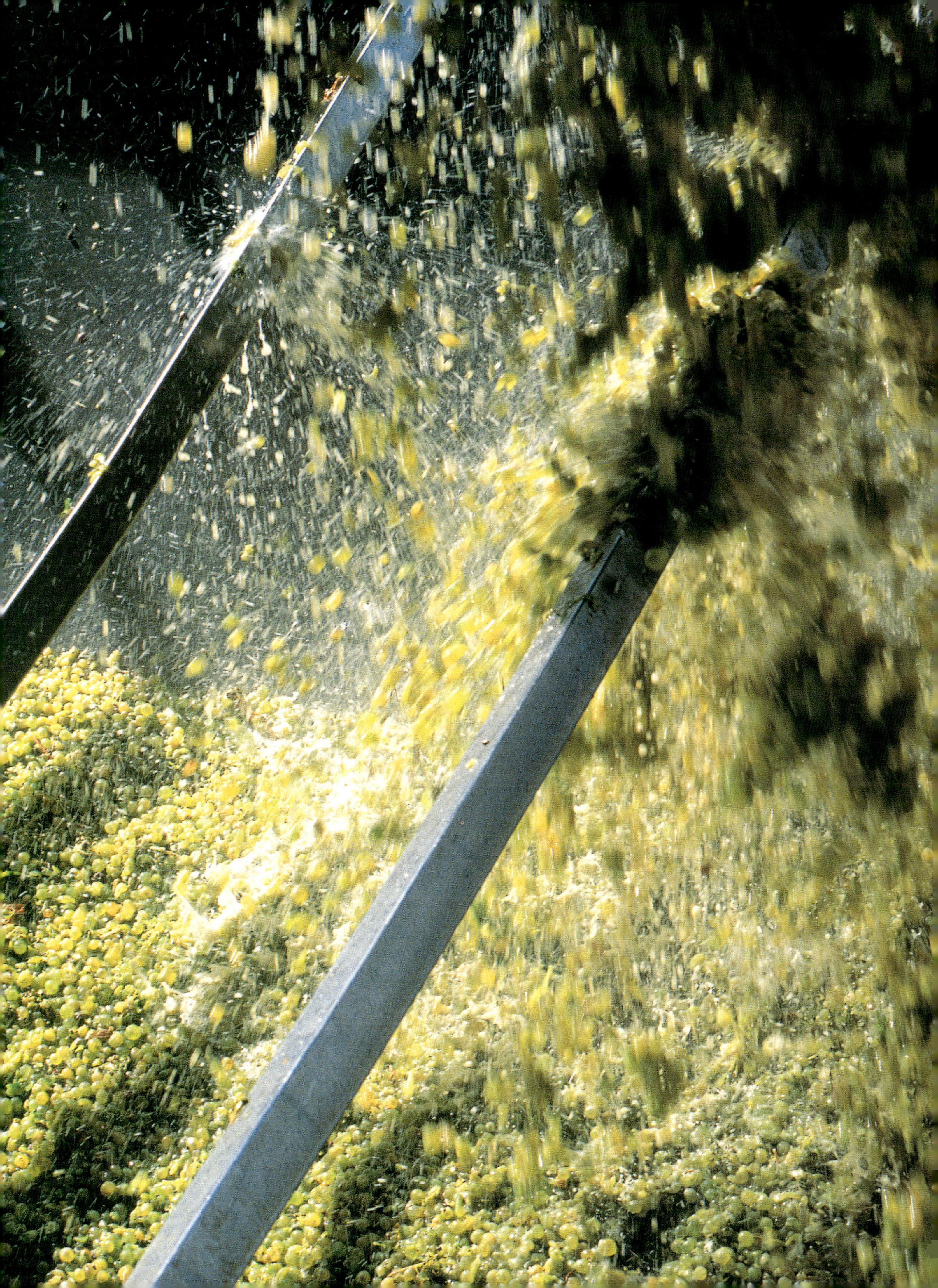

9. The great sites

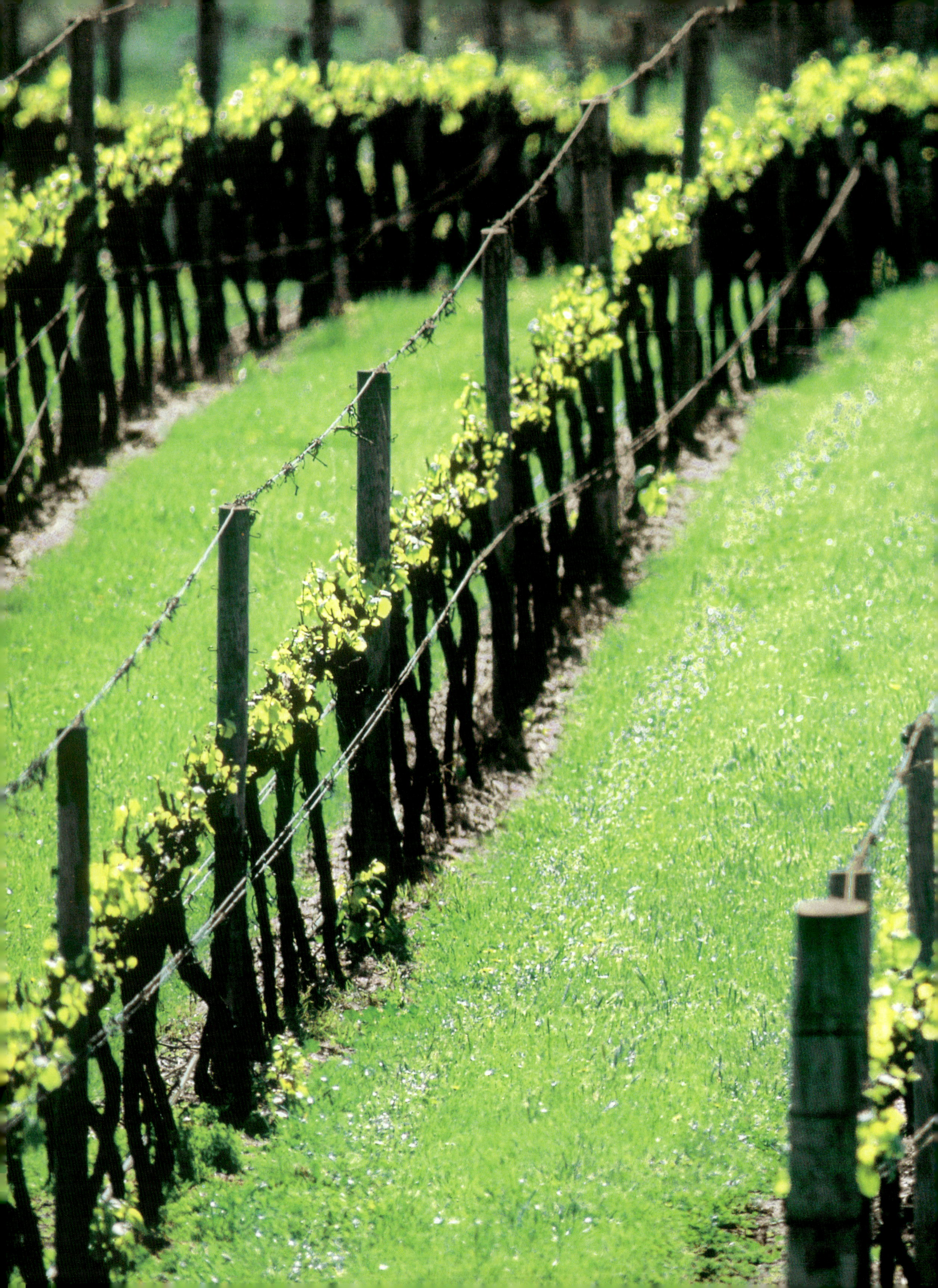

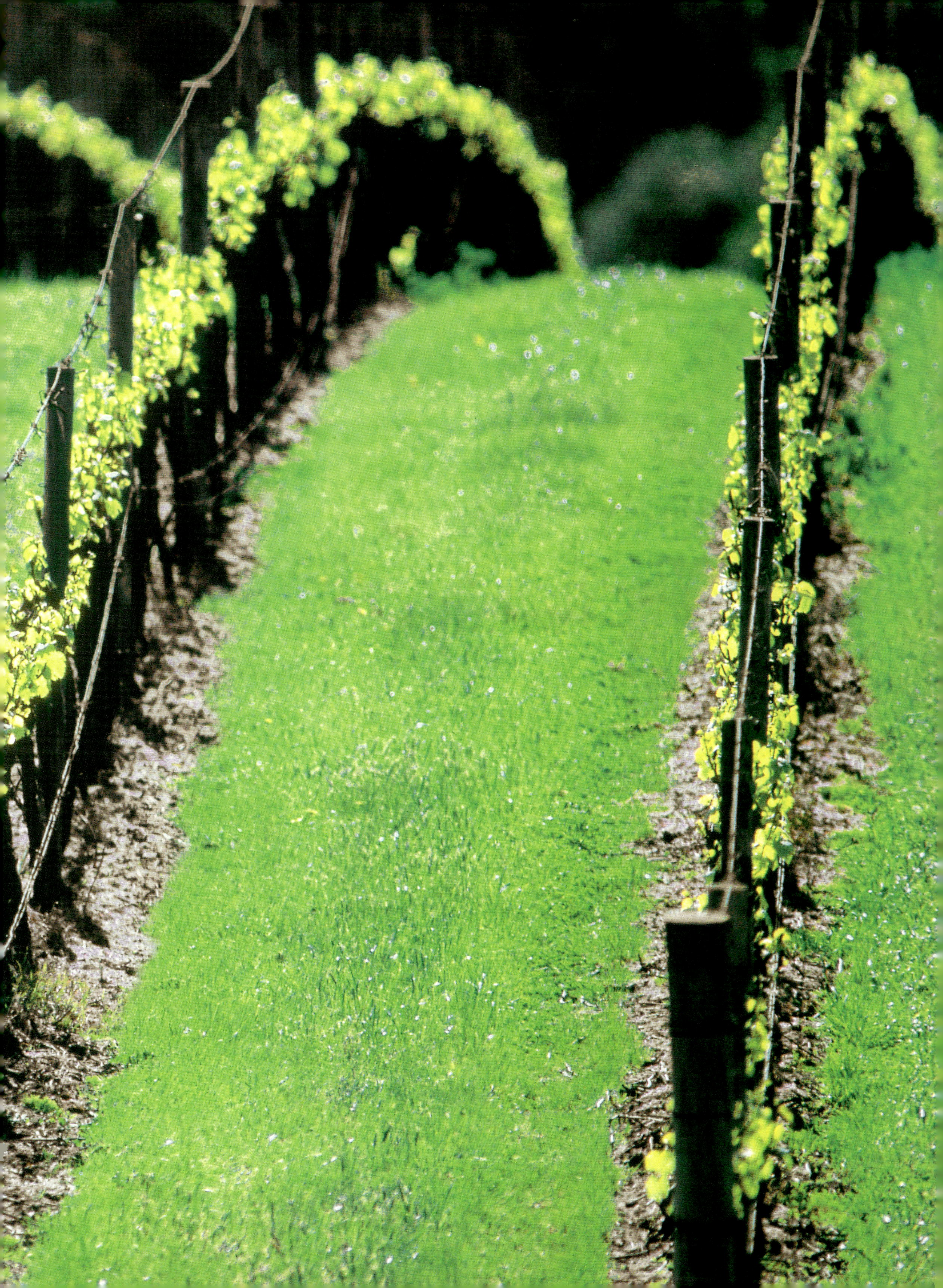

Margaret River wine has an individual character that puts its indelible stamp on each variety. There's the strength, power and intensity of cabernet sauvignon, the supple generosity of merlot, the rich savouriness of shiraz, the fine lingering intensity of chardonnay and a herbaceousness that draws semillon and sauvignon towards one another. These are the varieties that have carried Margaret River to the world and established its reputation. Although pinot noir and riesling have been grown with some success, they have not soared to such heights.

The quality of these wines confirms the predictions of Dr Gladstones and rewards those people who followed his guiding star into the district. In the viticultural world Margaret River is still an infant, yet already significant trends are emerging. Great wine styles have clearly been established and the most outstanding producers have set the standards over the years with wines that continue to reach new heights of sophistication and complexity.

Each year the region reveals more of itself. It may well be a very long time before we fully understand why some sites in Margaret River are better for viticulture than others, and why some grape varieties are more clearly suited to particular areas than others. However, we do believe that it is possible to make some interim comments based on our view that some of the region's greatest wines consistently come from the same sites.

Page 205: A cabernet sauvignon vine a week after budburst.
Previous page: The chardonnay vines in the Brookland Valley vineyard.
Above: Howard Park vineyard in the rain.
Right: A chardonnay leaf.

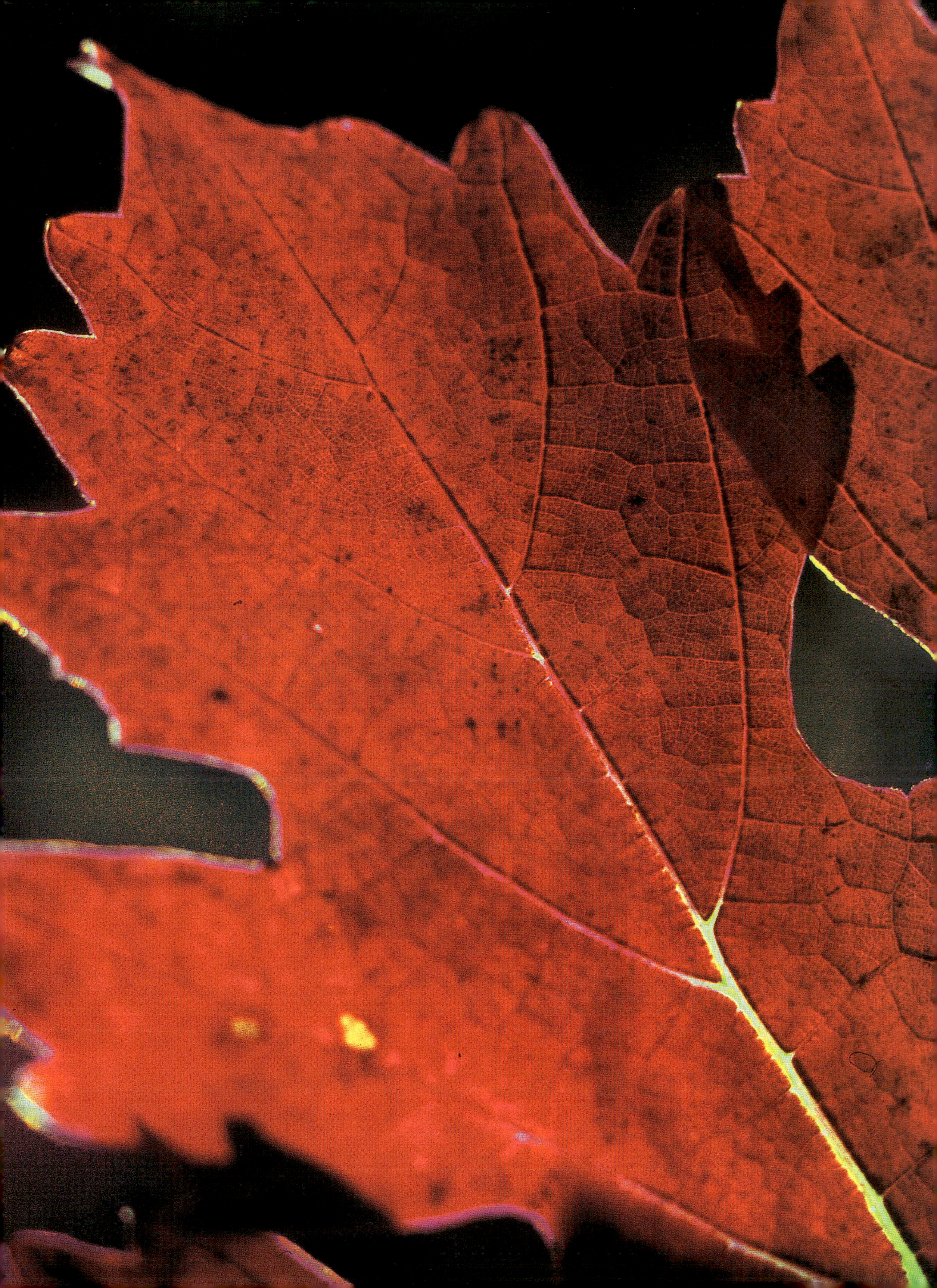

The Margaret River wine region

The boundaries of the wine region are those suggested by Dr John Gladstones. It is that part of south-western Australia to the west of longitude 115 degrees 18'E. The eastern boundary, now referred to as the Gladstones Line, runs from the coast just west of Busselton to the Southern Ocean near Snake Springs to the east of Augusta. The area extends about ninety kilometres from north to south and roughly twenty-seven kilometres west to east.

The climate is characterised by high winter rainfall — about 1150 mm average — and very little summer rain. Because it is close to the coast, frosts are infrequent, while cloud and hail are rare in the crucial spring and summer seasons. Although there are common climatic threads which run through this greater Margaret River region, significant differences can be found in some parts. Gladstones mentions the difference between the northern segment which faces Geographe Bay and is exposed to the warm, dry north-easterlies in summer, while the southern part near Karridale is dominated by the steady, cooler, more humid south-easterlies which bring some summer cloud.

Distance from the coast is often underrated in its effect. Although it is only a few kilometres between Bussell Highway and Caves Road, temperatures during the crucial ripening months of summer can vary by as much as 5°C.

These differences can make a substantial difference to viticulture. For example, a grape variety such as cabernet sauvignon may look leafy with red berry characters when grown to the south of the township of Margaret River and show weightier, denser, blackcurrant flavours when grown to the north in Wilyabrup.

In general, the cooler southern areas produce more elegant and less robust wines than those further north. But there are many other factors contributing to differences that are sometimes subtle and sometimes quite marked. Slope and aspect, proximity to the Southern Ocean or the Indian Ocean, soil profiles, wind exposure and other natural features all influence the quality and style of the grapes.

Soils can have a significant impact on wine. Viewing the region from the air can be revealing. The best soils often support towering red gums or are found along river courses: these are then useful pointers to ideal viticultural sites. Less suitable are likely to be those areas where deep gravelly loam contrasts visibly with lighter, grey sandy soils.

Generally the soils in the region are gravelly loam over a clay subsoil in which the ancient granite bedrock and smaller deposits of limestone have gradually broken down over centuries. Those which contain a high proportion of decomposed granite are commonly referred to as Wilyabrup soils, although

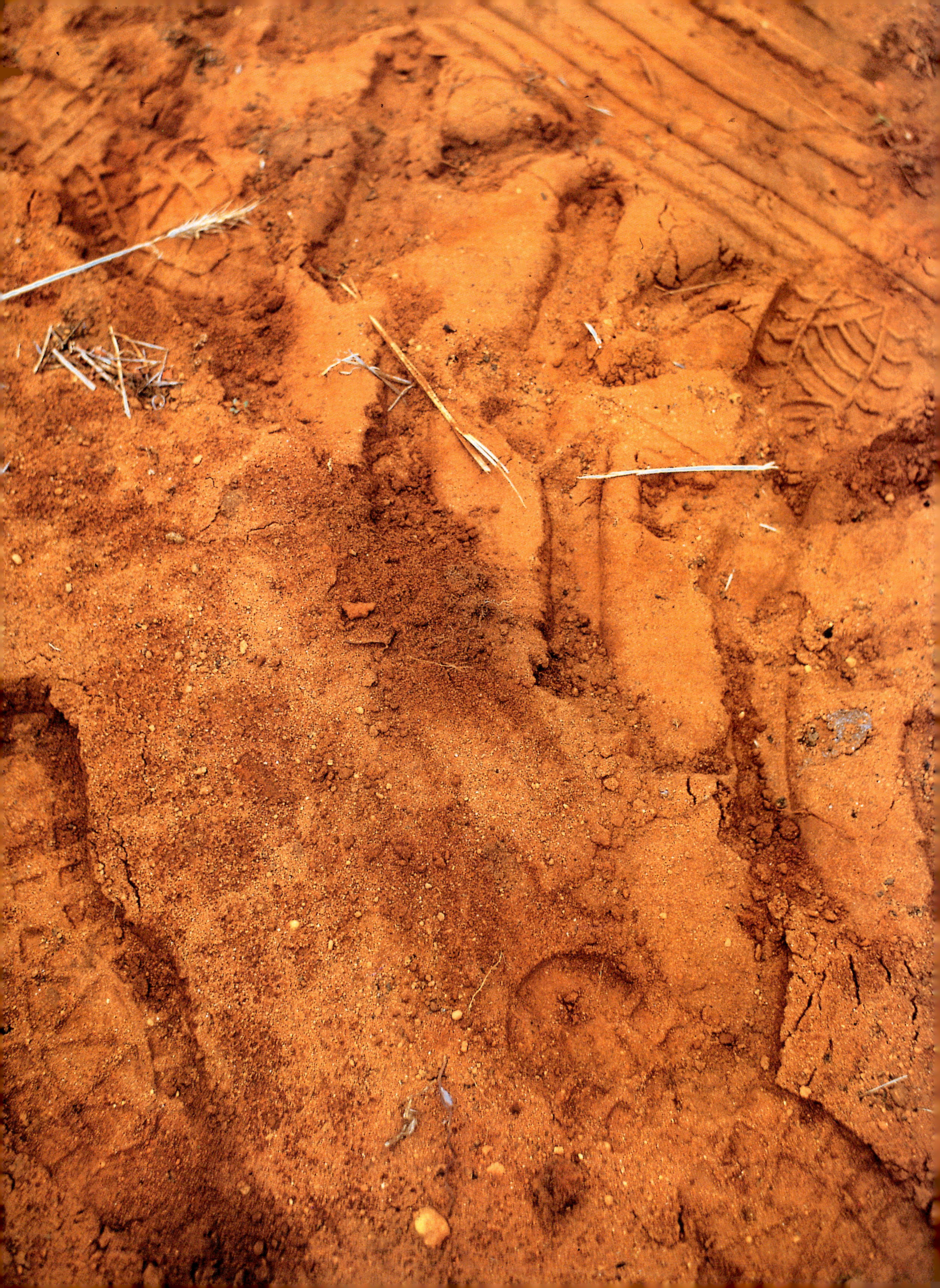

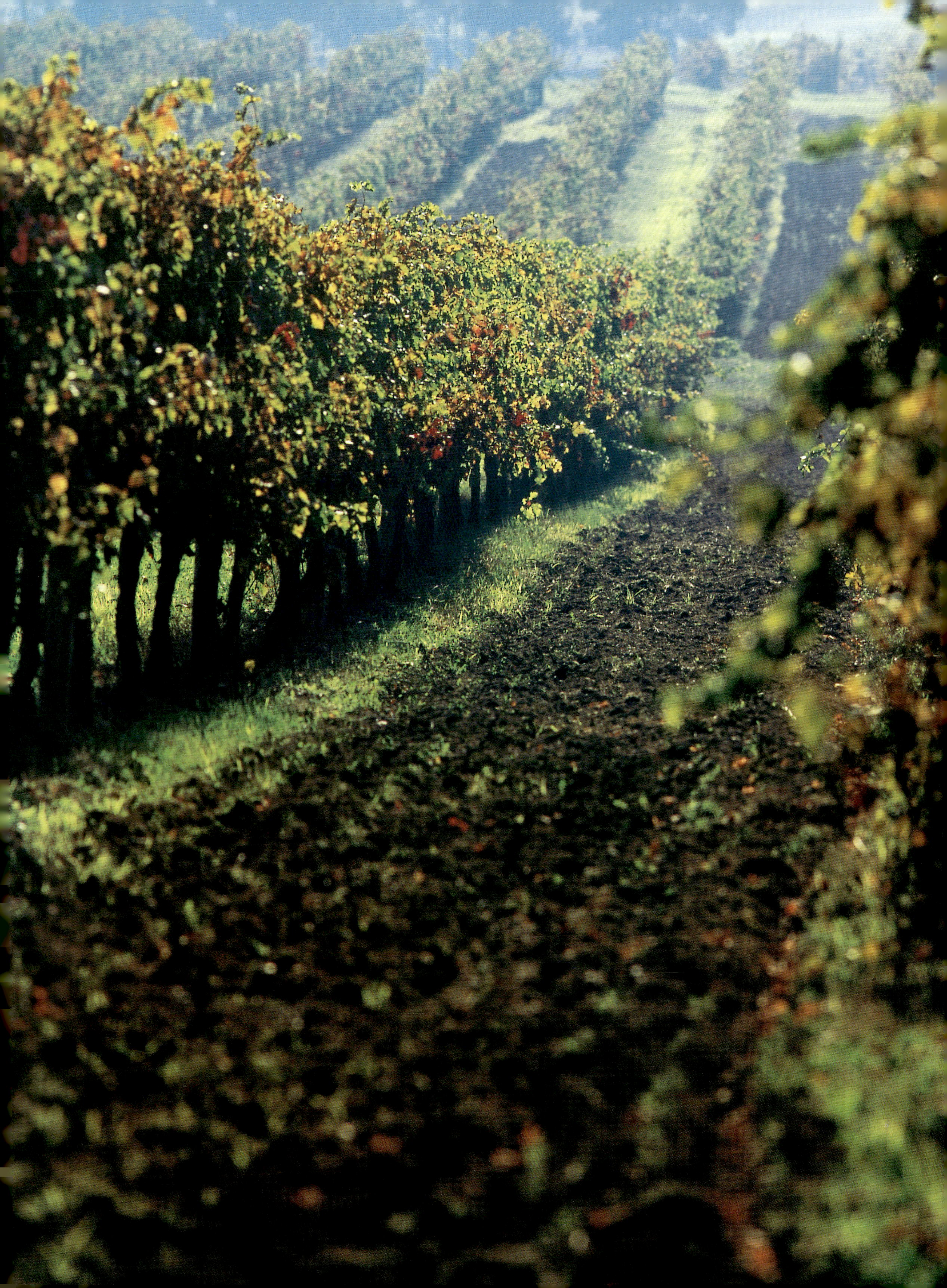

Previous page: In the merlot vineyard at Leeuwin Estate.
Left: Leeuwin Estate vines.
Above: Chardonnay grapes.

these are not confined to the Wilyabrup area. There is growing evidence that the greatest wines of Margaret River come off these Wilyabrup soils.

It is the physical, structural composition rather than the chemical make-up or its level of fertility and richness that determines the suitability of soil for viticulture. The best soils have depth to allow the roots to penetrate so they can sustain the vine in those critical months of late summer just before harvest. These soils help maintain the right vine balance by not taking up excess nutrients and water so that the leaf to fruit ratio is in the correct range. Vine balance contributes to fruit quality and ultimately the quality of the wines.

Gladstones suggested that it might be possible to divide the greater Margaret River area into six sub-regions, based on the different climatic influences and the natural drainage basins of the river courses. Running from north to south, the divisions are Yallingup, Carbunup, Wilyabrup, Treeton, Wallcliffe and Karridale.

At this stage, however, Gladstones' work on sub-regions represent only the start of an attempt to define the whole region more precisely and to consider which grape varieties will be most appropriate for specific areas. Science can only go so far because the final arbiter in all of this must be the quality of the wine. Much remains to be done.

Leeuwin Estate Block 20

Some years ago the authors were privileged to be part of a historic tasting of every vintage of Leeuwin Estate's famous Art Series Chardonnay. To put things in perspective, Australian chardonnay was in its infancy when Leeuwin released its first wine in 1980. Australian winemakers and wine drinkers were embarking on a very steep learning curve that continues to this day.

The most striking feature of that Leeuwin tasting was the freshness of the older vintages. As a result of that and other tastings, we can say with confidence that there is not a chardonnay in Australia that ages as well as Leeuwin. The Art Series Chardonnay needs at least five to eight years of bottle age before it approaches maturity, let alone reaches its peak. This ability to age gracefully is rare in Australian chardonnay and is one generally regarded sign of greatness in wine.

Long-time Leeuwin viticulturist John Brocksopp, who retired in 2002, describes the wine:

The fruit flavours are mirrored in the resulting wine which begins with delicate balance but has the capacity to age into something extraordinarily powerful and mouth filling while still maintaining its finesse.

I want to finish up tasting the fresh fruit, smell the scent of the vine flowers, taste and appreciate all the winemaking touches. I want to be able to dwell on the colour, remembering it is a reflection of both the ripening conditions and the winery care. The finished wine must taste full but alive in the mouth with all these things, but then, also have a lingering finish that must be the essence and harmony of it all.

So what is it that gives Leeuwin its ethereal qualities that make it stand so far above the rest? Put simply, it is about the whole being greater than the

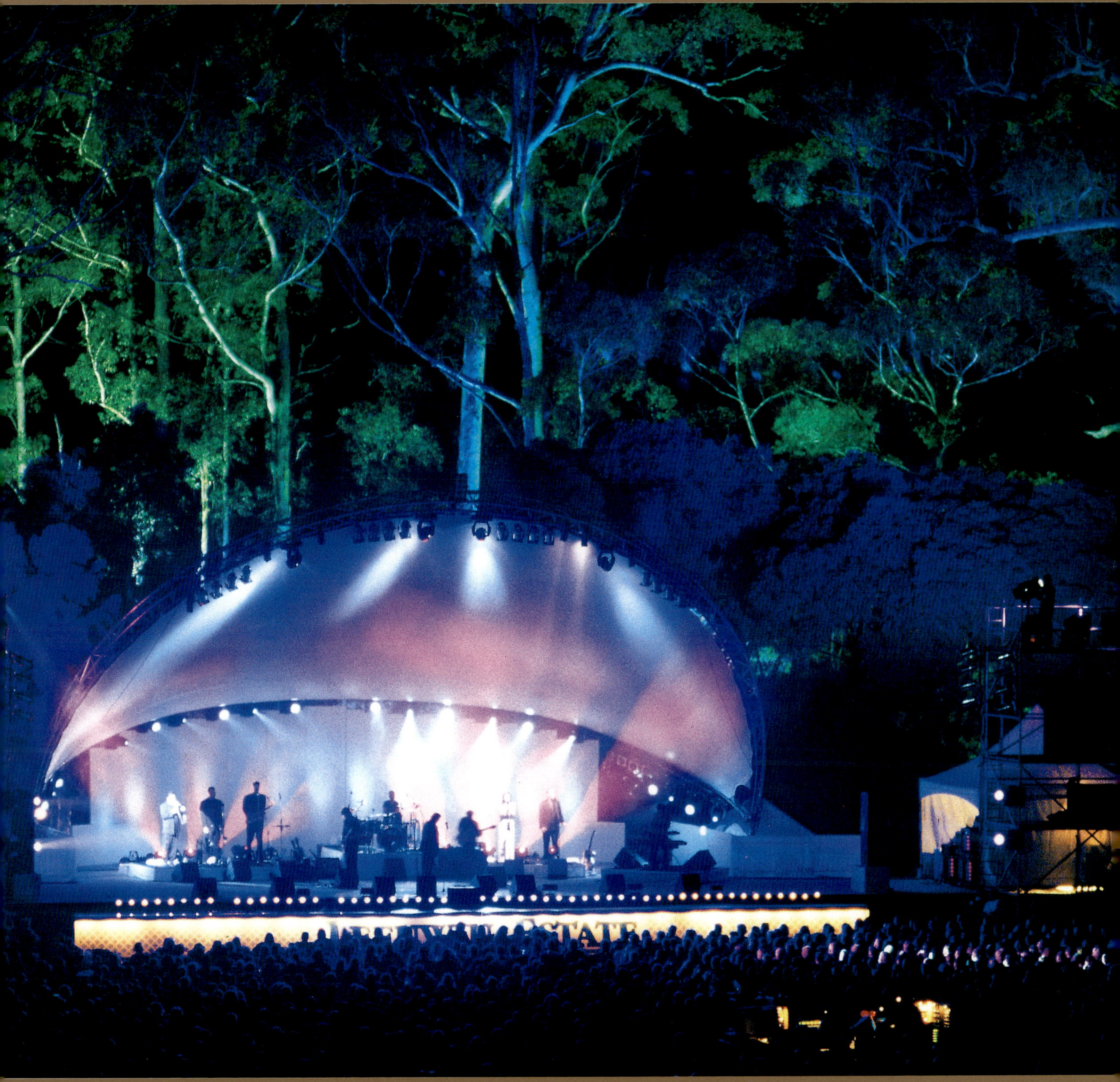

sum of its parts. More precisely, it is about the particular confluence of climate, soil, site and viticultural and winemaking practice.

The principal source for the Leeuwin Art Series Chardonnays is its Block 20 vineyard, established in 1976. Block 20 chardonnay has more distinctive flavour nuances compared to other sites at Leeuwin. When ripe the fruit has a strong pear character with its long flavours showing great delicacy, freshness and persistence on the palate.

Block 20, or the Front Gate Block as it is also known, like most of the vineyard land at Leeuwin Estate, is planted on the site of an ancient red gum forest. It is on a gentle undulating slope which was formed by the creek system which dissects the locality. The moderately deep laterite soils are ideal for growing grapes as they allow deep penetration for the roots of the vines. On this site, perfect balance is achieved. Leaf growth on the vines occurs up until the time that the grapes begin to ripen. At this stage, the vines concentrate on ripening the grapes. On less satisfactory sites, more vigorous growth occurs with the vine's energy split between growing and ripening grapes.

The vineyard slopes north-west to west with the rows running north-east and south-west so that they are open to the morning light and, in summer, are also gently lit in the afternoon. The early summer sea breezes push the warmer air out and provide good ventilation for the remainder of the day. Consequently, the site experiences mild temperatures and the warmth of the sun.

The combination of the soil, climate and the Gin Gin (or Mendoza) clone of chardonnay keep the yields on Block 20 moderate: less than two tons to the acre (five tonnes to the hectare).

The batches from individual blocks are kept separate during the winemaking process. The wine from Block 20, for example, is matured on yeast lees in one hundred per cent new Tronçais and Allier barriques for up to seventeen months while batches with lighter fruit flavours are taken out of oak after nine months. When the Art Series Chardonnay is finally blended, it is the Block 20 portion which forms the backbone of the wine with other batches being used to build complexity.

The adjacent Block 21 — Denis Road — shares many of the same attributes but the wine from it is invariably softer, sweeter and less intense than that from Block 20. Leeuwin has tried to determine the secret of this site, but without ever being able to replicate the quality that it produces. Block 20 is unique.

Previous page left: The diverse crowd relax and enjoy the Leeuwin concert.
Previous page right: John Farnham on stage at the Leeuwin concert.
Right: Simon Clarke picking merlot.
Overleaf: Melissa Manns among the vines at Leeuwin.

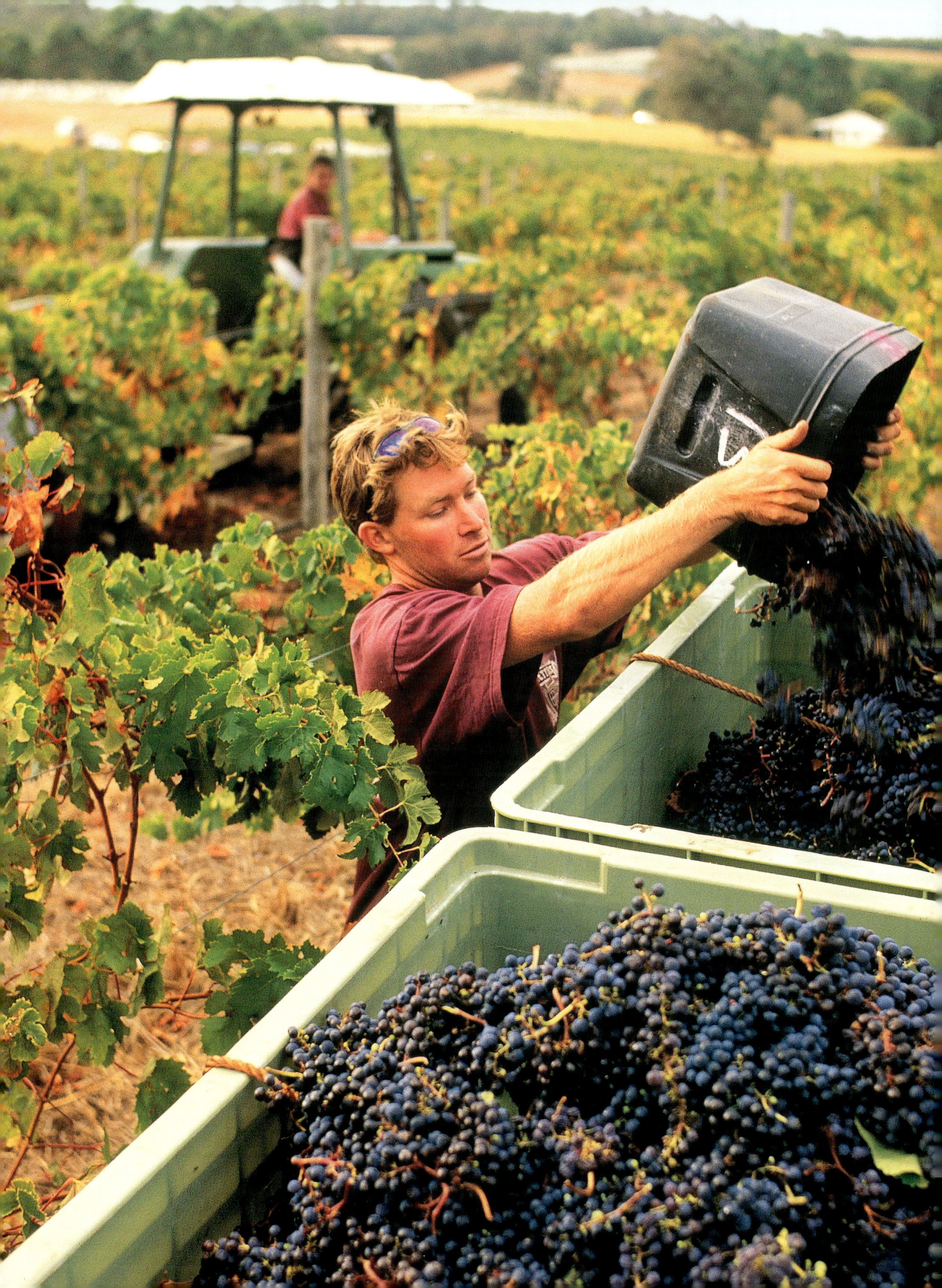

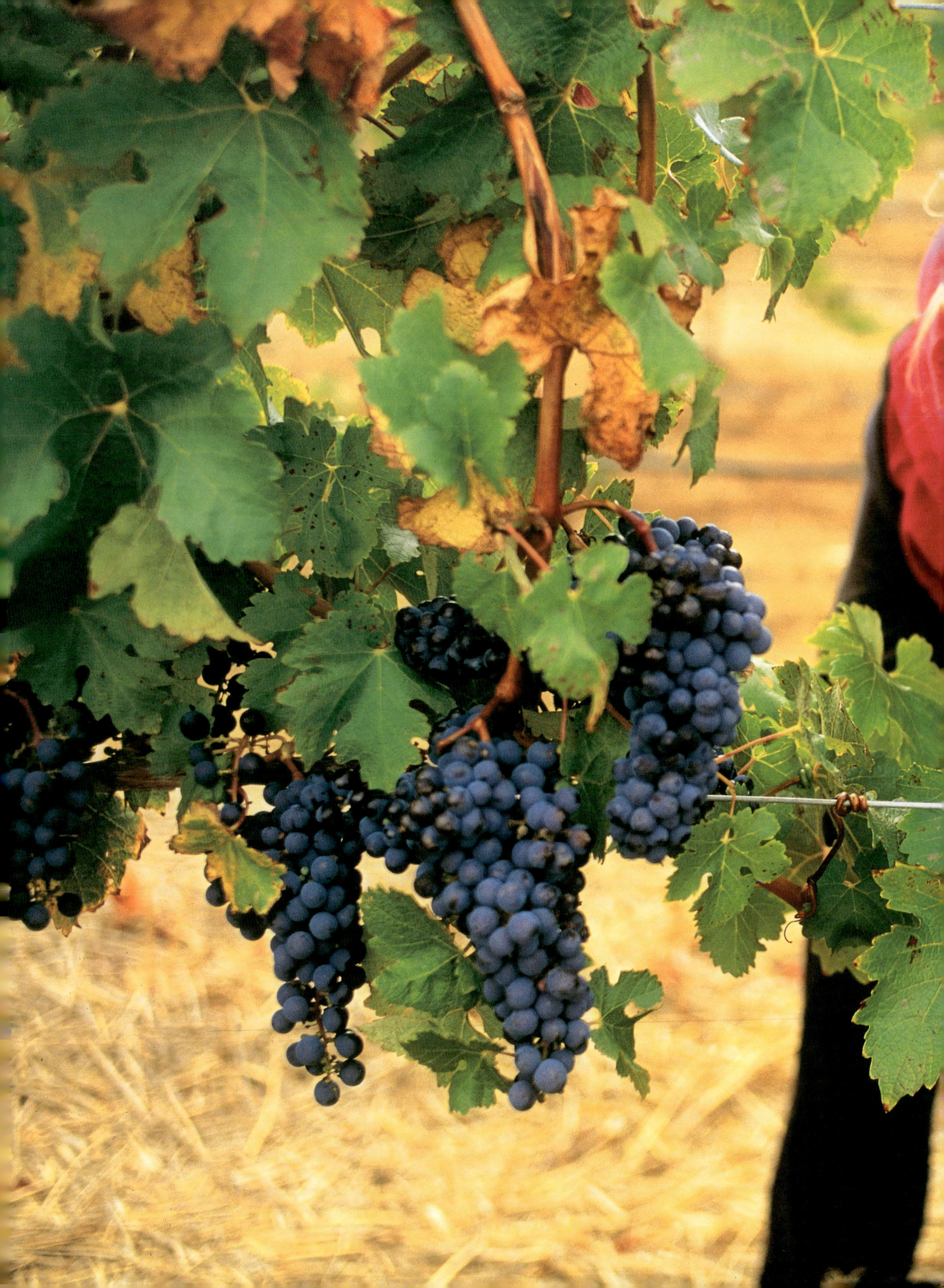

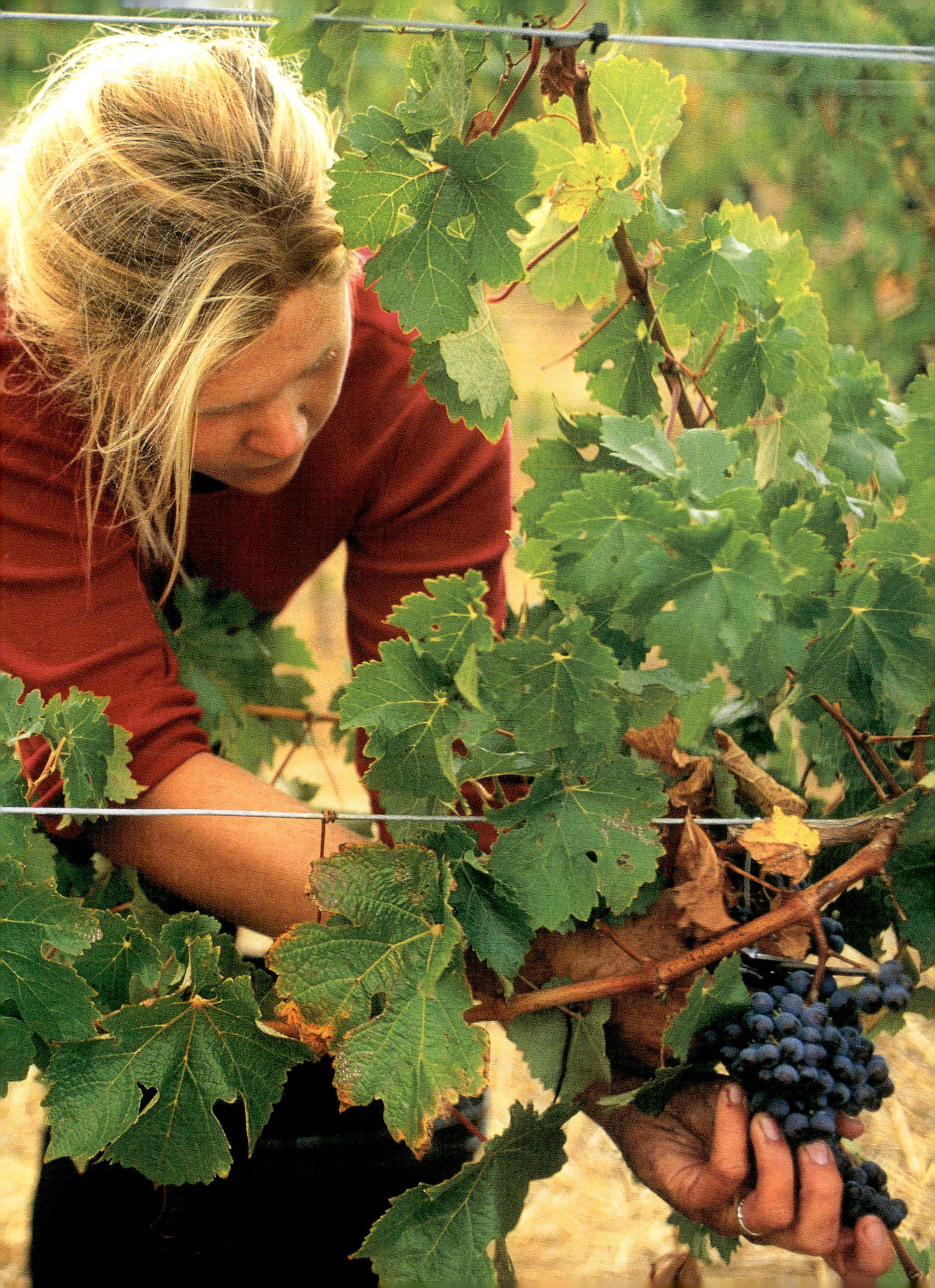

Pierro Caves Road Block

If there is one consistent rival to the great chardonnays of Leeuwin Estate it is Pierro, the small venture established by Dr Michael Peterkin on Caves Road. Peterkin is a thinker, who blends ideas and concepts with practical experience to create a residue rich in viticultural and winemaking knowledge.

There are three distinct plantings of chardonnay at Pierro, and about ninety-five per cent are the Gin Gin clone, which is the staple clone for Western Australian chardonnay. The vineyards are managed to maximise fruit, leaf and cane exposure to sunlight, minimise wind damage in spring and to obtain optimum flavour development in the ripening period. The three vineyard blocks are planted to high-density narrow rows on Wilyabrup soils that have a high proportion of granite rock, on steep slopes that run down to the Wilyabrup Brook. Rows in the first planting face west to north-west, while the other two face north to north-west. Tall jarrah and red gums provide protection from the prevailing winds.

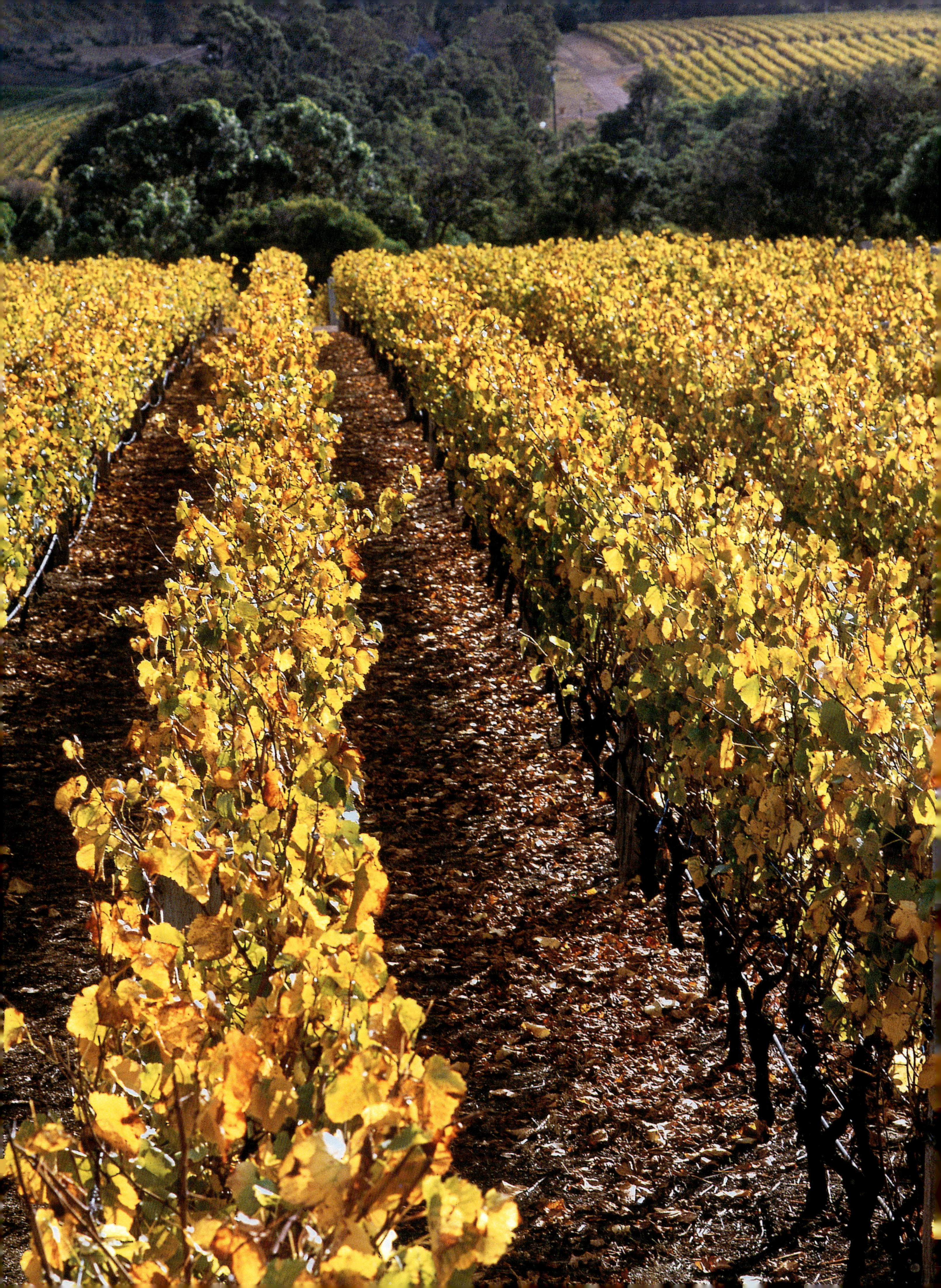

Watering at Pierro differs from that at most vineyards in the region. Peterkin uses his irrigation system to replicate natural rainfall, so that rather than trickle or drip water into the vines regularly, he gives them a decent drink when necessary, in much the same way as a good summer shower might put three inches into the soil and push right down to the roots. Like Dr Gladstones, Peterkin believes very strongly in balance, with vine management the key to achieving it. The concept of vine balance is about having the leaf vigour in balance with the optimum amount of fruit for the vine. When the vine is out of balance, with either too much or too little fruit, the resulting quality of fruit — the final arbiter of how well the vine has been managed — will suffer. Australian winemakers haven't had the centuries of experience to really understand how to manage vine balance on particular sites, yet they are learning rapidly.

Unlike Leeuwin Estate, Peterkin puts his great chardonnays through one hundred per cent malolactic fermentation, which, he maintains, contributes to better texture and mouth feel with a longer more refined palate.

Previous page left: Guinea fowl at work protecting the Pierro vineyard from predators.
Previous page right: Chardonnay vines on the Caves Road block at Pierro.
Right: Michael Peterkin and Jackson Gerard check the marc following the pressing of the grapes.

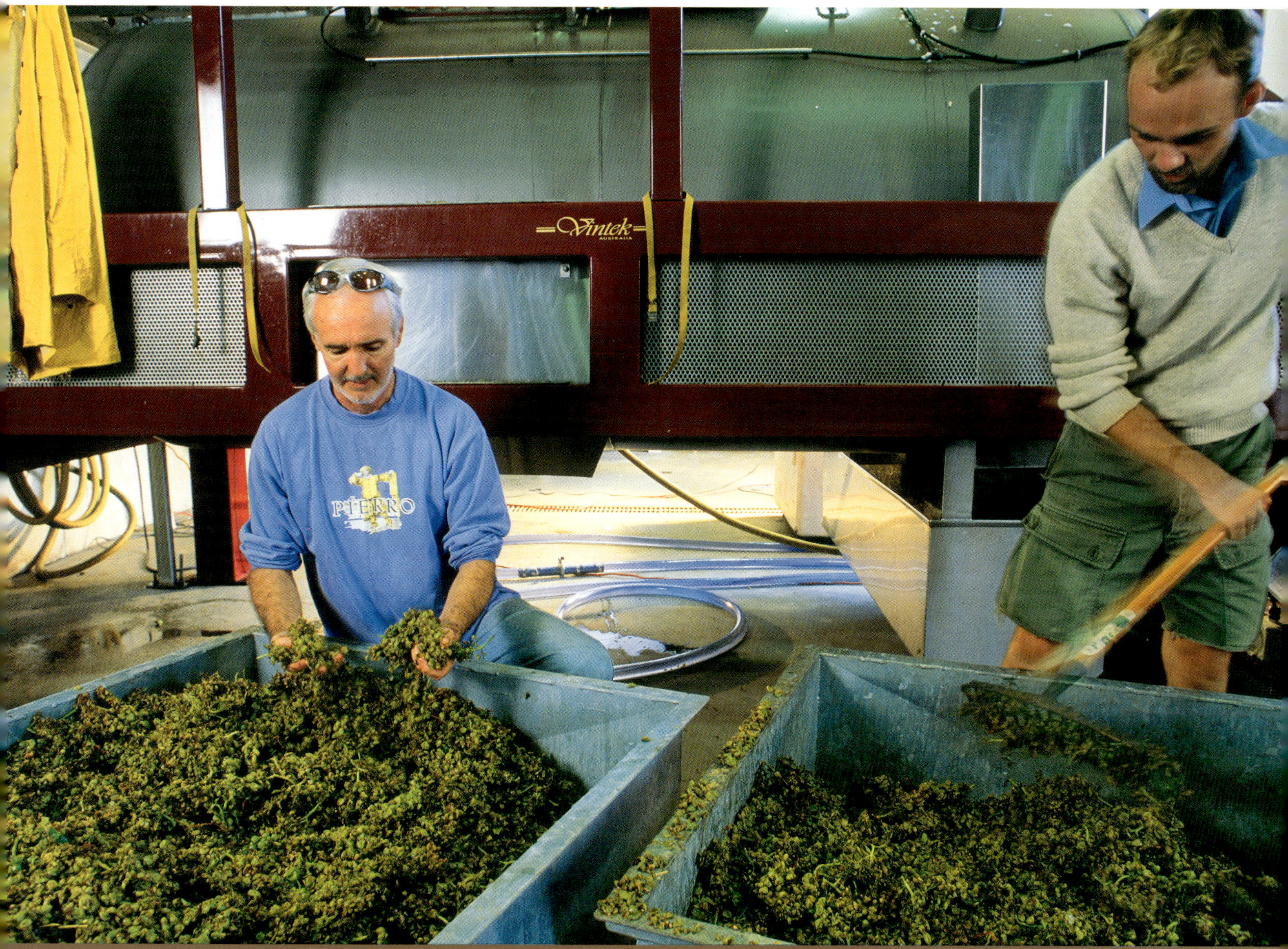
Vintek
PIERRO

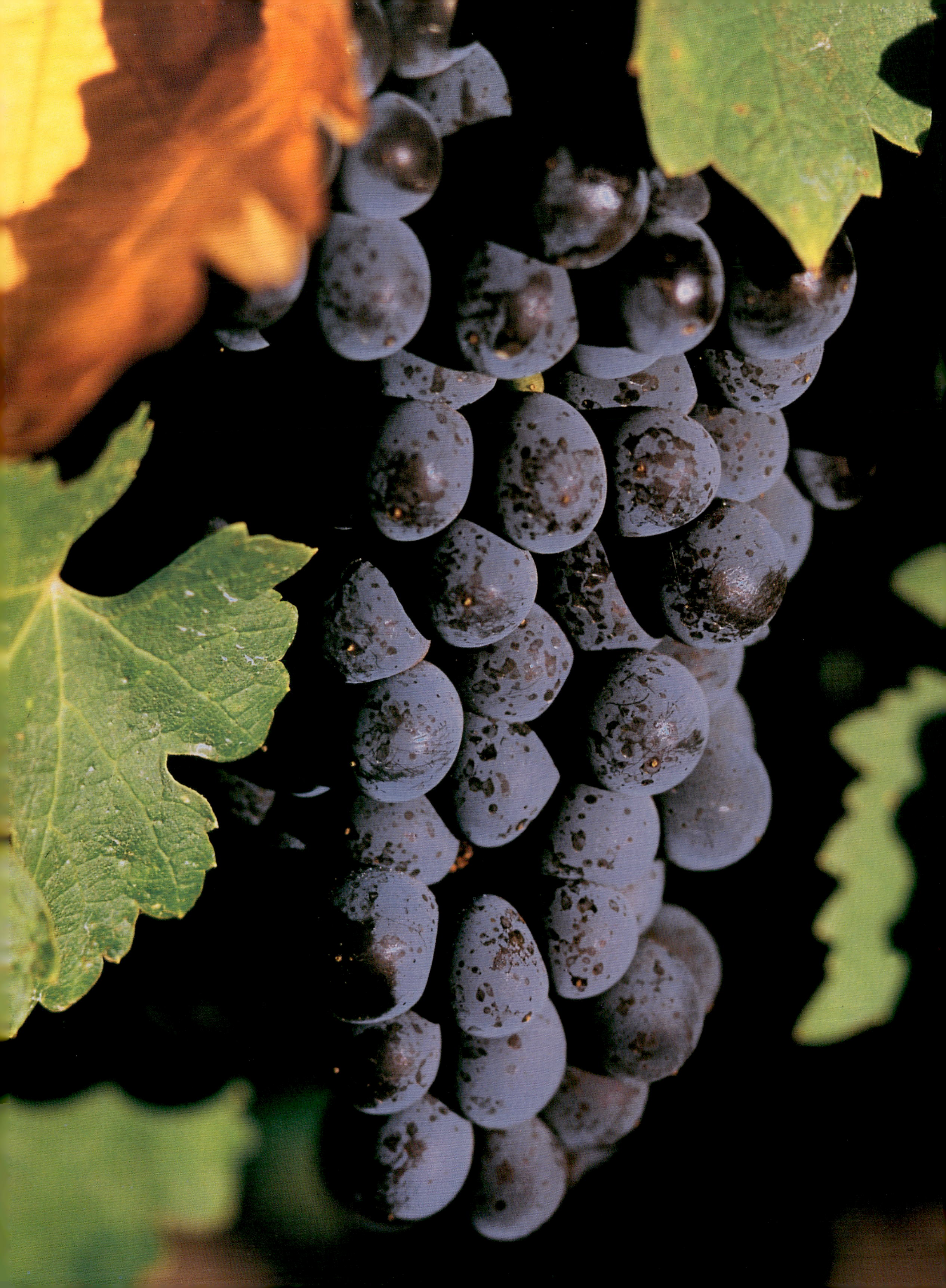

Left: Cabernet sauvignon grapes.
Overleaf: Plunging the cap. During the fermentation process, plunging takes place to mix the skins into the wine to allow alcohol to break down the skins and extract tannins and colour.

Cullen Cabernet Block

One of the great wines of Margaret River is the Cullen cabernet sauvignon merlot. This is consistently Australia's finest blend of these two varieties, rising to great heights in seasons where the gods add that little extra dimension of intensity and power.

Di and Kevin Cullen selected the site after a three-year search. It is a 7.7-hectare jewel, which features most of the characteristics associated with the great sites of the area.

The soil is forest grove gravel and decomposed granite with a sandy topsoil on to laterite and then to clay. These ironstone soils are particularly well suited to cabernet sauvignon, giving a minerality to the wine and the necessary firm tannin structure. A gentle north-east facing slope helps drain off the water and stops waterlogging, while it also provides protection from the weather, especially the strong gales in September, and subsequently helps ripening later in the season.

To maximise the advantages of the slope the rows are planted north-south, so that the vines get a healthy dose of morning and afternoon sunshine. And because the vineyard is close to the ocean, the cooling effects of the sea breezes play a key role in moderating the temperature while still enabling fruit to achieve maximum ripeness. As a result the grapes rarely 'cook' on the vines as they can in less moderate areas. This is particularly important for cabernet sauvignon in Margaret River because even at high alcohols the flavours do not tend to go jammy when riper.

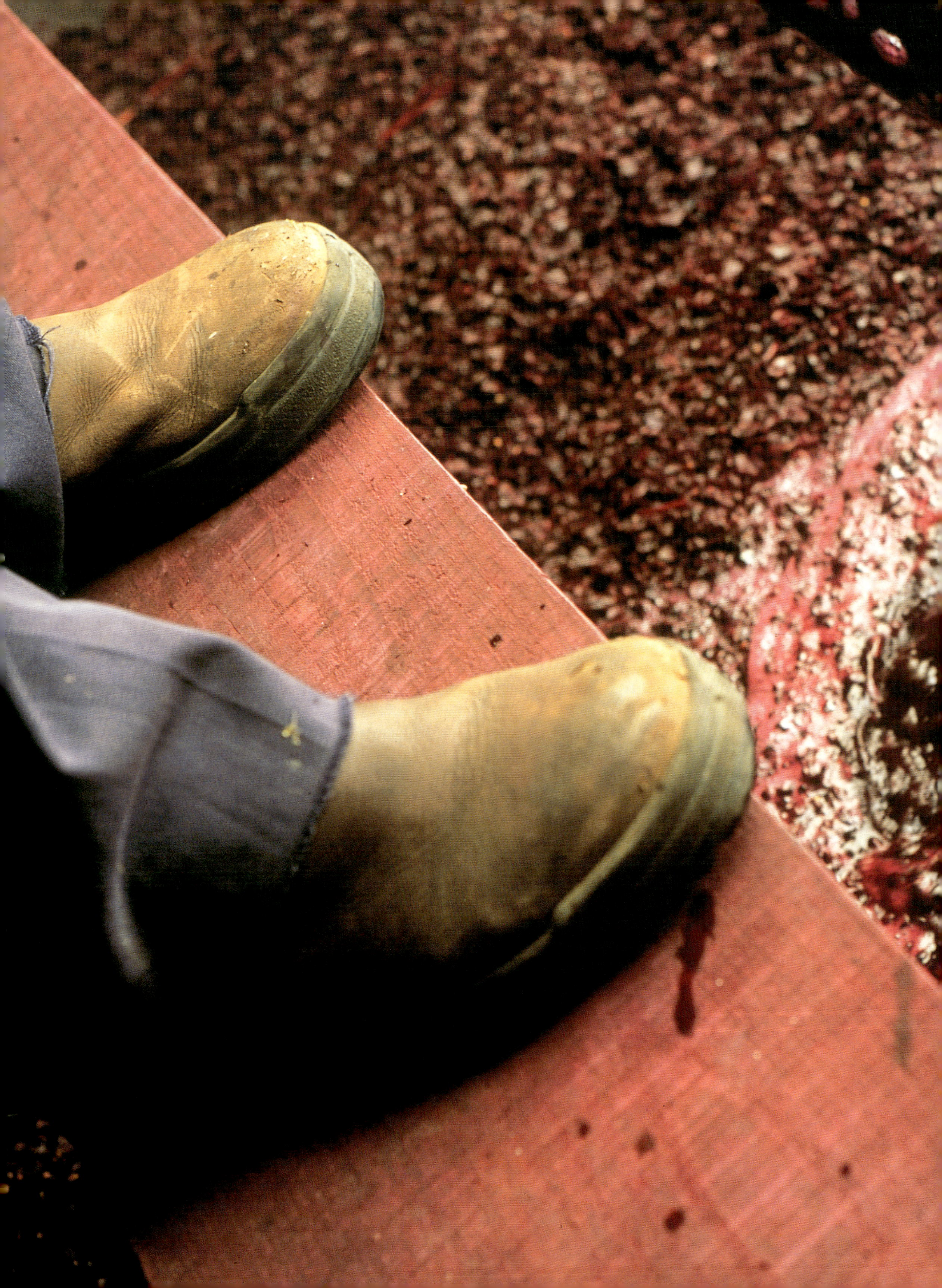

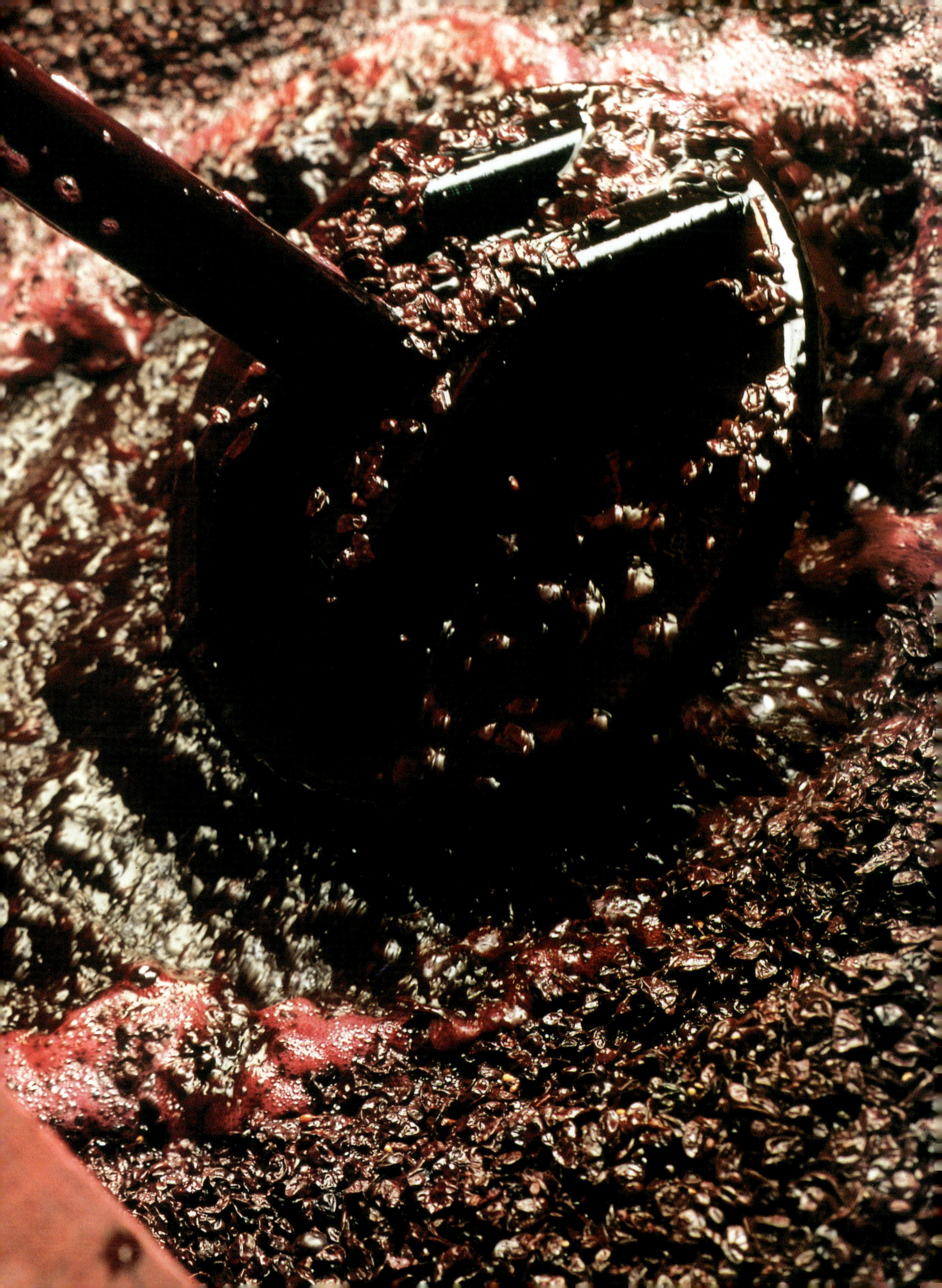

Above: The Cullen vineyard adjoining Gralyn.
Right: Di and Vanya Cullen with Rosie and Pookie.

The Cullen vineyard is managed according to organic principles. These contribute to improved vine health and lead ultimately to better overall balance and resistance to disease, while the vines achieve a physiological ripeness at lower sugar levels. The block is not irrigated and the vines appear to have found their own balance without requiring supplementary water, giving a yield of about two tonnes per acre.

The Cullens use the Scott Henry trellising system, which they believe contributes to better colour, riper flavours, better quality and riper tannins, and deep texture. Trellising was identified by Dr Gladstones — among many others — as a key determinant of vine balance and vine management. It enhances light exposure and contributes to the fruit remaining in balance as it ripens through summer.

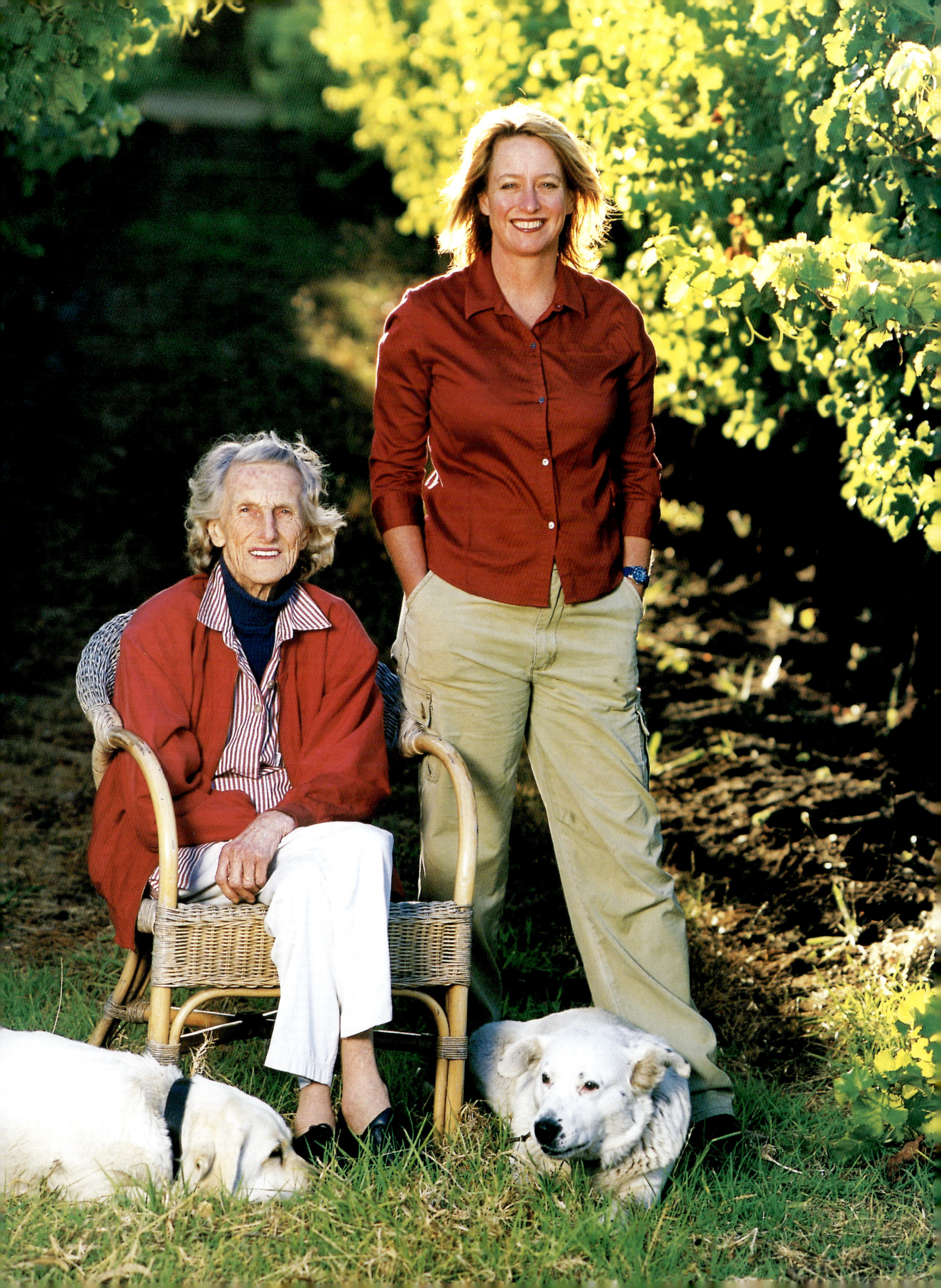

Moss Wood Cabernet Blocks

There is no small vineyard in Australia more synonymous with great cabernet sauvignon than Moss Wood, the vineyard established by Dr Bill Pannell and now owned and managed by Keith Mugford.

If Cullen consistently produce Australia's greatest cabernet merlot, and Leeuwin its greatest chardonnay, then just as surely Moss Wood consistently makes its greatest cabernet — a wine with remarkable softness and subtlety, yet with a structure and fruit quality that allow it to age for many years. It was a criticism of early Moss Wood cabernets that they were too soft to last. How wrong those prophecies now seem as we taste Moss Wood cabernets that are twenty or more years old and still going strong.

The Moss Wood cabernet sauvignon block is divided into three sections, known around the winery as the Old Block, Long Rows and Short Rows. The Old Block was the first Moss Wood planting, in 1969, on Wilyabrup gravelly loam on a south through north-east facing slope. The original trellis system was Sunraysia 'narrow T' (originally developed for sultanas), with limited shoot positioning and fixed foliage wires, and hand trimmed. The fruit from the Old Block always causes plenty of excitement around the winery: the legendary 1975 and 1976 wines were made exclusively from fruit off this block.

The Short Rows and Long Rows blocks were both planted in 1970 on north-facing slopes of Wilyabrup gravelly loam. The original trellis type of single fruiting wire was replaced with Scott Henry in 1993 in the Short Rows block and in 1997 in the Long Rows. With the new trellis, the quality improved significantly and this appears to have contributed to a strong run of very good vintages.

After working the new trellis systems, it seemed possible that some of the differences between the blocks were due to the old trellis system. The Scott Henry system was introduced to twenty per cent of the Old Block between 1989 and 1993, but the quality change was not deemed sufficient to justify the expense of converting the entire block, and thus a large part of the block remains a monument to history. Although it still forms a sprawling canopy, it is relatively effective in allowing sunlight to the fruit and leaves.

The north-facing blocks share two characteristics: the fruit ripens about a week earlier and it has the ripest fruit aromas and flavours. The Old Block provides delicate fruit aromas and flavours and a softer tannin structure, especially off the east-facing section. This appears contradictory because it suggests lower fruit ripeness but riper tannins — logically not possible, but that is one of the curious things about this exceptional site at Margaret River.

Right: Keith Mugford, Moss Wood, in contemplative mood.

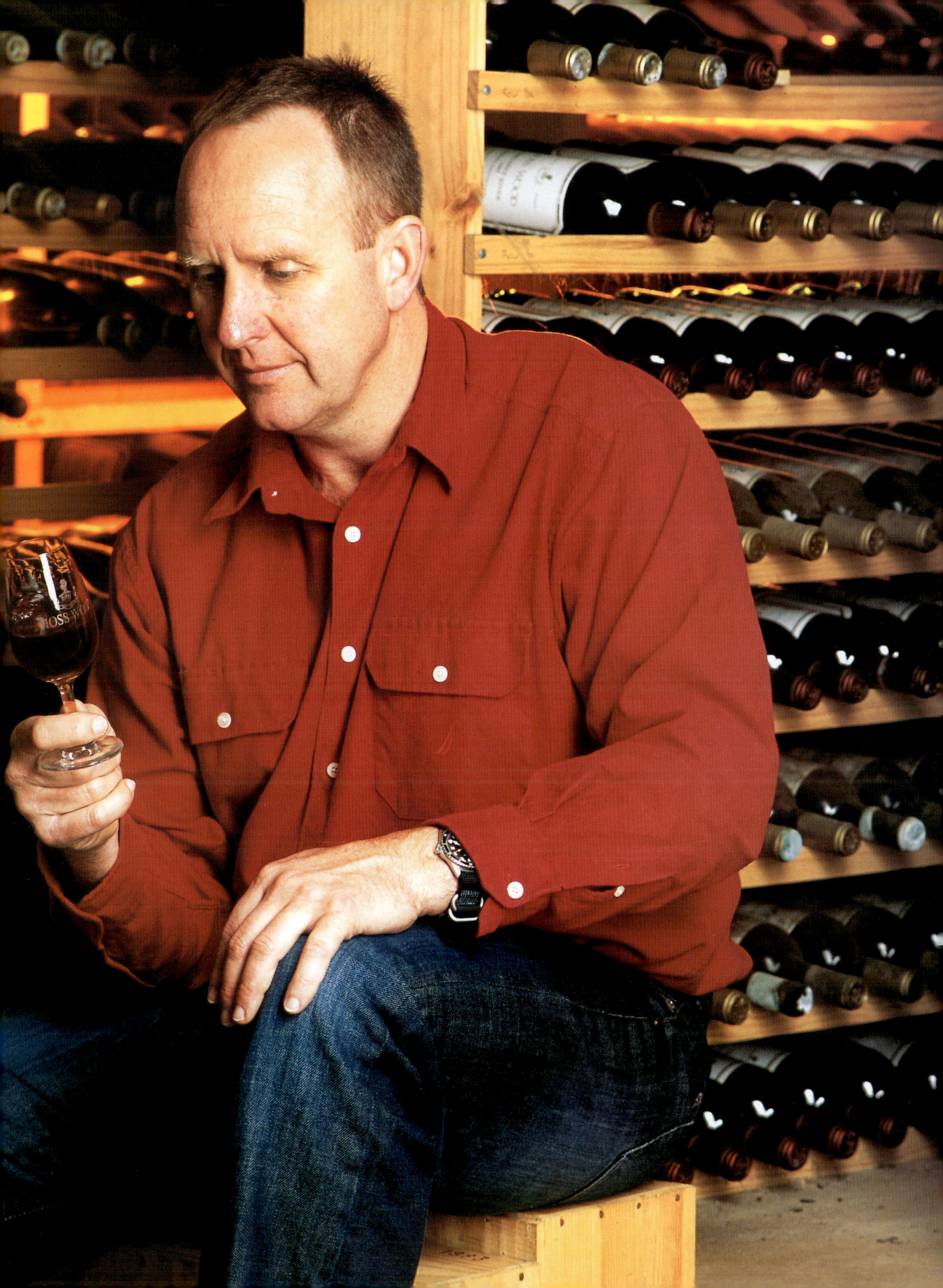

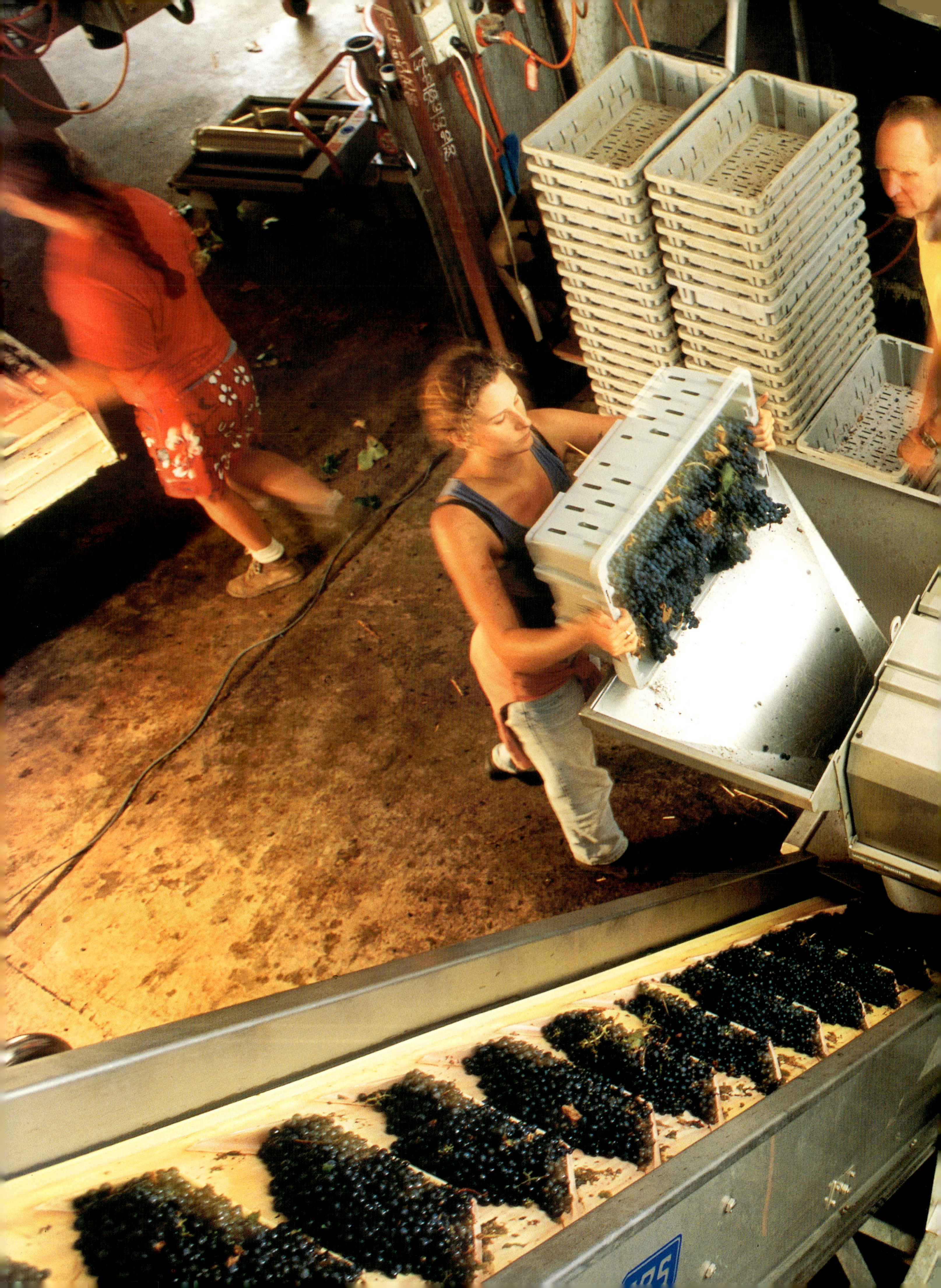

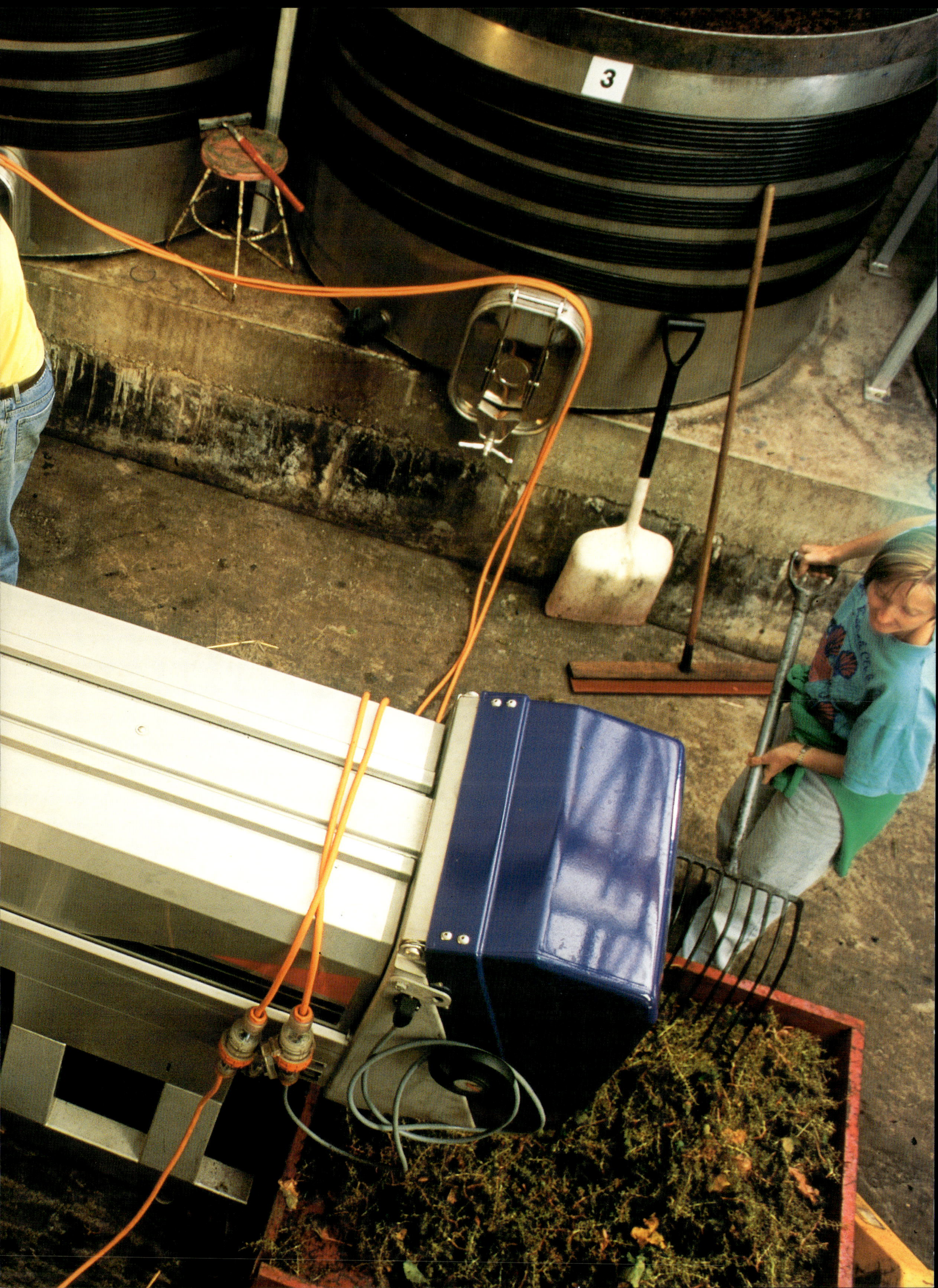
3

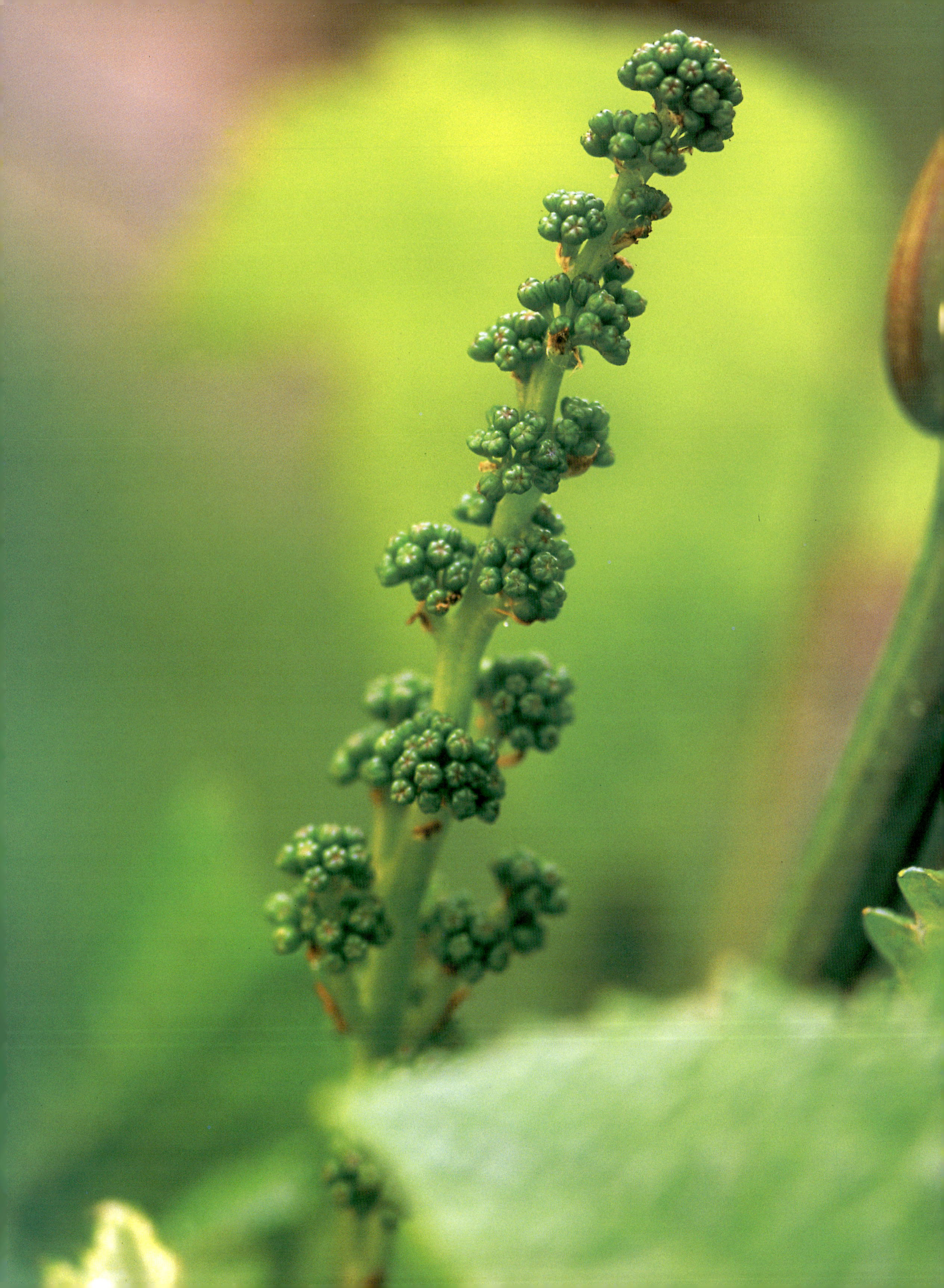

The Moss Wood team has made a number of important observations on the impact of all of these factors on the vineyards and the fruit. It seems that on the north-facing slopes sugars develop more quickly, as do flavours and tannins, largely as a result of better sunlight and less impact from the prevailing winds. The Old Block has a mix of flavours that comes from the range of slopes. Even ripening on the south slope is not impeded, principally because it is sheltered from the prevailing wind.

In all of this the Wilyabrup soils appear to be important. The gravel allows good drainage and encourages moderate but not excessive vigour. There is also a belief that the gravel content keeps the soil warmer at night and this encourages respiration of the malic acid, therefore possibly increasing the concentration of the flavour compounds, responsible in cabernet for those mulberry and violet characters. There can be problems, though, if the gravel content is more than fifty per cent. The vines may stress if they are not irrigated, leading to lower quality.

Previous page: The vintage in full swing at Moss Wood. Bunches of grapes enter the destemmer to the left of the picture; the grapes are carried up the conveyor belt to the fermenter; the useless stalks emerge to the right of the destemmer.
Left: Vine prior to budburst.
Overleaf: Cabernet sauvignon vines.

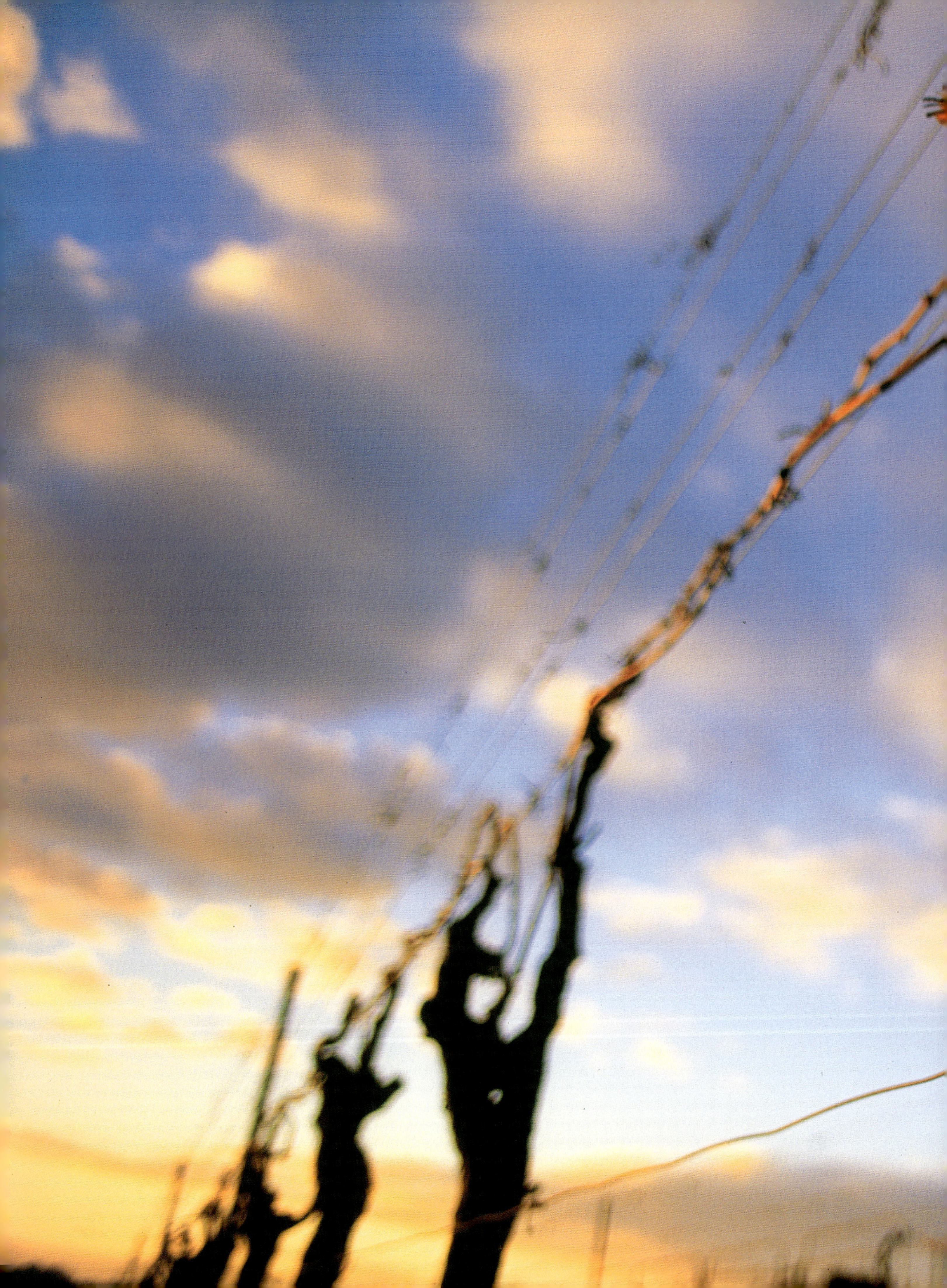

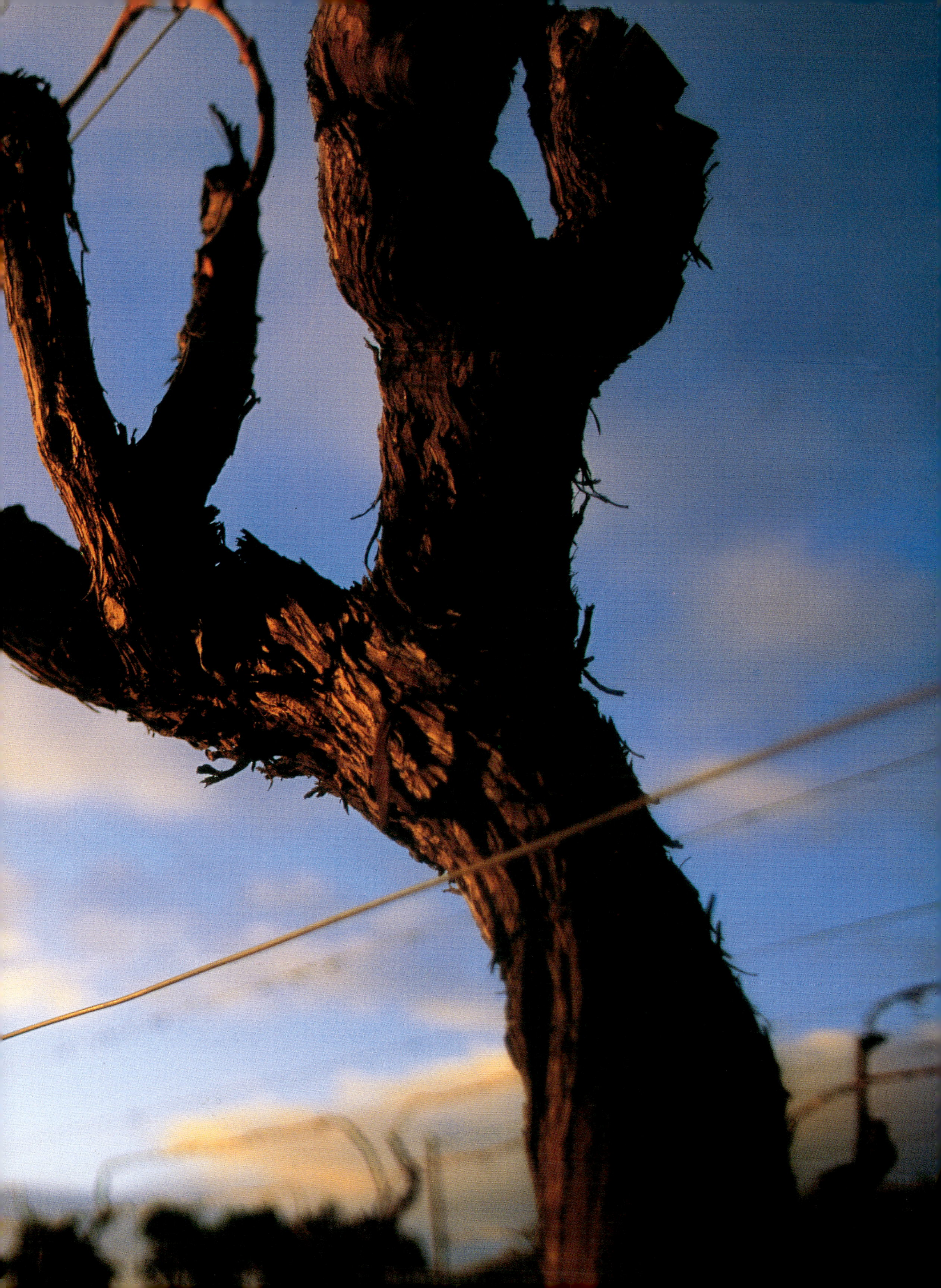

Cape Mentelle Wallcliffe vineyard

Since those twin Jimmy Watson Trophy triumphs in the early 1980s, Cape Mentelle founder David Hohnen and chief winemaker John Durham have refined their cabernet style into something consistently better than those early wines that shot it to prominence. Their focus has been on the vineyard, where they have been working hard to ensure greater ripeness of the cabernet grapes so that the wines are richer, riper, more densely flavoured than before, with a tight structure and supple, fleshy texture.

The predominant soil type on the Wallcliffe Cabernet Block, planted in 1970, is a free-draining ironstone gravel laterite. It is moderately acidic to neutral, with low fertility. The addition of lime and compost are important to improving drainage and, more importantly, the capacity of the vine to extract nutrient from the soil. Although the sub-surface clay becomes quite hard in summer when it dries out, it cracks open to encourage the development of a deep root system. This buffers the vines well against stress and, with judicious irrigation, allows them to grow and mature the fruit.

The focus for Cape Mentelle is achieving harmony between ripening sugar, flavour and tannin. In a perfect vintage on an ideal vineyard site, the wine will be richly flavoured with full ripe tannins and balanced alcohol.

The south-west aspect of the Wallcliffe site allows full sunshine exposure during the long afternoons as the sun sets in the western sky, resulting in better skin colour as the grapes ripen. Cool conditions which extend the ripening period are ideal for vines as they slow the rate at which grapes acquire sugar and give tannins and flavour time to fully ripen.

Like all other winemakers, Durham believes that balance is the key, maintaining that soils which encourage balanced vine growth will always produce better wines. Conversely, ordinary wine will be produced if the vines are planted on marginal or excessively fertile soils and winemakers resort to watering or fertilising to excess.

Right: Tipping grenache into the hopper.
Overleaf: Joe Italiano pruning at Cape Mentelle.

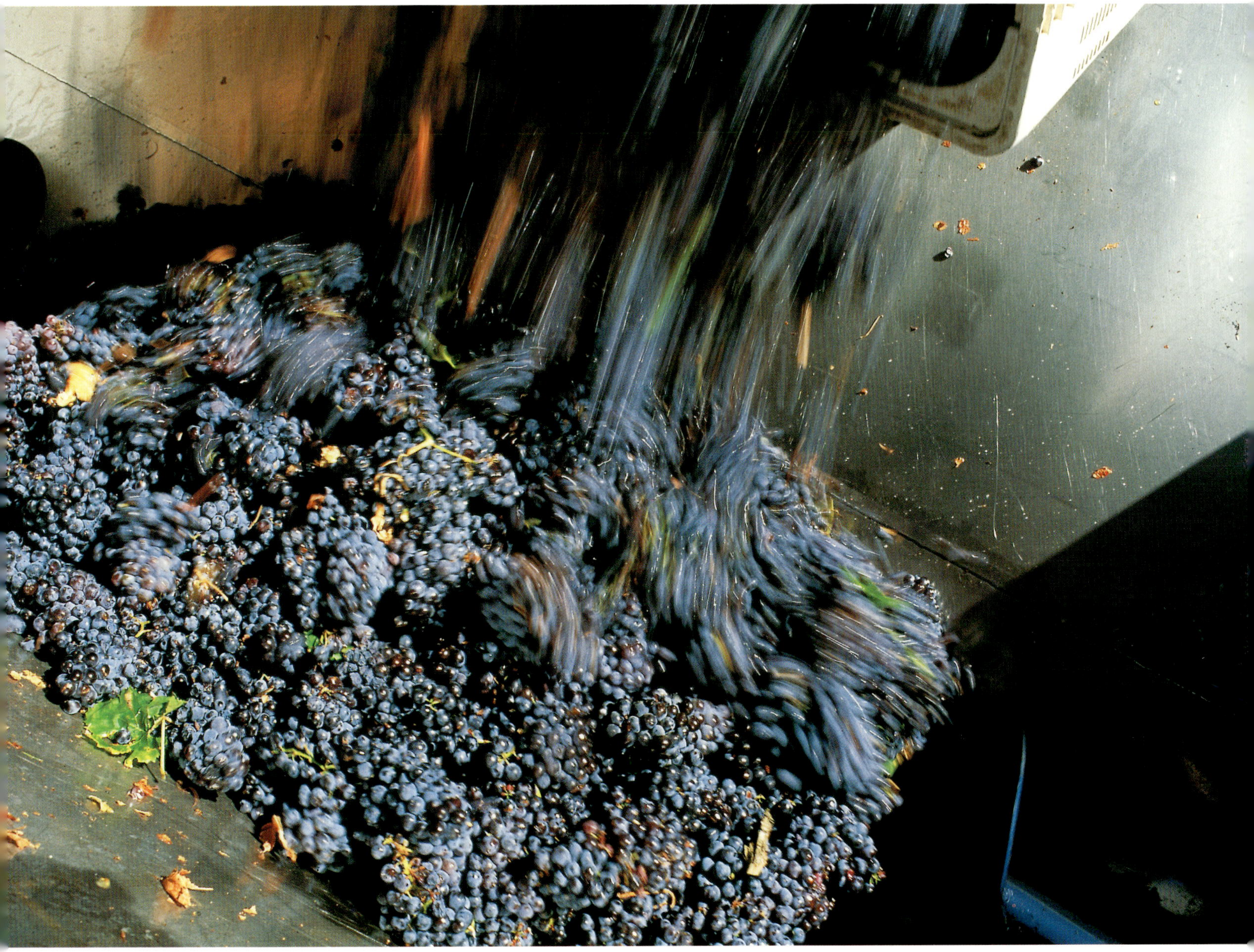

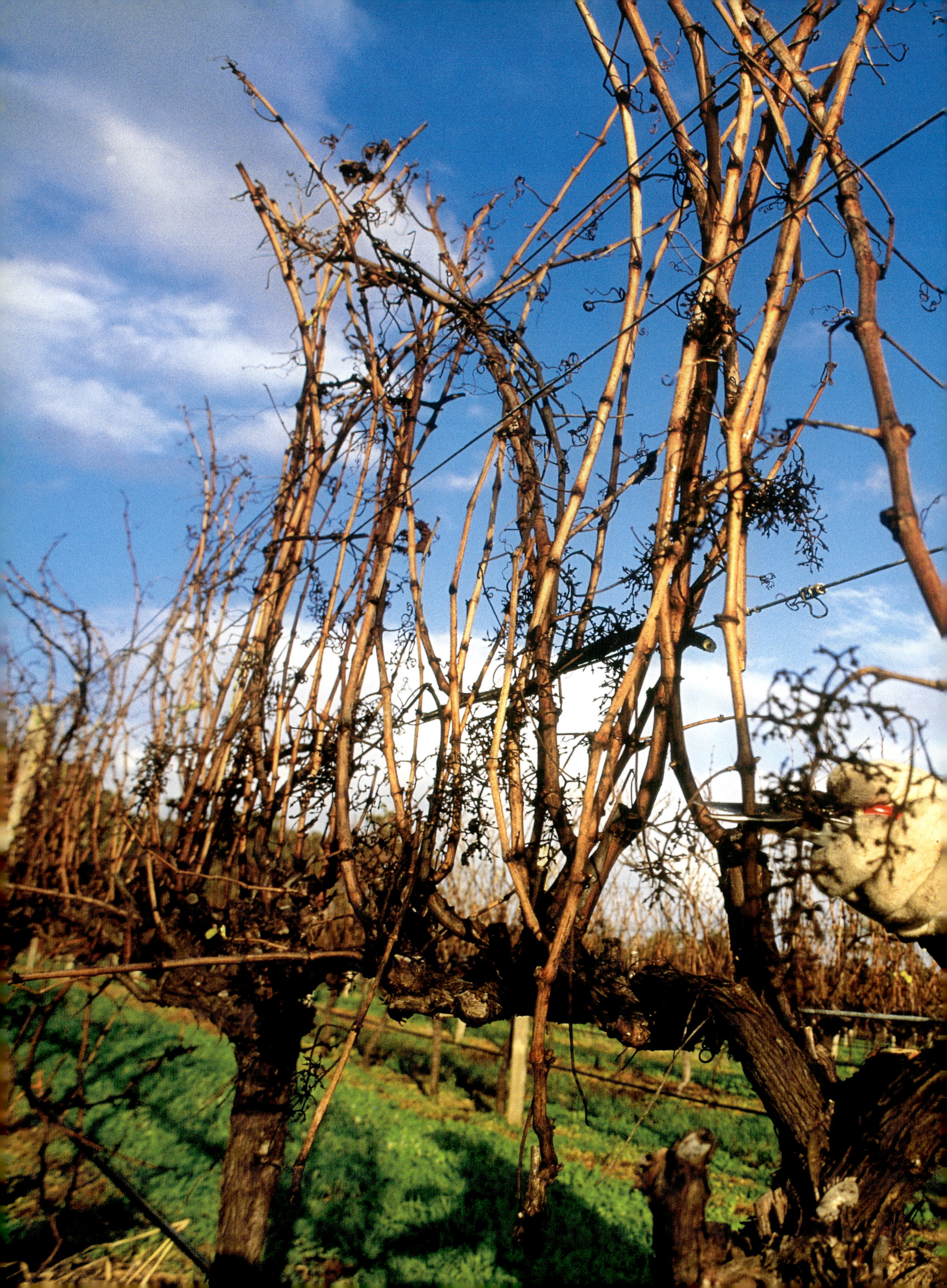

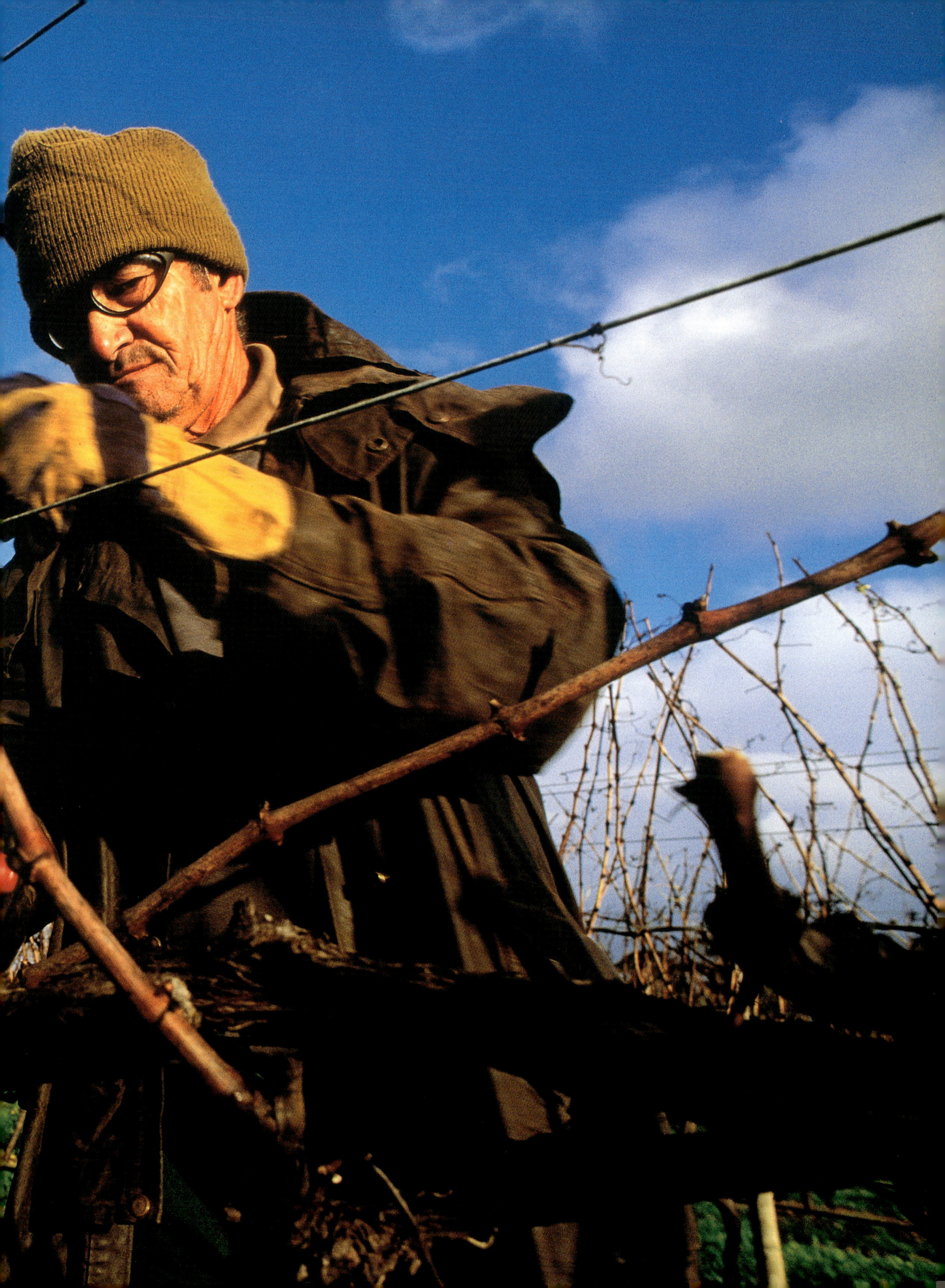

Vasse Felix vineyard

The Vasse Felix vineyard planted in 1967 by Dr Tom Cullity sits on the Leeuwin-Naturaliste Ridge on the banks of the Wilyabrup Brook. It is about four kilometres from the coast and so it receives the cooling effects of the ocean, with the afternoon sea breezes that prevail through the ripening period contributing to the build-up of full flavour and colour intensity. The gravelly loam over clay soils enables the vines to be grown on their own roots without supplementary irrigation. The outstanding feature of these soils is the ability to drain excess moisture early in the growing season, while retaining enough moisture to sustain the vine through to harvest. This special *terroir* has produced excellent natural vine balance, with vines that are not excessively vigorous and yields that are moderate. The vineyard has been planted according to the contour of the land. The north-south rows allow sunlight to penetrate the canopy, which means the fruit can ripen fully without the green characters that often mar shaded fruit. The east to west rows produce some fruit shading with cooler minty flavours and the selected blending of fruit from these blocks creates a distinctive vineyard character, which adds to the complexity of the finished wine.

Over the years trellising has been changed. Originally it was the double 'T' trellis and then later a single 'T'. However, trial and observation over the ensuing years have shown that a vertical shoot position type trellis, with a single fruiting wire and two sets of movable foliage wires, gives improved fruit exposure to sunlight and better airflow, both important in the pursuit of fully ripe fruit and the elimination of disease.

Vine age is a major contributor to fruit quality at Vasse Felix. The vines have adapted to soil variations and achieved a natural balance, which contributes to even ripeness across the vineyard. But within the vineyards there are idiosyncrasies, which must be managed to accommodate the different ripening times, generally related to soil profiles. Each vine is treated as an individual. They are pruned by hand so that bud numbers can be set in line with the vine's ability to produce and ripen a crop. Hand operations such as green shoot removal and leaf plucking enhance the sunlight exposure to fruit and are undertaken to improve quality.

Vasse Felix, the first commercial vineyard planted in Margaret River, remains one of the region's premier sites for growing grapes. The richness and concentration of flavour which its vines still produce owe much to Tom Cullity's choice of the site as well as to careful management by present day vignerons.

Right: Enjoying a glass of Vasse Felix.
Overleaf: Vineyard at Vasse Felix. Riesling in the foreground with shiraz behind, the original vines at Vasse Felix planted in 1967.

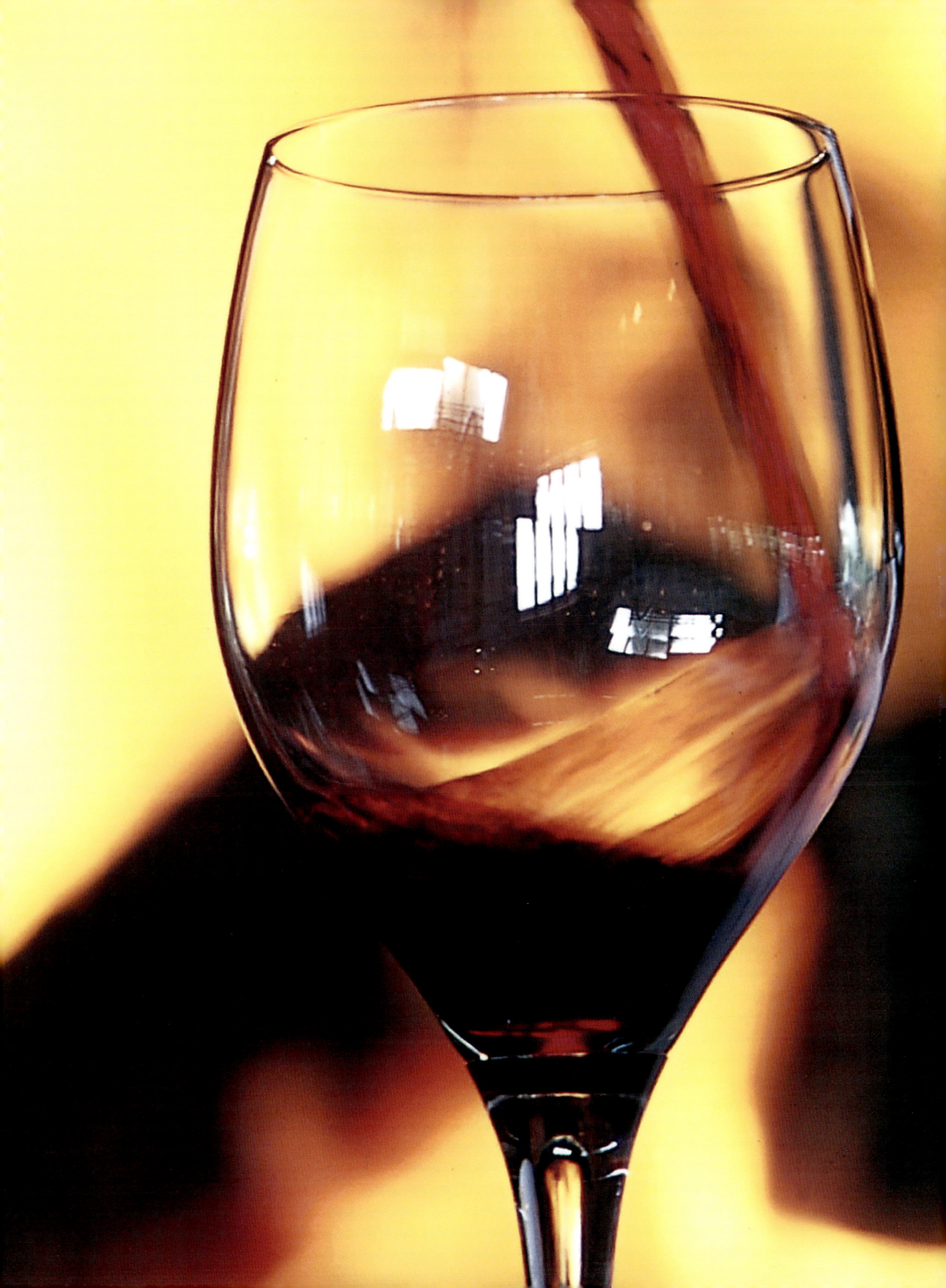

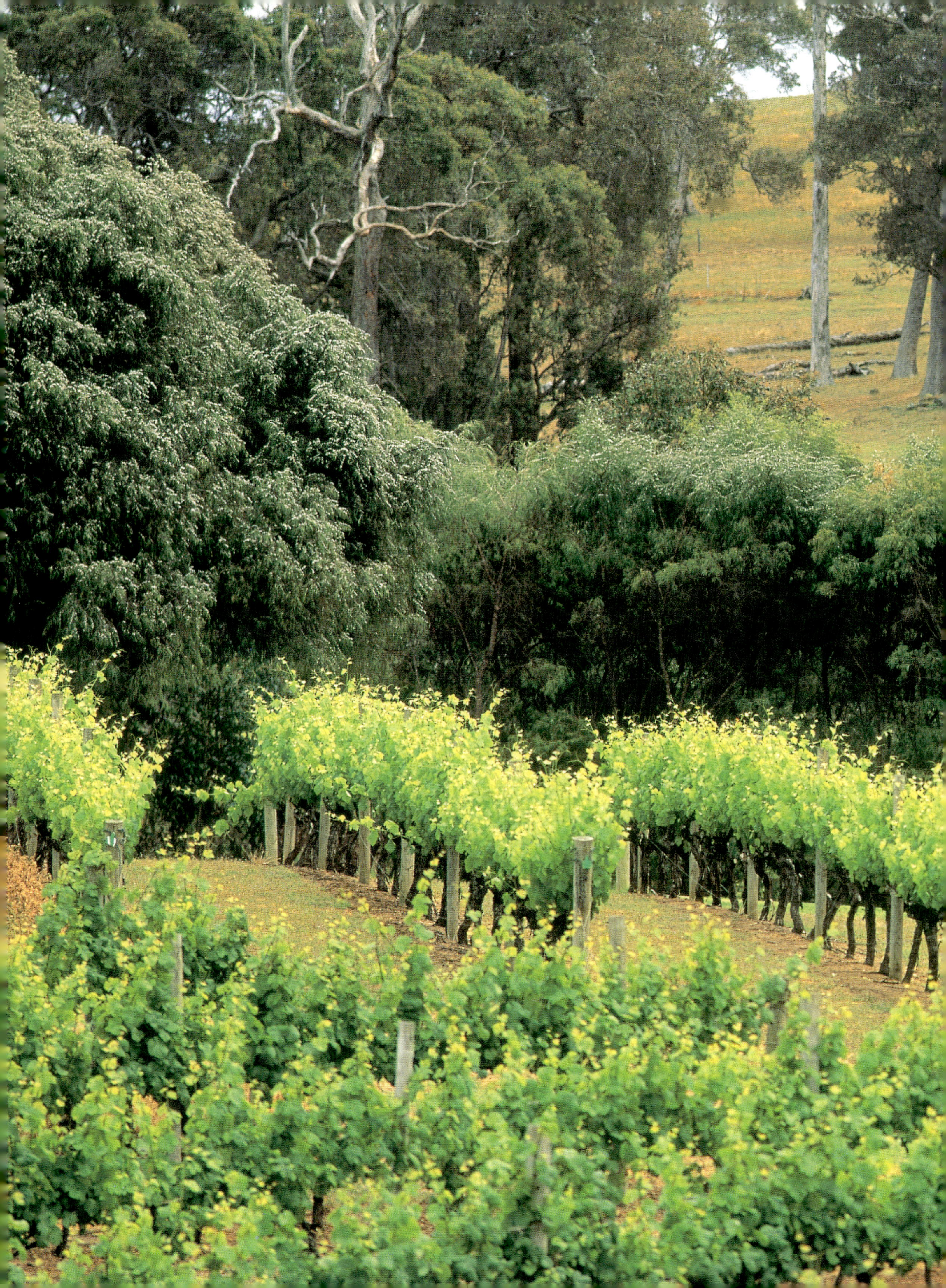

Frances Andrijich is predominantly an editorial photographer contributing to fourteen magazines, including *The Weekend Australian Magazine*, *Time*, *The Bulletin*, *The Australian Financial Review Magazine*, *The Good Weekend*, *Australian Gourmet Traveller*, *Australian Gourmet Traveller WINE*, *The West Magazine*, *Australian Geo*, and *Harper's Bazaar*. Frances has won numerous awards, has been involved in six books, and her images have appeared in the prestigious Fuji ACMP Photographers Collection six times. In October 1999 Fuji Film, Tokyo, chose four of her images for the worldwide promotion of their new colour film Provia 100F. She is a member of the Sydney based Wildlight Photographic Agency. Born in Croatia in 1956, Frances now lives in Perth and has two daughters.

Peter Forrestal is a Perth-based freelance wine writer and founding editor of *Australian Gourmet Traveller WINE*. He is currently editor of the *Oxford Companion to the Wines of Australia and New Zealand* and co-author, with Max Allen, of *Quaff*. His twenty-five books include *The Global Encyclopedia of Wine*, *Discover Australia: Wineries* and *A Taste of Margaret River*. Peter has been a member of the Top 20 tasting panel for *AGT WINE* since its inception and has judged at wine shows, including the Sydney International Top 100.

Ray Jordan has been writing about wine for twenty-five years. He is currently wine editor for *The West Australian* for which he writes regular mid-week and weekend columns. He has also judged at a number of wine shows including Barossa, Swan Valley and Sheraton. Ray hosted his own radio wine show for three years, and in 2002 produced the guide *Wine: Western Australia's Best*.

Technical notes: 35mm Nikon F4 bodies and Nikon lenses — Nikkor 20mm f2.8, 24mm f2, 28mm f3.5, 35mm f2, 85mm f2, 105mm f4 macro, 105mm f2.5, 135mm f2 and 180mm f2.8, 600mm f4; Hasselblad C/M 500 camera bodies, using 40mm f4 Distagon, 50mm f4 Distagon, 80mm f2.8 Planar, 120mm f4 Planar, 180mm f4 Sonnar, 250mm f5.6 Sonnar and a Fuji Panorama G617 camera. Other equipment used included Gitzo tripods, Minolta Flashmeter III and IV, Lowell Tungsten lighting, Bowens lighting. None of the photographs in this book have been digitally manipulated or enhanced in any way.

Film used: Fuji Velvia, Fuji Provia 100F, Fuji Provia 400F. Frances Andrijich prefers Fuji transparency films for their extraordinary sharpness and dramatic colour saturation.